1981

VERDICT ON SCHWEITZER

GERALD McKNIGHT

VERDICT ON SCHWEITZER

The Man Behind the Legend of Lambaréné

Illustrated

THE JOHN DAY COMPANY
NEW YORK

 Published by The John Day Company, Inc., 62 West 45th Street, New York 36, New York.

Library of Congress Catalogue
Card Number: 64-20467

MANUFACTURED IN THE UNITED STATES OF AMERICA

"It is the man who is the missionary,
not his words . . ."

HENRY DRUMMOND
The Greatest Thing In The World

DOCTOR SCHWEITZER'S HOSPITAL AT LA

NUMERICAL GUIDE

1. MAIN "TAPE-WORM" DISPENSARY
2. OPERATING THEATRE
3. DR. SCHWEITZER'S CONSULTING ROOM
4. DENTIST'S ROOM
5. FOOD STORE AND RATION ISSUEING BUILDING
6. DR. SCHWEITZER'S ROOM
7. SENIOR STAFF QUARTERS

8 & 9. DOCTORS' AND NURSES' QUARTERS (ALSO VISITORS

10. DINING HUT
11. STORE ROOMS
12. HELPLESS CASES
13. SERIOUS CASES

É BASED ON A SKETCH BY THE AUTHOR

4. POST-OPERATIVE CASES
5. WARD
6. MENTAL CASES
7. VIOLENT MENTAL CASES
8. BELL
9. LEPER VILLAGE
20. NEW OPERATING THEATRE (IN CONSTRUCTION)
21. NEW ROAD (STILL NOT COMPLETED)
22-23-24. CARPENTER'S SHOP, ANIMAL STORES, ETC:
25. "WHITES'" LATRINES
26. VEGETABLE GARDEN
27. CEMETERY
28. GRAVES OF MME. SCHWEITZER AND NURSE HAUSSKNECHT

CONTENTS

ACKNOWLEDGEMENTS

I MUST withhold public acknowledgement of my most helpful sources in this book. Not grudgingly. Not because Dr. Schweitzer might be upset by them, for the Doctor observes a lofty tolerance toward all his critics and denigrators. But because the little legendeers, the sycophants' chorus line, the adulators and image-makers of this great man are as sensitive as squeezed asps.

For the sake of the *status quo,* let us say, I shall therefore merely "think" my thanks to a number of truthful, trusted and unprejudiced observers.

I am grateful to those publishers who have kindly allowed me to reproduce passages from their books; Messrs. Allen & Unwin Ltd., A. & C. Black Ltd., Peter Davies Ltd., Harper and Row Publishers, Inc., George Harrap & Co. and Messrs. Hodder & Stoughton Ltd. In all relevant cases, I have credited the quotations in the script. I also thank the following for permission to reproduce their photographs in the book: Agence Dalmas, Paris; Camera Press, Ltd.; Dr. Joel Mattison.

Such valued, if unwitting, informants as Dr. Fergus Pope, Mrs. Clara Urquhart, Mrs. Jane Rouch, Mr. Henry Friedmann, Dr. and Mrs. Joel Mattison, Miss Olga Deterding, Nurses Silver and Lloyd, Miss Bernhard, and the redoubtable Mrs. Joan Clent will, I hope, accept my gratitude whether or not they sympathize with my motives.

Finally, let me thank Dr. Albert Schweitzer O.M. and his staff for their hospitality.

GERALD MCKNIGHT

PREFACE

HALF A century ago Dr. Albert Schweitzer and the dutiful woman he had married set out by steamer from Bordeaux to practise medicine and healing among the primitive, and sometimes cannibal, tribes of that part of West Africa where the coastline, having turned south and crossed the Equator into the Southern hemisphere, is broken by the mouths of great rivers such as the Ogowe and the Congo. About 130 miles inland from where the Ogowe discharges into the Atlantic Ocean, Dr. Schweitzer set up his first consulting-room in an old fowl-house at the Lambaréné mission-station, unpacked his few instruments and began a labour that has since stirred the world.

From that day the name and reputation of this Alsatian doctor have grown steadily, until today he is regarded almost universally as one of the noblest, greatest, most self-sacrificing men—if not *the* example of these qualities—in the world. With wearisome repetition books have been written about him, about his jungle hospital and the work that goes on there under his control. These, in the main, have raised a hymn of adulation and hyperbole to Schweitzer higher than the towering mahogany trees of the Gabonese jungle surrounding his hospital.

In surprising discord, the occasional dissenting voices have growled lamentations that Schweitzer's kingdom is unnecessarily primitive; that he refuses to treat with progress, or to move forward on any wings other than his own; that Lambaréné is no more than a shrine of the sentimental and the vicarious do-gooder; in reality, a jungle sore suppurating into the fresh body of emergent Africa, hampering the advance of clean, clear-minded and progressive

Africans who are now building modern and fully-equipped hospitals in the vicinity.

Shocking? Yes, but these assertions, like rusty cracks, persist in corroding the shining legend. The fact is that if Schweitzer's hospital were to vanish tomorrow, no leper or other sick African presently being treated there would go untended. That, in a word, Schweitzer's Lambaréné may well be redundant . . . an old man's private dream-world overtaken by realities he refuses to accept.

In view of this paradox, it seems urgently necessary to take a fresh and impartial look at the legend of Albert Schweitzer *aside from* the man who—whether intentionally or not—has created it. Time now, in this his ninetieth year, to weigh the full measure of his experiment in living against the values of our more material life outside which he has so often vehemently deplored. It is also proper perhaps that this re-appraisal should begin before his death; for at the time when Schweitzer is no more, the lustre of his name and of his legend will be unassailable.

There will be men, and more doubtfully women, who will attempt to straighten the picture after his death, often from personal experience of working with, and sometimes in opposition to, the Doctor. But their voices are certain to be drowned by the sycophants' chorus. If the question is to be asked: is Schweitzer's legend out of all proportion to the man and his doings? then let it be asked now, while it can still be answered.

It is a question demanding a certain attitude of mind on the part of the asker. For, though scientific analysis may be purely objective and unbiased by preconception, literary analysis may not. This is so for the simple reason that the writer poses a question to which he is about to supply an answer already known to him, while the scientist does the opposite.

So far as is in my power, I have tried to open my mind and my senses to the truth about Lambaréné. I have come to this subject neither to praise Schweitzer nor to bury him. But I have come to report on him. For it was as a reporter, that I was first attracted to the subject of Schweitzer many years ago. Since then I have discussed it with many visitors and workers from Lambaréné, and have read what Schweitzer and others have written. In January 1963, while in Africa, I stayed at the hospital as Dr. Schweitzer's guest. On my return, I completed my research.

The result is a feeling of even greater need to see Schweitzer set on the scales of our time, together with many of the facts about him which only a handful of his closest followers know exist; to express the failings of this man as well as his extraordinary virtues. Indeed, to show him "in the round" for perhaps the first time, starting from the premise that legend is rarely true to its subject even in the most inspiring of cases.

Yet is it fair to re-valuate a man who has done, and is doing, a greater amount of good for others than most families perform in several generations? What right has anyone to suggest that Dr. Schweitzer, his life, his work, his aims, his achievements and all those who so selflessly devote themselves to his hospital should be examined afresh to decide whether or not they have been over-valued? Let the answer be as simple as the question: why not? If Schweitzer's legend has falsely created a "jungle saint" out of a humble, dedicated doctor, then he will be well rid of the distortion. So will his true friends. If there are aspects of his credo, his philosophy and motivation, which seem exceptional then they will surely be better weighed in the open.

For, if Albert Schweitzer were a god, or a self-convinced Messiah, there would be nothing more to be said. The question: what can be added to his story that has not already been told? would answer itself. His eccentricities, his "benign dictatorship" over a flock of adoring disciple helpers, supporters and admirers would fall into place as comfortably as the miracles of the New Testament. His curiously autocratic attitude to the African Negroes he heals might be excused, if not actually respected, on the grounds of some super-human ethos. Even the manner in which he brought the woman he had married to the sickly heat of Equatorial Africa, always giving priority to his work, his mission, and finally leaving her alone in Europe when illness prevented her returning with him, could perhaps be understood. So, too, could his behaviour to his only daughter, Rhena, whose upbringing he barely knew of.

But Schweitzer, for all that legend has ascribed to him an ethereal stature, is neither a deity nor a man fitted with the cloak of saintliness in the full meaning of the term: that quality of exceptional holiness through which an individual may win a high place in heaven and veneration on earth. On earth, he is revered by many and held in awe by others. But he has his critics and, for valid reasons, his detractors.

As to holiness, it is easy to see how Schweitzer has come to be regarded as among the supreme human beings. It is harder to visualize his situation in heaven, should it exist and should he enter it. There are some who find his theological beliefs un-Christian as well as unorthodox. And there is the moot question whether service or self-advancement was the reason for his astonishing self-sacrifice in giving up a brilliant career to become a humble, Negro doctor. This perhaps more than any other aspect of the Doctor is the one on which our verdict will have to be given. For in plain terms the question must be asked: is Schweitzer a saint or a fraud? When we come to consider this, it will be wise to have studied most carefully the facts of Lambaréné where, for half a century, the wood has been hidden by strange trees.

ONE

THE MYSTIQUE OF LAMBARÉNÉ

IN LAMBARÉNÉ, there is an almost tangible aura of mystery and suppression. It is there because those who surround Schweitzer want, no doubt with excellent motives, to protect him from intrusion, from criticism and from interference likely to tire and distract him. This is not to say that Schweitzer is a recluse; far from it. He sees all those who visit him, from young Paris typists whose fares have been paid by popular magazines (the one whose story appeared in France last year had taken a live sparrow from a Paris park to ease the Doctor's solitude. Regrettably, it had not survived the journey, but she wrote at length about it, and about how touched Dr. Schweitzer had been when she mentioned her intended offering) to such obviously sceptical visitors as myself. He spends as much time as he can allow with each person, and has a well-balanced machinery for making them feel both at home and, finally, well favoured in his presence.

The form this takes should command the respect of protocol setters in Whitehall, Washington and the Quai d'Orsay, to say nothing of Red Square. It is a form of flattery, both subtle and discreet, which begins by suggesting respectful indifference to the visitor from the outer world, then continues by providing unexpected prizes, such as interviews with the Doctor offered suddenly in the middle of his busiest working hour. It rises to its zenith with a farewell scene reminiscent, depending on the susceptibilities of the departing, of the most hilarious of Gilbert and Sullivan or the most stirring of Verdi.

As the visitor's canoe is paddled away from the hospital bank, nurses and doctors in dazzling white clothes and sun-helmets stand in groups, or singly, raising white handkerchiefs in gentle waves like magnolia blossoms in a spring breeze. Their relaxed wave is not merely a sign of the equatorial heat. It is a means whereby the see-ers-off can keep up their polite performance for as long as it takes the retiring visitor's craft to pass out of sight around a headland in the river system, some ten minutes, and often in the full, blazing sunshine.

If the departing visitor is somebody of importance, or a member of the staff (even if only leaving temporarily), the *whole* hospital team, as many patients as can walk or hobble, the cured lepers who work as handymen, and even Dr. Schweitzer himself will congregate in this courtly and disarmingly unrehearsed manner to wave the voyager on his way.

The extraordinary corollary of this custom is that those who have once left Lambaréné seem to be erased from memory. Dr. Schweitzer does not discuss the departed, nor does he respond to discussions about them. For him, the world of Lambaréné and the world outside are so separate and distinct as to be incompatible, and his interest in people follows them no farther than the headland round which they disappear from view.

The effect of this obliteration is that nothing in Lambaréné remains for very long a monument to those who may have struggled and suffered to create it. The most unselfish and unstinting work of surgeons, pharmacists, nurses and others is ignored during a visitor's conducted tour of the wards and buildings. Lambaréné is always on show to anyone who cares to visit it, but what is seen will appear as a shrine to the work, the direction and the creative talents of one man alone: Albert Schweitzer. Whether or not he is completely at ease with the legend created by his admirers in the world, it is clear that the Doctor has no wish to see it challenged by those he has permitted to share his toils.

I enjoyed many conversations with Schweitzer and his closest staff, and spent several hours in private discussion with him, yet never once did he refer to Dr. Percy, the assistant he once hoped would take over the hospital but who left him recently. Nor to Trudi Boschler, the nurse who became known as "Lambaréné's

Lady With the Lamp" for her work in the leper colony at all hours. Nor, indeed, to anyone who had served the hospital who was not physically there.

It is often Schweitzer's custom to seat his visitor at a distance from him when he or she first arrives. The proper seating position is respectfully pointed out by one of the staff and a napkin, with its own case, provided. The uninitiated will expect to find the napkin at the same place each time, but this will not occur. Showing a fine understanding of human psychology, his host will have arranged for the visitor to, as it were, "work his way up the ranks" of the table. As meals succeed one another, he will find he is being placed nearer and nearer to the great man, until finally—eureka!—he is opposite to him, in the place of honour. This mark of respect may be bestowed only on the final day, when a packet of sandwiches and bananas will also be placed beside his plate, a kindly thought for his journey. At this point, Schweitzer will appear at his most genial and engaging, talking merrily to the visitor whom he had previously all but ignored, except during formal interviews. The procedure is again deliberate. Once knowing he is safe from over much attention, the Doctor feels free to be companionable. To be so earlier would be to lay himself open to the risk, which he never takes, of becoming too familiar with a person from the world outside.

This matter of two worlds plays a definite part in the mystique of Lambaréné, for Schweitzer believes that there are those who are with him, "insiders", and those who are not with him (though not necessarily against him), "outsiders". He can bestow no greater compliment on his staff than to admit them into his small circle of "insiders" and he will do this whenever somebody comes to work for him whom he finds useful and congenial. From then on, the helper feels elevated to a special position which demands loyal behaviour and respect. One result is that the Doctor has little difficulty with any of his staff so far as their discipline or moral behaviour goes.

To be an "insider" in the court of Schweitzer's kingdom is a proud situation to occupy, but it must not be taken to imply an intimacy at any depth with the Doctor. Nor even an assurance of notice and friendliness from him at all times. In social terms, Schweitzer is an ungiving man. His charm is a finely focused beam rather than a beacon. It is part of his complex machinery of domination that he can direct a warmth of attention towards an individual at will, then switch it off completely so that the temperature appears to drain out of the association. Yet, when the subject has been reduced to imagining his responsibility for some breach between them, the beam will again flash on and thaw away the ice.

There is consequently no guarantee of endurance in Schweitzer's favour; no means of knowing how his mood will be half an hour hence. Nor can the "insider" tell his position in the social structure of Lambaréné, because there are several interlocking and eccentric spirals in the domestic and political world of the "Schweitzerines". Where one lieutenant will hold an almost total power over one aspect of the kingdom, another will occupy a similar position in another, related field. The result, since only Schweitzer holds the key to both, is total centralization of all control and only the most carefully—one might say grudgingly—delegated authority.

I have touched on some of these quaint customs more as a signpost than anything else. The way to Lambaréné is paved with good illusions. One of these is that the hospital is primarily busy with the curing and tending of black and poverty-stricken lepers. In fact, it is not mainly a leper hospital, or leprosarium, at all, but a sprawling general and surgical treatment centre for most ailments (excepting sleeping sickness, which is dealt with by one of the Gabonese hospitals farther down the river). Wounds, complicated hernias, pregnancies and fevers are treated with the same attention given to sick animals, many of these also being brought to the crowded compound. A good deal of healing goes on, and many of Schweitzer's helpers, particularly his staff of young doctors, work unstintingly at it. But it is an open question whether the recovery of his patients is as fundamentally important to Schweitzer as the fact that he is there, tending them. That it may be the effect of a personal experiment in Christ-like living, rather than its cause.

In his attitude to those who serve him he adopts the manner of a strict, aloof, though kindly schoolmaster. For many of the more impressionable, this is a manner which they both know and respect from their own childhood; that of an aging and occasionally testy grandparent. Already disposed to revere the utterance of his name, they are totally charmed by his patriarchy and quickly take their places at his feet as part of the chorus of adulation which surrounds him. Such offensive matters as might upset them on arrival are quickly rationalized, either by the older workers or by their own wishful thinking.

The hospital, it is Schweitzer's contention, *has* to be kept in a simple state in order not to jar or distress backward patients. Lack of clean water, electricity, a balanced diet, or hygenic sanitation can be blamed on this. Finally, the novice finds that these shortcomings become so much a part of the entire universe of Lambaréné—which ends at the river front for most of them, since few even visit the near-by towns or villages—that they are easy to ignore. Only when a sensitive visitor shows some evidence of shocked surprise (even, occasionally, nausea) do they return to the notice of the denizens.

Before I went to Lambaréné, I had been told of a visit made there by Dr. Adlai Stevenson which amused the eye-witness who confided in me. Stevenson had apparently crossed the river in the usual laborious way, following a long, hot flight in an aircraft lacking all but the most simple amenities. Having met Dr. Schweitzer, and exchanged pleasantries, the American statesman asked if he might "visit the men's room". This request, translated, was sympathetically acceded to by his host who had him shown to the single, solitary-standing timbered hut which serves the community as its *only* white, male latrine.

Inside, Stevenson found a scrubbed unpainted wooden seat over a trench in which chickens and flies swarmed. The trench led towards the hospital vegetable garden. The effect on Dr. Stevenson was, according to my informant, a rising feeling of sickness which showed greenly in the sallowness of his cheeks when he returned to the Doctor's side.

The exact reason for this primitive and unpleasant form of sanitation is in some doubt. But it is certainly Dr. Schweitzer's whim, if not wisdom, that retains it. One visitor was told that it was because the Doctor is unable to bear the thought of introducing water-borne drainage out of deference to the insect world. "Dr. Schweitzer knows that a large number of ants and other insects would be drowned and swept away," the visitor was told. "He finds this quite out of the question." Another reason put forward by an observer who spent some time at the hospital is that the aged Doctor is a man who has known and experienced great need and want. He cannot bear to see anything wasted; not even the excretions of his staff, when these can be used to manure his crops. It is more likely that, lacking piped water, the Doctor has a choice between the method he now employs and that of using a chemical disposal system which *would*, presumably, destroy some insect life.

In his main philosophical credo, the belief that Reverence for Life is the most important virtue in living, Schweitzer goes to lengths which at first strike the casual viewer as mildly absurd. It is well known that he prevents ants from being squashed by those who find them intruding on their persons. He makes a deliberate little pantomime of saving one of these insect's life when he encounters it on a visitor's face, or on his own.

Though this may be inspired by either showmanship or a desire to give evidence of his belief, the substantial attitude is deeply rooted. While at the hospital, I spoke to a young man, a German architect, who is serving Schweitzer as a carpenter/helper. He told me of the difficulty there is in attempting to put up new structures under Dr. Schweitzer's control: "We must not creosote, or protect with chemicals, any of the footings of the timber," he explained to me, "because the Doctor is anxious not to pollute the earth and damage the insect population."

A large-scale building operation was in progress, adjoining one of the huts where members of the European staff sleep. This, I was told, was to house the operating theatre, when built. And when would it be completed? Ah, I was informed, that is impossible to say. It depends on . . . well, many things, including what we find as we go along. As I discussed this further with the worker, I learnt that *all building work must stop* whenever insects are encountered which might be damaged by its progress. "For instance," I was told, "whenever we come to an ants' nest, we down tools until the ants—who always move out the moment they are disturbed —have all disappeared." The delay can take up to three hours, but time is Dr. Schweitzer's servant.

He does, in fact, make his own time. When he first came to the jungle he found it tiresome to use mechanical time-pieces which are unreliable unless checked against some master time-piece. He learnt to tell the hours by the sun's shadow and still uses a sundial set in the ground near his dining hut, which contains the only clock. From this he no doubt decides, roughly, when work may begin or end, meals be served, etc. But it is far more likely, and vouched for by many of his staff, that he has the gongs struck when his own purpose is most suited. The fact that he persistently used the sundial pointer, an iron bar, as a boot-scraper adds some weight to the suspicion that he has only contempt for time of any sort. Even at its most efficient, indeed, the hospital sun-time is usually half an hour ahead of that in the town of Lambaréné, a mile or so down river, though presumably that is based on such standards as latitude and the mean of Greenwich. It is an example of Schweitzer's omnipotence in his own sphere that even time stands still for him. How many of the world's most illustrious princes can say the same?

Charmingly quaint as these idiosyncrasies may seem, it is the purpose of this book to study them in relation to the use and value of Lambaréné as a hospital for healing the sick, and to weigh them in the balance where they contribute to Dr. Schweitzer's personal stature. Can it truly be said that a sufferer is better tended by nurses who are working to a time-schedule which may vary at the arbitrary disposition of its maker? In modern hospitals, time is a vital part of the rhythm of healing, as evidenced by the careful programming of all functions. Only in Lambaréné is it allowed to flow like a jungle stream, ebbing at one moment and accelerating the next. To subjugate the clock is the aim of nearly every prisoner of civilization, the most triumphant act of the all-powerful; but it surely is not the most perfect symbol of humility and service to others.

Admittedly, the effect of a properly stream-lined schedule on the primitives who are Dr. Schweitzer's patients could well be disastrous. For many of them, as he would say, time has no more meaning than an expression of their appetites; a wish for food or drink at certain points of day, for rest or relaxation at others. With this backwardness constantly in mind, Dr. Schweitzer has persisted in refusing to bring his methods up to date throughout the fifty-one years that he has been in Africa. It is open to question whether the rise of the African situation, from cannibal savage to self-governing citizen, has affected his attitude of mind at all. The suggestion is implicitly there that he does not wish to see the natives as anything but lowly lesser-beings; for to do so would be to acknowledge that his own position among them might well have grown anachronistic.

I believe he has never trained any of them to do more than the simplest tasks. A handful is able to give injections. Three or four work occasionally in the operating room. But none has been allowed to qualify as a real assistant or regular nurse, although the operating theatre records show that certain native helpers did once assist with surgery, quite successfully.

Thus, Dr. Schweitzer stands today as a relic of what used, half a century ago, to be considered the absolute standard of missionary behaviour to the *indigènes* or native-born people of Africa. He is contemptuously scorned by some of their more educated citizens I have spoken to, though much of their depreciation is excessive and due to impatience with old ties. The value of his work, and the need for it, will be analysed in this book, but perhaps already it can be seen that there is more than one side to the question.

TWO

SAINT OR BIGOT?

THE CHISEL blade dividing those who believe Dr. Schweitzer to be a saint from those who suspect he is no more than an exceptionally bigoted man is forged out of the question whether or not he has advanced with the times in a way which would bring the full advantages of medical science to bear on his cause. There are critics who insist that he deliberately and implacably stands in the path of progress, allowing only those modern facilities which he can, himself, control and operate; retaining the standards of his hospital at the level of a Victorian country doctor's consulting-room. These detractors assert that Schweitzer is more interested in personal domination of the colony he has created than in healing the sick. At best, this is an emotional and not wholly balanced theory which tends to judge by superficial considerations.

Nevertheless, there is reason to believe that Dr. Schweitzer does find difficulty in distinguishing between those aids which give real help to his work and those which merely modernize and, in his opinion, bring distress and perplexity to the primitives among his patients. Since many of these are *fetichist* in their religious beliefs, i.e. followers of tribal witch-doctors, he may possibly be right in rejecting a number of modern innovations. But, though the use of elaborate machinery might upset these backward folk, they can see for themselves most Western appliances functioning in the town of Lambaréné.

Schweitzer is an old man who has spent most of his life cut off from a civilization he basically distrusts. It would be surprising if he did not attempt to preserve the customs and principles which once helped him to triumph over the jungle. A more important consideration is whether, in doing so, he is deliberately holding together a kingdom over which he alone can hold sway.

During the visit of the celebrated South African plastic surgeon, Mr. Jack Penn, F.R.C.S., to Lambaréné in 1956, Schweitzer answered one of his visitor's inquiries in a way that illuminates the point very clearly. Penn had raised the question, never popular with Schweitzer, of what would happen to the hospital after his death. Schweitzer was non-committal (indeed it is doubtful whether he bothered to acknowledge the question, his usual custom being to ignore what he does not like to hear). But Penn persevered, assuring him: "If you would only say the word, you could easily, in America alone, raise thousands of pounds with which a teaching and training, as well as healing, hospital could be built to your memory at somewhere like Brazzaville in the Congo . . . why don't you do it?" Schweitzer, Penn later told friends in Johannesburg from whom I heard the story, paused to deliberate on this suggestion, then said, "No. I am too old to be able to run such a place." If at first glance this seems an innocuous enough reply, it should be considered again in the light of what Penn had actually suggested, i.e. a hospital *to perpetuate Schweitzer's memory*, and not a hospital which he himself would run. From the Doctor's reply it seems fairly clear that he can only envisage a field of operations in which he is the supreme master.

The temptation for Schweitzer to see Lambaréné as a place cut off from the world, in which he can preserve its original forms and so reject any theory of treatment or life other than his own, is understandable when one considers the enormous achievement he has attained in his lifetime. He came to the Ogowe in 1913 when horses drew the buses of London and leprosy was considered an incurable scourge. Housed originally in the grounds of a mission, he chose to leave this comparative sanctuary for the unknown and forbidding regions of the jungle near by. No doubt a wish to have absolute dominion over his hospital drove him to this course, linked with the inner purpose which had brought him to Africa, but it was none the less heroic. Today, the hospital has grown, entirely under his hand and direction, into a sizable colony where between five and six hundred people live in reasonable comfort.* No greater tribute to his abilities as a conqueror of the jungle need be cited than the fact—regarded locally as something of a miracle—of his own survival. Though here, too, details are worth noting which reflect the particular value he puts on his own contribution.

At Lambaréné, the white staff are provided with three meals a day in the communal dining-chamber, a brick-walled hut set high above the ground beyond the reach of flood waters in the rainy season which begins in October. These meals, to the casual visitor, seem adequate, indeed plentiful and nourishing. But a dietician who had spent several months in the hospital told me that they actually lack sufficient protein to sustain healthy life for more than a reasonable period; and that, had Dr. Schweitzer restricted himself to them, he could not have reached his present age without considerable debility and sickness. Apparently this is due to the extreme conditions of heat and humidity which make equatorial Africa a breeding ground for all manner of bugs and bacilli. Schweitzer knows this fact, I was assured, and protects himself against it.

The Doctor has his baths prepared for him from specially boiled cans of partially sterilized water, while his staff and patients content themselves with the risky use of water drawn from Lambaréné's single, hand-pumped well. Contaminated by the fever-ridden water of the Ogowe, this well is the colony's sole supply of running water. To wash the whole of one's body, one must take cans of its water to a shower which consists of a bucket with holes in the bottom. By filling the bucket repeatedly, it is possible to cleanse oneself; but the danger of infection accompanies the pleasure. A doctor who recently left Lambaréné told me: "Everyone working there for any length of time contracts something or other; either Bilharziasis or some other ailment. Nobody leaves Lambaréné unscarred."

Except Dr. Schweitzer. Though even he suffered severe illnesses

* A count taken on Aug. 9 1962 showed 451 adult and 116 child patients: total—567. As only 342 beds were available, this meant 1·65 patients to each! There were also 120 to 130 lepers in the Leper Village (which holds 200). These figures do not include "consultants", or out-patients, who come in far greater numbers.

in his youth, doubtless before he learnt how to avoid the marauding pests. He has now provided himself with an equally well thought-out protection against malnutrition, by having two hens' eggs specially reserved for him each day. The rest of the staff are lucky to see one, let alone two, at any time except for a ceremonial "birthday egg" once a year and a very occasional omelette. Thus the jungle doctor whom the world sees as a saint ensures that his strength is kept up whatever happens to anyone else.

Ah, but he is an old man, it will be said. He has a particular need to guard himself against the perils which threaten all white, civilized mortals who spend more than a brief spell in this climate. A dangerous truth this, for if one is to accept that Schweitzer is holier than the average man, one has a right to expect in his behaviour a consistent pattern of putting others before himself.

At Lambaréné, every other human life but the Doctor's radiates outward from his as the spokes of a wheel extend from its boss. He is mother, father, priest, doctor, teacher—and frequently confessor—to his assistants. They may not accept this domination completely, and I have been told that not all of them, by any means, do so, especially not the men of the community. But, in public, they must either conform to the strict code of observing deference in all things to the Doctor, or leave. In return, he gives them a reasonable life in which work and austerity are not always as hard as outside admirers of Lambaréné imagine.

The first impression of the hospital complex is one of languid bustle. Europeans who visit it are often struck by this easy-going rhythm which at last appears to predominate among the wards and work rooms. No one seems to be overdoing his labour, though some are engaged in heavy duties such as building roads and buildings. In the humid climate, where the temperature stays permanently in the eighties both night and day, though with the slight breeze common to regions close to the Equator, concentrated effort is hard to maintain. But visitors from both New York and Durban, South Africa, would testify that these cities have periods of far more exhausting climatic conditions, yet men are forced in them to work to the maximum.

One gets the impression that Schweitzer believes in pottering toward his objectives rather than in striding towards them. His perseverence has been marked throughout his life, and on many occasions has robbed his wife and others of his companionship; yet there have been few books he has tackled which he has not found tedious to write, as he has often said. Much of his final literary work lies unfinished in tin trunks within his room at Lambaréné. Utterly indomitable where a principle is at stake, Schweitzer has been less inclined to force himself to accept more temporal challenges, with the result that Lambaréné, certainly at this advanced age in its creator's life, has assumed a somewhat sleepy air.

The score or so of solidly constructed buildings stands as a monument to his physical activity, nevertheless. To imagine how the jungle looked where now the hospital colony stands is to force realization of the stupendous nature of an achievement inspired and largely carried out by one man. A doctor from one of the near-by French-built hospitals told me: "You must not look at Lambaréné as it is today, and at Dr. Schweitzer as he is today. If you want to judge the task this man tackled, imagine it as it was, an impenetrable, savage wilderness. See him as a tall, broadly-powerful, young man with a shock of rich, black hair, enormous moustaches and a look of piercing determination in his bold eyes. *Then* you have the forces that met to do battle together."

It is a formidable thought. The jungle at this part of the Ogowe rises fairly densely from the banks of the river and possesses few natural clearings. Where Dr. and Mrs. Schweitzer chose their site (the hospital is named the "Albert Schweitzer-Bresslau Hospital" as a tribute to Mme. Schweitzer) there were huge, pale trees rising from wing-like roots at intervals of only a few yards. Undergrowth swarmed prodigiously over everything they had cultivated, if they were forced to leave it untended for more than a few days. While Schweitzer built his leper colony, at some distance from the hospital, the jungle over-ran his orchard to such an extent that he was forced to transplant it and start again. The present huts and hospital rooms came into being as individual triumphs in his constant struggle against heat, rains, exhaustion, sickness and the elaborate task of bringing vital necessaries of existence to the spot.

Today, the colony can entertain a visitor in simple but acceptable comfort. There are rooms for all white people and no more than two share accommodation in cubicles, all of which are contained within five or six long, metal-roofed huts bordered by covered verandas. Native patients, on the other hand, are crowded beyond anything they are likely to endure in their villages; but as they may bring to the hospital their relatives and animals, their cooking utensils and even furniture, they are perhaps fortunate in finding any sort of accommodation at all. What they get is a tiered and partially unwalled shelter area wherein they must camp on a form of rough bed-space at ground level, or on wire bunks above. Outside the native "wards", wide stoeps are bordered by drain-like ditches into which the women pour all the refuse of the daily cooking and washing.

Since Lambaréné's domestic economy does not allow for feeding the patients but merely provides them with foodstuffs for which they must queue in the mornings and cook on their own open wood fires, the ward area is probably the most unusual of any hospital run by Europeans in the world. Unlike the Gabonese town hospitals, Schweitzer insists on allowing his patients to bring their homes with them; the result is a bleating, lowing, clucking swarm of goats, chickens and other animals roaming freely abroad among patients and nurses. While some of these do provide nourishment, in the form of occasional eggs and manure for the vegetable crops, it is hard to understand their inclusion in a place of healing. They constitute a potential source of tetanus. A doctor there told me he had treated four cases of the disease in little over a year, three of them fatal. "Wherever you find farm-yard animals," he pointed out, "you find tetanus spores."

To the unqualified visitor, of course, the inclusion of animals adds a charmingly barn-yard flavour, so that suffering does not show up against a background of orderliness and white paint and starch, but melts into an aura of animal rusticity. Also, the habits of some natives in dealing with their animals can be amusing. Five years ago, when a visitor was being shown over the wards, an old native was seen sitting in bed on a clutch of eggs laid by the hen which shared his sleeping quarters. He apparently boasted of his success in hatching out more than one of these. Regrettably, there are few such examples in European wards of patients putting their enforced recumbency to some useful purpose.

The trouble with all this intermingling of animals and humans is that it makes the policing of ditches and ward-rooms almost impossible. A type of modified patrol is carried out by a native armed with an authoritative stick, but he would be a watchful observer indeed if he could be sure that no undue fouling of the quarters takes place. One is told that the natives are naturally clean in their persons and in their homes. Yet it would seem inhuman if there were not among them some who were more prone to carelessness than others. In fact, from the ditches where the cooking is done arises a stench that is indescribably nasty (as I well know from having been forced to bend my head over one while taking part in a Sunday morning church service) and the general conditions are constantly bemoaned by the otherwise tolerant nursing staff.

Dr. Schweitzer cannot be told that these standards of hygiene and nursing comfort are inadequate. His reply is constant: what would these poor primitives do with bedpans and temperature charts? In his experienced view, the people who dwell in the jungle, even today when many of the villages have radio sets broadcasting dance music beside the village "tum-tum" or ritual dance-and-message drum, do not expect Western comforts; indeed, they would be upset by them up to the point, he maintains, where they would cease to bring themselves in to be healed and treated.

One of the ailments most rife in this part of mission-infiltrated Africa is venereal disease, and the Doctor may be quite right in assuming that few of these sufferers would voluntarily come to hospital were there the slightest obstruction in their path. But his attitude seems to be slipping steadily into the past, as far as the reality of the situation is concerned. More and more natives of Africa's new republics are becoming emancipated and familiar with Western methods and modes. For them, the Schweitzer Hospital is a slightly humiliating reminder that the white man still believes them to be a backward, near-animal race. At present, sick Africans still choose to come to Schweitzer past other, better-equipped, modern hospitals, but the reasons why they do so are not always what they appear to be, as will be shown later in this book. Fundamentally, it seems that there is some reason for supporting the outraged cries of the critics who deplore Schweitzer's deliberate "primitiveness".

One of the most uninhibited of these is an American woman who visited the jungle hospital a couple of years ago and later wrote an article which was printed in the French-language, nationalist-sympathizing journal *Jeune Afrique*. It appeared in September 1962, entitled "The Scandal of Lambaréné". Mrs. Jane Rouch, the author of the article and in private life the wife of a French film director, stated that ". . . The Gabon is one of the richest countries in Africa in hygienic equipment. For 445,000 inhabitants, it has 4 hospitals, 30 medical and treatment centres, 22 radiological units, 9 mobile decontamination and sanitary units and 2 maternity clinics. Systematic vaccination there has practically eliminated yellow fever and smallpox. Leprosy, the terrible sleeping sickness, and malaria are in full retreat. In the midst of this surge of modernization, the Schweitzer hospital must be regarded as a sore, a cesspool, connected as it is with typical racist theories. The sick enjoy distinctions of label: *indigènes* for Africans, *européens* for the half-castes."

Mrs. Rouch was attacked in European newspapers for her expression of these views. She told me she was unrepentant; in a talk I had with her before I went to Africa she said: "If you saw the paper, and the pictures they printed with my article, there is surely no doubt. The pictures are convincing enough in themselves, and it is much more difficult to lie with pictures than with words."

Continuing her article, Mrs. Rouch wrote: "The most favourably inclined of Dr. Schweitzer's visitors admit that his hospital is the most backward in the world. Main drainage, a proper sewer, is still not installed (after forty-nine years and in spite of the donations). Taking its place is an open ditch. Large clumps of surgical dressings, thick with coagulated blood, flow slowly down it.

"Dr. Schweitzer's principle is that 'it is right for the black to suffer, recover, or die in his natural surroundings'. So they come to the hospital with their families and their animals—no better off for this contagious promiscuity—and then they prepare their own meals. 'I give them the food,' says the great white Doctor, 'they cook it themselves. That way, they can't say it isn't good.' "

Schweitzer has always damned rum and cheap spirits as the cause of having destroyed most of the will to work among the missionized Africans. His distrust for the "lazy negroes" is so ingrained that a visitor told me wryly, some years ago: "The busiest man there is the locksmith." Thus he expects no ordinary gratitude from his black patients. What he gives them, either as food, treatment, accommodation or medicine, he apparently provides in support of his belief that such charitable work must be done in order to glorify a man's own soul.

This out-moded belief is responsible for many of the practices which Mrs. Rouch found upsetting. A photograph printed alongside her article showed the notice in the Doctor's dispensary which reads, in French: "Drugs must be paid for in cash." Schweitzer has admitted that he believes in charging the natives for their treatment and medicaments where possible. "Before the war," he wrote, "I had begun to make a small charge for the medicine to those patients who seemed not to be absolutely poor, and this brought in something like 200 francs [$22] a month. Even though it was only a fraction of the real value of the medicines dispensed, it was something . . ."* Today, he says that he has no idea what the profit and loss account of his hospital is, but the charges go on.

Mrs. Rouch claimed that her reason for publishing this candid report on Lambaréné was that "an international taboo" exists, protecting Dr. Schweitzer and his work from the inquisitive world outside. "Some thousands of visitors have been to Lambaréné," she alleged, "and all have seen what we are showing you here today

* *On the Edge of the Primeval Forest*

in photographs. Yet no one has said a word. A love of low standards is kept alive by an enormous amount of publicity. Good souls are touched by 'the incessant efforts of the poor Doctor who sacrifices his life to heal the blacks'. Old ladies, to ease their souls, send postal orders . . . We know of one state in the U.S.A. which regularly pays $200 a month to Dr. Schweitzer. He constantly receives gifts of drugs, surgical supplies and such things as an operating theatre . . ."

Winding up her argument, this critic stressed three aspects of the Schweitzer affair, as she called it: "The mystique . . . the whole world imagines that Lambaréné is the only corner where one can be cured in Africa, when in fact the Schweitzer hospital heals less well than every other hospital in Africa. The anomaly . . . when Gabon is trying to modernize its medical system, and is succeeding in doing so, the persistence of this form of treatment becomes scandalous. The mystery . . . what is done with all the donations of money sent to Lambaréné?"

There are clear answers to each of these accusations, as any of Dr. Schweitzer's staff would insist. The Doctor, they would say, has never tried to pretend that his is the only healing oasis in Africa. He has not sought the publicity lavished on him by the world; far from it. Indeed, he has always tried to avoid the limelight which his growing reputation has focused on him. Equally, his methods are not in any way "scandalous" to the hundreds and thousands of Africans in the "modernizing" Gabon who voluntarily show up at the hospital for treatment despite the attractions of the State run hospitals. Nor is there, they would add, any mystery about the donations subscribed to Dr. Schweitzer's Fellowships throughout the world; the money and supplies received are placed at Dr. Schweitzer's disposal and used by him for one thing only, the furtherance of his healing mission.

We will return to these points of argument, fundamental as they are to the understanding and evaluation of Dr. Schweitzer's experiment. At present, the aim is simply to put them down as two opposing viewpoints, both of which are beginning to marshal supporters throughout the world. I have been asked in many odd corners what my own appreciation is of the true value of Lambaréné. In view of criticisms, such as the one by Mrs. Rouch which I have taken the liberty of retailing at length, there is growing scepticism about the Doctor's ultimate value as an instrument of human salvation. This leaves aside the tremendous respect in which he is universally held for having sacrificed his career to his cause, but it does demand an impartial re-assessment.

So often, the disturbing particles seized on by his detractors appear outrageous to the world of Schweitzer's followers, yet they could easily be explained by those on the spot. Mrs. Rouch stated, for instance, that "cartons and cases (of drugs and surgical supplies) are dumped in the bush and never opened". One doctor, who was at Lambaréné recently, told me he had actual photographs of large crates of drugs being dumped in the river. But in Johannesburg I met a man who was able to refute the worst of these allegations from the most personal and expert knowledge.

Henry Friedmann is a chemist, a Jew, and one of the most humbly charitable men I have met. In 1957, he was asked by Mr. Jack Penn, the South African surgeon who had just returned from Lambaréné with a vivid impression of the need for supervision of its stores and supplies, if he would undertake the task. Mr. Friedmann agreed and since then, he told me, "I've been going up there for the love of the thing." During his visits, he has managed to co-ordinate and arrange the hospital's use and storage of its most vital supplies, but he has been unable to stop the arrivals of quite useless drugs and other materials.

Mr. Friedmann told me: "I've seen cases of stuff arrive from big drug firms plainly marked 'Not for use' after a date that had already passed by. Why do they send such useless consignments, which might actually be dangerous when used?" One answer could be that the big drug firms find, in Schweitzer's distant hospital, a perfect dumping ground for products they have been unable to dispose of elsewhere. It is not impossible that, in giving their goods to charity, they are able to obtain sizeable tax concessions.

"In 1959," Mr. Friedmann recalled, "the Doctor received a big Spanish shipment of cortisone and aspirin—both drugs which he can use in large quantities at Lambaréné. But they weren't separated, they were in the form of a mixed preparation which meant that they could only be used together for the treatment of special rheumatic conditions. We had to throw most of the stuff away."

Waste is foreign to Albert Schweitzer. At meals in his hospital I was struck by the care with which every article of food was husbanded, not even a crust of bread being left by those of the staff who had learnt the first rules of the place. "Nothing is ever wasted here," I was told by a senior nurse, in a tone of voice that suggested absolute conviction. But the Doctor has many things on his mind and only limited time in which to organize every detail of his colony. "The secret," said chemist Henry Friedmann, "is that you may criticize him if you like, but never forget that it is humanly impossible for one man to take care of everything."

Thus, and for no more culpable reason, occasions sometimes arise when visitors see what they believe to be examples of wasteful inefficiency. Mr. Penn told a friend, after his visit, that he had noticed a certain ulcerated condition of the feet being habitually treated with the wrong substance. He asked Schweitzer for the correct remedy and was told that none existed in the hospital. But when the surgeon inspected the stores, he came upon case after case of the medicine, at which Schweitzer was both astonished and delighted. "I had no idea of their existence," he said. The stores were then in a hopelessly chaotic state, with cases of drugs donated from all over the world left unopened and unused. But since Mr. Friedmann's visits began, these conditions have improved to the point where a trained young American doctor at Lambaréné while I was there, Dr. Joel Mattison of Florida, told me: "We have all the drugs I was familiar with at Duke University (in the U.S.A.) and some I didn't even know."

If wastage of human endeavour were as easily explained away as the "scandal" of Dr. Schweitzer's rotting drugs, then the legend would stand aloof from any criticism. But, in re-assessing the failings as well as the virtues of this great man and his work, we must look very much deeper.

THREE

THE IMAGE

THE TRAIL of belief, self-doubt and rebellious re-adjustment that led Albert Schweitzer as a young man of thirty to break his links with a world on which he had already made distinguished marks as a theological, musical and philosophical scholar—to say nothing of resigning his post as a college principal—so that he might take up the study of medicine and go to Equatorial Africa as a doctor, is explained in his writings in two ways. They differ but they are not unsympathetic. He says that: 1. He wished to execute a plan "which had been in my mind a long time" to give something in return for his own ideally happy life. 2. He sought to "stand and work in the world as one who aims at making men less shallow and morally better by making them think". Whichever of these we choose to regard as closer to the realization he has since attained at Lambaréné, they are equal pointers to the brand image with which we are concerned. But in one important aspect they clash.

Where the first motive, expressed by Schweitzer as the revelation that came to him one brilliant summer morning in 1896 at Günsbach that "I would consider myself justified in living till I was thirty for science and art, in order to devote myself from that time forward to the direct service of humanity" suggests nothing but unselfishness and the altruistic purpose of a purely humble man, the second has an egotistical and authoritative ring. For Schweitzer, thought has only one end: a pursuit of the mysteries of life; following this, he asserts that man must come directly "and almost irresistibly" to Reverence for Life, his pet creed. "Because I have this certainty," he writes, "I oppose the spirit of the age, and take upon myself with confidence the responsibility of taking my part in the re-kindling of the fire of thought."

Where is the humility in that? The statement has a crusading tone, far more in keeping with the image of a young and sturdy German intellectual, fiercely maned and moustached, seeking his personal grail and defying, as Schweitzer so often had done before, all that stands in his way. For whether or not this detail is blurred or even unknown in the minds of his millions of admirers, Albert Schweitzer is and always has been an anti-establishment tornado. In his youth, he scandalized the theological world by turning its interpretation of the New Testament upside down. He went on to trounce the musical world for playing Bach all wrong. By middle age, he was ready to denounce the achievements of Western civilization as hollow. And in his old age he now campaigns against the nuclear menace.

Where, in all this, is the true man? Selfless healer, bent on re-paying his debt to society and to God? Christian medical-missionary, using the primeval jungle as his show-case example of self-sacrifice? Or stubborn rebel determined to gain a sensational platform from which to dictate his views to the world? What he has done at Lambaréné is not exceptional enough *in itself* to justify the reverence attached to his name. In Africa, as elsewhere in underdeveloped areas, not a few devoted people have built and run hospitals and the like in spite of fantastic difficulties, yet we rarely hear of them. As they do not claim to have made a gesture of renunciation such as Schweitzer made, or to play an organ-pedalled piano in the depths of the jungle, they remain relatively unknown, while Schweitzer is one of the best-known names of our time. Why?

The answer, at least in part, is that Dr. Schweitzer is a superb self-propagandist, far excelling even George Bernard Shaw who used to be known as the most remarkable proclaimer of the great "I Am" alive. Schweitzer has achieved the feat for which T. E. Lawrence was credited, of "backing into the limelight" and with far more telling result. It was in the early twenties that he first exploded into popular consciousness, when, having attracted the attention of the press during one of his visits to Europe, he insisted

"I am a poor, small negro doctor." The legend of his humility was created at that moment. "This most modest of men," wrote a reporter, "is only concerned with easing bodily and spiritual ills of humanity and will not talk about his great achievement . . ."

It is easy to see how this Image fits neatly into a popular mould. But a closer look at his life shows that he has himself directed, aided and encouraged its circulation. In fifteen or more books and extensive lecture tours and recitals he has maintained the same humble, dedicated mien; rarely giving a hint of the purpose and egotistical strength which dominate every facet of his thought and behaviour.

Today he is far from poor, in fact a fair estimate of the wealth which has poured into the coffers of his many Fellowships places him among the richest men in the world. Nor is he small. If he wanted to, he could extend his hospital to treat far larger numbers; it is already filled to capacity. It is even doubtful whether he can primarily be regarded as a negro doctor, since the greater part of his time is now taken up with the problems of atomic devastation. We thus have a rather different picture from that which first released the legendary aura around him.

Nobody would say that there is anything morally wrong with the design Schweitzer has followed. But it is open to question whether it corresponds to the popular image of him as a saint among men. He holds views which are completely opposed to our civilized way of life and are based on the conviction, expressed in another of his works, that "the suicide of civilization is in progress".* He begins this book by stating, unequivocally, that "We are living today under the sign of the collapse of civilization", yet he encourages us to think! This seems to remove even the anaesthetic from the fatal operation to which, in his stated opinion, we are foredoomed.

Meanwhile, despite the approaching holocaust, Schweitzer continues to build. At Lambaréné, the work of repair and renovation goes on alongside the construction of new buildings and roads. He has increased his staff by some 20 per cent during the past five

* *The Decay and the Restoration of Civilization*

years and sees little prospect of the need for his hospital and its services shrinking as the Gabon Republic increases its medical services.

In this he may be ahead of popular ideas about Africa. Some African states are stumbling badly along the path towards total self-administration of hospitals and healing centres. As this is being written, both Uganda and Ghana are voicing strong expressions of concern, through their leading statesmen, about the lack of proper nursing facilities. In London, *The Times* has commented in a leading article: "Only ten years ago the mass of Africans were suspicious of modern medicine and—upcountry at least—avoided hospitals. Now almost everybody wants their benefits." Schweitzer's Lambaréné may well be a popular sanctuary for the sick as long as it remains.

As he increases his dominion, Schweitzer becomes more noticeably an overlord. When I was there, he had twenty-seven white women helpers (of whom ten were qualified nurses) and five male doctors. He treated them all with marked, though gentle, autocracy. In the hospital, it cannot be over-stressed that there is only one rule, one method of doing things and one opinion that can be sustained: Schweitzer's own. He may believe in teaching people to think, but it seems that he prefers them to think in his way.

Before my arrival, I had wondered if he might feel more need today, when the world can visit him without difficulty, to keep a tight rein on the underlying principles of his experiment. If so, it does not appear on the surface. Lambaréné continues to operate entirely as though it belonged to another planet, another century. In this, it is no more out of this world than many of the surrounding villages and *kraals* which house its patients, so that it synchronizes with *their* world rather than ours. Yet Dr. Schweitzer remains both civilized and European amidst his choir of white helpers, eating food sent specially from Switzerland, baking European style bread, and even—on high days and holidays—serving beer, chilled from the single large refrigerator. Nobody could accuse the doctor of having "gone native" in other than the rhythms of time.

The difficulties of reaching the hospital from Europe or America have decreased sharply in recent years, since the surrounding states have obtained independence. One of the first considerations of any republican government seems to be the provision of a modern airport; with the result that the traveller can now leave Paris on a fast and superlatively comfortable jet one evening and be helped aboard the native dug-out *pirogue* canoe on the Ogowe River the following midday. The service I chose, and which seems most efficient, was U.T.A., the African affiliate of Air France. In one of their planes I flew out of a freezing Paris blizzard at 10.30 p.m. on Friday, January 18 1963 and landed at Douala, in the Cameroon Republic, only seven hours later. It had been a smooth flight with one brief stop at Kano in Nigeria, and I remember I sipped good champagne after dinner and wondered what my next meal might be. In fact, it was a very satisfying French breakfast in the air-conditioned restaurant of Douala airport, while waiting for the much smaller plane to take me on the "jungle hopping" trip to Lambaréné.

This flies one, at an interestingly low altitude, via Libreville and Port Gentil, to the landing strip of Lambaréné town. Five years ago, I was told, the seats aboard these aircraft (operated by Air Afrique and Trans-Gabon Airlines) were hard metal; one squatted along the side of the plane, rather like a parachute trooper awaiting the jump. Now, they are fully fitted out, but about the hottest conveyances I have ever endured, both on the ground and in the air. At 2,000 feet, the air rising from the jungle is obviously as sun-baked as it is at ground level, with the result that we sweated with fully open ventilators. As one of the planes I was in had a family of inquisitive cockroaches exploring my baggage on the canvas rack above my head, and occasionally journeying down past my left arm towards the vicinity of my perspiring feet, I cannot truthfully say that this was the most enjoyable part of the journey; but it was soon over. One had some relief from the extreme heat while on the plane by the circulation of air from small electric fans placed over each seat. And at the three stops, including Lambaréné, it was possible to buy refreshment.

A word here about the economics of the land where Dr. Schweitzer

—who claims to be incapable even of thinking about money, but is reputed to drive as hard a bargain as any Alsatian peasant—has to shop for supplies and necessities. Gabon and the surrounding Equatorial African states have found a simple escape from an inflation brought about by their presently unbalanced economies: they give outside currencies just half their world market value. In the case of French francs, which I was carrying, these are legal tender but at only 50 per cent of their normal currency rate. Hence a small, though iced, bottle of Coca-Cola cost 2·50 local francs, or 5 NF in French money, i.e. approximately 7s. 6d. in English cash. A bottle of beer was less palatable and equally expensive. But after the Turkish bath conditions of the aircraft, and the enforced walk in glaring equatorial sunshine across the tarmac to the airport buildings, a passenger is more than ready to pay the price asked.

Dr. Schweitzer, on the other hand, takes a strong line with local profiteers. I am told by one of his ex-doctors that he insists on paying *his* price for bananas, which form the staple diet of the natives at the hospital and are eaten roasted, fried and in other novel ways. As his price is only two-thirds of that offered freely by the local towns, it might seem strange that he is able to survive; the reason pays tribute to his strength as a negotiator, but it also casts a strange light on his ability to extract measure for measure from the primitives he heals.

Dr. Schweitzer, so I was told by one of his assistants who had spent well over a year at the hospital, sends his lorry into the jungle on "rounds", during which it calls at several near-by villages. At each of these, the Doctor's representative offers a price per kilo for bananas—knowing full well that the price paid by the town merchants, who will also call and collect in a truck, is a third higher. The villagers, if they know the rules of the game, usually comply, offering huge bunches, or "hands", of unripe bananas to the hospital. And the reason why they do so is that, when the time comes for someone from that village to fall sick, they can be sure that he will be taken in on the lorry with the bananas. Should the village prove unco-operative, it is probable that the patient, unless in a serious condition, will have to make his own way to Schweitzer's domain.

To our way of thinking, this may seem an amusing piece of blackmail by the wily old jungle Doctor; but it is part of Schweitzer's wisdom that he can apply the methods understood and respected in his district. This form of bargaining is fully accepted by most of the sixteen or so tribes he has to deal with, and many of them would regard Schweitzer as less of a man if he failed to use such means to attain his ends.

The backward natives know little of Schweitzer's universal reputation; only those among them who are learning to read and write in the new schools and universities are now fully aware of his fame. Some are deeply suspicious of his charity since they have read of the many donations subscribed by people all over the world. "Where does all the money go?" I was asked when talking to natives outside the hospital. Inside it, there was no opportunity to talk with the patients, few of whom speak anything but their own obscure tribal dialects.

One exceptionally primitive woman patient, or visitor, spoke a language—mainly clicking sounds with her tongue and teeth—which was meaningless to everyone (though at least sixteen tongues can be understood at Lambaréné). Dr. Schweitzer told me: "She came here like a little dog, following the others along the road." The woman smoked the stub of a small clay pipe and seemed contented, but she would accept only a little of the hospital's free food, prefering to collect nuts, berries and roots which she cooked in a small pot she had brought with her. At night, she wormed her body under the exposed roots of a huge tree and slept. The doctors, who had so far been unable to persuade her to let them examine her or get her to take even the mildest medicine, nicknamed her "Madame Sans-Nom (without name)". Such oddities are not exceptional under the Doctor's roof.

Among the patients he takes in are raving, murderous madmen brought down river by native police or warriors from inland tribes; there are also occasional victims of fearful accidents which sometimes occur during mining and road-making works going on in the interior. Animals and men are sometimes brought to him suffering from strange wounds which suggest that the witch-doctor has been busy with them. And some of the native Africans who work for him in the hospital know that they do so at the risk of their lives. If their superstitious fellow tribesmen regard them as having been contaminated by the white man's *juju*, they will certainly be put to death when they return home. It is a risk few Africans will take, and an indication that Schweitzer's fifty-one years of dedication have made a slighter impression on the peoples he has given his life to save than on the world he has turned his back towards.

At first sight, however, Dr. Schweitzer's "primitives" seem peculiarly uncolourful; they are obviously at home in European clothes and with Western customs, and the visitor's first encounter with them is likely to be disappointing. He will come through the customs and immigration departments of the Gabonese administration at the airfield (one large, quietly mannered African when I was there). His baggage will appear for the first time since leaving his place of departure, covered with sand-coloured labels of U.T.A. and looking suddenly sophisticated among the crates of livestock and merchandise off-loaded from the plane that brought him. If bareheaded, he may get a foretaste of the danger, which Dr. Schweitzer never underestimates, of sunstroke from the piercing rays of this equatorial blaze, making him glad to stay in the shade of the corrugated iron roofed buildings of the airport. Meanwhile, he will notice, in contrast to his noisy plane trip across the jungles, the sudden quiet in which only occasional native voices shout slumbrously to each other. Outside a Land-Rover is being slowly loaded by one or two young men in khaki shorts, and he will be told that this will take him as far as the ferry, where he can either go on to Lambaréné town, spread along the opposite bank of the Ogowe, or make his rendezvous with the hospital's canoe.

The *pirogue* is a dug-out canoe, presumably carved out of the trunk of a single tree. It has blunt ends and shallow draught, but when controlled by four skilled paddlers makes an efficient, though slow, craft. While aboard, during the forty or so minutes which the voyage up-river to the hospital takes, the visitor may wonder why his transportation is so slow and antiquated when the river is teaming with motor-boats of all shapes and sizes. This, of course, is an idiosyncracy of the Doctor's; the funds to meet the added cost of such transport have been donated by his benefactors many times over with precisely this purpose in mind. But what was good enough for Schweitzer and his wife fifty-one years ago is good enough for his staff and visitors today. This is his attitude, and it is another example of his stubborn refusal to treat with the times. In fact, when presented with a brand new engine and boat by the Evinrude Company of the U.S. recently, he promptly gave it away.

Nevertheless, the slow journey has its interest. Provided the sun is not unleashing its maximum ferocity, the visitor can idle the time away studying the jungle flora (fauna is harder to come by, and he must be persistent and far-seeking if he hopes to encounter any of the terrors of the bush, i.e. crocodiles, hippos and snakes). He can also observe the four "rowers" as the paddlers are called by Schweitzer's helpers, seeing them bend their backs to force their blades against the strong current. These men wear ragged, faded khaki. They have grubby bandages round their feet, and ugly gaps show where leprosy has claimed more than one of their toes and fingers. If acutely sensitive, the visitor may feel a slight prickling of the skin at the base of his skull remembering how he cheerfully shook hands with the native who greeted him, and how the others had taken his baggage in their incapacitated hands to load it into the boat. He has yet to learn that leprosy today is no longer one of the most serious scourges of the jungle, such as sleeping sickness, venereal disease and tuberculosis, but can be cured or at least arrested and held in a harmlessly negative condition by a new drug. These men, bending to their paddles, are no more contagious than a fellow commuter on a suburban line in Britain or America would be.

As they paddle, they talk. Their voices are low and vibrant, carrying for long distances across the placid surface of the river. Another canoe might approach and, before it is near enough for the visitor to distinguish the features of the people inside, the paddlers will be conversing, having opened conversation with the conventional greeting of that part of Africa: "*bolo*" or hallo. A chorus of deeply felt grunts will be heard from both boats whenever somebody makes a particularly strong statement. During the more intense of these exchanges paddling will stop while the listeners pay strict attention. Then, with a deep, melodious "Ooooh" or "Aaah" they will slice the blades back into the water and proceed.

Thus it is that one comes to Lambaréné, a clearing of the jungle seen on rounding a headland some half a mile away and slowly expanding and taking detailed shape as the canoe approaches. At first, it seems small, but this is an illusion. In fact the river frontage extends for well over 100 yards at the main part and is linked to other developments of the Doctor's along the bank. For about the same distance, the clearing extends inland without interference from buildings, and with only a few shady trees covering the bareness of this forecourt. Then, somewhat huddled, the buildings which Dr. Schweitzer has largely built with his own hands begin to rise on brick piles and timbered stilts.

First seen is a long, large pharmacy building—the biggest single structure in Lambaréné—once nick-named by native patients "the tape worm". It is here that Dr. Schweitzer has his time-worn and insect riddled desk-table, and where he sits when daily prescribing methods of healing and diagnosing ailments. In this building, which spreads its width at the edge of the forecourt clearing, there are several of the hospital's most vital organs: the operating theatre (presented to Dr. Schweitzer by Prince Rainier of Monaco), the delivery room, X-ray chamber, laboratory recess, dispensary, dentist's chamber and main consulting rooms. From his wire-screened window, Dr. Schweitzer can see the arrival of any guest. Having done so, he takes off the muslin sleeves he wears to absorb perspiration from his forearms when writing, slips on a formal, black bow-tie, takes down his old sun-topi and walks out to greet him.

This first meeting is unforgettable. Schweitzer, growing deaf, walks bandy-legged towards his visitor, one hand cupping an ear to catch what is said in whatever language used and whether or not he understands it fully. He is accompanied by a smiling interpreter, probably Nurse Ali Silver, his trusted, English-speaking lieutenant, who smoothly effects the introduction while Schweitzer takes his visitor's hand in his own large fist and shakes it warmly. His skin is soft and pale. Age shows in the sagging lines of his body, white hair curls at the nape of his neck and the awkwardness with which he now moves shows at every step. Yet the eyes are bold and alert, seeming to tease while remaining serious at the same time. Nobody can meet Schweitzer without liking him, without responding to some instinctive respect and regard for this great individual. His power to disarm remains immense.

A cured leper takes hold of the visitor's bags and Nurse Ali soon escorts him to his quarters in one of the communal dormitory huts behind the "tape worm" and its surrounding wards. These sleeping quarters are ranged on the higher ground, so that they have an uninterrupted view of the whole vista spreading forward from the hospital, the forecourt and the river beyond.

What does the new arrival find? A simple, pleasant room similar in every piece of its furnishing and toilet equipment to those occupied by the nursing staff. But also a cleverly constructed and well-ventilated chamber, which may surprise him by its coolness and softly stirring air. The bed, or beds in the case of double cubicles, is of plain, black iron but the mattress and springing are not unyielding. There is a chair and table for his writing. On the latter stands an oil lamp with a wide green shade over its glass.

The room has only two solid, timbered walls. The others, at either end, are composed of frames covered by wire mesh through which the least breeze flows gently into and through the room, cooling and purifying it. On another table an enamel basin and jug provide washing facilities, though the water in the jug has a greenish-grey tinge and more than a trace of river mud in its depths. For drinking, a litre wine bottle of boiled water stands corked alongside. This too has a sediment of moss-like mud, but is presumably potable (I suffered no stomach problems during my stay). A soap dish, a tumbler and towels complete the toilet facilities.

Until he realizes that there is no familiar drain hole or lavatory

Does he imagine that the spiritual devotion of his flock would be suborned by such recreations? Or that light in the darkness of Lambaréné would frighten away his patients? It seems more probable that he has declined to install into his self-created hospital something which he alone would not be able to run; for which he would require the assistance of a skilled assistant, superior to him, at least, in the knowledge of electricity. In the world of Albert Schweitzer there is no room for such autocrats.

only between relatives, intimate friends, or when addressing children. Under the French colonial administration, use of the more polite "*vous*" rather than "*tu*" was enforced by legislation in French African states. Schweitzer has ignored such advancements.

"*Tu*, the singular and intimate form of *you* in French, had through long usage become a symbol for all that was distateful in the relations between European and African. It represented the social and psychological gulf between black and white. It became synonymous with an inferior position. It was like whistling your dog . . ." This description of the slur which Schweitzer's familiarity casts on the African was given some years ago by the American journal *The Saturday Review*, surprisingly in an article written by the magazine's editor, and Schweitzer's great admirer, Norman Cousins.

It is strange to reflect that Schweitzer, whose own childhood must have been microscopically small and who has since had little time for gaiety or relaxation, insists on seeing the majority of the people around him as little children. In the hospital, I watched him demonstrate the water pump to a visitor, demanding from an African woman waiting in the queue to fill buckets that she should give up her place in the line and bring him her bucket. He addressed her curtly, like a stern father, and "*tu'd*" her throughout. The woman showed typical African indifference, but plainly was not pleased.

In an early book Dr. Schweitzer wrote: "The Negro is a child, and with children nothing can be done without the use of authority. We must, therefore, so arrange the circumstances of our daily life that my authority can find expression. With regard to the Negroes, then, I have coined the formula: 'I am your brother, it is true, but your elder brother.' "* In the book's sequel, Schweitzer observed: ". . . inability to exert and adapt themselves to difficult circumstances is typical of the natives of Equatorial Africa, and makes them pitiable creatures . . . starving natives sit in their huts and wait for death just because it is famine time. One cannot say in

* *On the Edge of the Primeval Forest*

this country: 'Need stimulates invention.' It has to be: 'Need paralyses into idiocy.' "*

My next question to Dr. Schweitzer, as we sat knee to knee at his desk, was more general. Did he feel satisfied that he had accomplished what he had set out to do in his lifetime? Schweitzer shrugged and answered without any real feeling. "Yes. Because my work is to show Reverence for Life." But is it not true, I asked, that sometimes one must be cruel in order to be kind? As a greenfly must be killed to spare a rose, or a slug to save a vegetable, isn't it equally necessary to take life at different levels so that other forms of life more useful to us, indeed our own, may survive? Thoughtfully, Schweitzer replied to this: "The important thing is that man should be humane to all living things. He should never take the smallest life, say a fly on this table, without regret and compassion."

Such an attitude, which in present-day Europe and America and other civilized countries is almost unthinkable, is ostentatiously practised by Schweitzer. He delights in showing visitors his "pet ant" and begs them not to brush it off his sleeve, "for fear of breaking its leg". He has small, hinged hatches let into the screens of his main rooms at Lambaréné so that a mosquito, if caught under a tumbler, can be gently released without harm. He once found himself pitying the bacilli of sleeping sickness exposed under his microscope when a new drug had been discovered capable of destroying the disease.

Yet one man who knows and admires Schweitzer well, an American named Fergus Pope, told me of another side of the great humanitarian's character. Schweitzer, says Pope, will knock the brains out of litters of kittens and puppies at the river edge rather than see the hospital over-run. He boots the backside of a rooster when it comes to steal the corn he puts down for his pet hens. These actions compare strangely with the saving of a dangerous mosquito or a fever bacillus. Reverence for Life appears to have its boundaries, like other panaceas.

We turned to the problems of the world he barely knows at first

* *More From the Primeval Forest*

hand, the world of space travel and the Russian launching pads, of air conditioning and miracle drugs. Why did Britain, he asked, tie herself to the warlike defence policy of the United States? Was it not plain to us that American intentions were more dangerous even than the Russians today, refusing as they persistently do to put a brake on atomic tests? No, I told him, this was not understood to be so in my country. In fact, we had come round to the somewhat grudging acceptance of America as our protector and, especially since the Cuban crisis, to rely on her might, knowing our own weakness. To turn the question, I explained that few great thinkers, other than Bertrand Russell, had tried to lead us away from reliance on the biggest Nuclear Brother, and Dr. Schweitzer himself had been remarkably silent. Why had his voice been so little heard?

As Schweitzer talks, he uses a curious form of physical code, emphasizing points by gripping his listener's arm and pinching it lightly, or nudging him in the ribs. His deeply-rutted face mirrors his feelings, changing rapidly from complete indifference to the most lively and passionate interest in a topic. The eyes are paramount, and their signals can be understood even though one knows no word of German. When the Doctor quotes other people's comments, he smiles jocularly, with the clear implication that he doubts the value of what he is saying. When he disbelieves entirely, he winks. In our meetings each wink was forced on my attention by a pinch, or a nudge. The effect was rather as, back in my childhood, I was forced to sit on the lap of some bibulous uncle and react to his pleasantries. However, it certainly was not dull.

Now, because my suggestion that he avoids the fray had provoked him, Schweitzer gripped my arm tightly. "It does no good to talk too much," he said. "Nobody will then listen to you. I have one thing more to say but I have not yet decided when to say it. I must find the right occasion."

The code signals were working. To stress his own convictions, Schweitzer leaned back, closed his eyes, and nodded and swayed in time with the rhythms of his strong, guttural voice. I realized that he was completely serious about his decision to make one more—perhaps final—statement to the world; that he believes it to be of deep significance. I said that man in the West no longer feels free to choose his own destiny. Schweitzer opened his eyes and bent towards me: "Then he is doomed," he said harshly. "The answer is in himself, and he *must* develop more humanity. Each individual has to stand on his own feet in this matter."

I suggested that, in real terms, we could only say that so far the nuclear bomb had shortened the Japanese war, thereby saving lives. He said with great sincerity: "Shall I tell you what really happened? Truman wanted to use his bomb, not to end the Japanese war but to show Russia that he had it. The scientists were against its use; they were horrified, but powerless. The allies were told, not consulted." He looked me deeply in the eye for a moment, then added: "Einstein was a friend of mine. I know!"

So how, I asked, could his philosophy hope to succeed in an increasingly material world? He replied softly: "If everyone will turn to humanity and to humane thoughts, it will succeed. Just as Christ's teachings succeeded after his death."

After a general discussion on his theological research which I propose to mention later in this book, the conversation came back to the nuclear age. I asked: "Does Germany have the bomb?" It was, on the surface at least, a naïve question since I knew well that Germany does not possess nuclear weapons. Yet from one or two of the Doctor's observations I had gained the impression that he either has some special sources of information denied the rest of us, or is misled on a number of more worldly subjects such as this. His reply was startling. "She has small bombs," he said, "though nothing much yet." But wasn't Germany's control of atomic weapons limited to their carefully prescribed use under NATO? Dr. Schweitzer made no mention of this. I asked whether he believed that Germany was surreptitiously financing France's nuclear development in the hope of becoming her partner in the nuclear "club". The Doctor said: "Not now. The cost is too high. Where it used to take 40 per cent of a nation's wealth to join the nuclear 'club', now it can take 60 per cent. And before you have completed tests on your own weapon, it is already obsolete."

At this point in our discussion Dr. Schweitzer astonished me with a statement about the Polaris missile, promised to the British by the Americans at the Nassau conference and not due for operational service in British atomic submarines until 1965 or 1966. "You will see," said Albert Schweitzer, "Polaris is about to become obsolete. It will come as a great shock to the British."

Was there any weight behind this disturbing assertion? Does Schweitzer, who seemed throughout our talk to be stressing the more humane and generally worthy cause of Soviet Russia in comparison with the West ("warlike", "dangerous", etc.) receive information from iron-curtain sources which have given him this impression about the short-term value of Polaris? This question was to bother me for a long time after I had left Lambaréné.

Meanwhile, we turned to the issue of radiation and the problems of our increasingly polluted atmosphere. I knew in advance that Dr. Schweitzer felt extraordinarily strongly about the menace of this, having been told at the hospital that he had already found evidence that radiation has affected the soil of his vegetable garden. The Doctor, I was told, also believes that equatorial sunshine is becoming more dangerous as a result of recent atomic tests. He told me: "The reassuring statistics being put out by scientists and government departments are all big lies. The effect of the pollution is already being felt in the number of miscarriages. And still the doctors have no idea what the damage will be to the third and fourth generations."

With increasing severity, Schweitzer pursued his dismal line of thought: "When two radio-active people marry," he said, "the results, if they have children, can be very bad." I ventured a comment that, as the pollution situation was so gloomy, the question of whether or not we used the bomb might well be academic. Schweitzer nodded to agree. "Yes," he said, "but we must return to humanity, sanity and the destruction of the bomb first, before we try to cure the other thing." For Britain, he added with crusading zeal, "The important first step is to break off your defence ties with the U.S.A. Only by doing so can you stop the nuclear weapons being dumped on you. When you are free of these, then perhaps you can recover your individual rights and your common humanity."

Before we got up from our seats, Schweitzer from his soft couch of foam rubber and I from the hardest stool I have ever had to sit on for over two hours, Dr. Schweitzer gave me a word of advice about the writing of this book. "Write your book," he said, "but be prepared to go to prison. In this I am very serious. Those who believe in ethics, like Russell whom I know well, are never popular. They will be hounded." I took this dire injunction as a compliment from the man who has opposed so many conventional theories, though never to the point where he would be likely to be imprisoned for expressing his opinion himself.

Quite the opposite; after Churchill and Eisenhower, Schweitzer probably holds more honorary degrees and the freedom of more towns and cities than any man alive. He has won the Nobel Peace Prize and been admitted into Britain's distinguished Order of Merit, in which he, Eisenhower and President Sarvepall Radhakrishan of India are the only non-British members. Before he was forty he was already a triple doctor: of philosophy, theology and medicine. As a non-conformer, he is remarkable for having carried the conformers with him while scaling their most select peaks.

As a figure of controversy, in fact, he seems to have been swallowed up long since. Nor has he done anything to discourage the world from accepting him, complete with rebel doctrines. In February 1922, when he came to Britain to deliver the Dale lectures in French at Mansfield College, Oxford, and to give a series of Bach recitals at Carr's Lane Chapel, Birmingham, Schweitzer lectured on the gospel of Jesus in the light of history. He did this at Selly Oak College, Birmingham, and as a result of what he said was heralded as a dynamic rebel in theological thinking. His book *Quest for the Historical Jesus*, which had appeared in 1906 was dug out and re-investigated; so, too, was the criticism of his work included in Dr. Sanday's *The Life of Christ in Recent Research*, which had appeared the following year.

The result of this interest was that the young and handsome jungle Doctor was raised in most European minds to the level of a self-sacrificing martyr who had found in conventional, civilized life only exasperation. For this reason, it was assumed, he had gone to Lambaréné to shut himself away from this distasteful world, to work out his example of unfettered living.

But some proved less easy to please. Sandays had said in praise of his book on Jesus: "It is the most striking work of its kind I have read for some time. The author is young but, if he has something of a weakness he also has in full degree the strength of youth. He knows that he is one-sided, but he glories in his one-sidedness." While it was said that some English scholars like Professor F. C. Birkett of Cambridge were "disposed to go a long way with Schweitzer", others "regarded the whole thing as a trick". The most damning and withering denunciation of the Schweitzer theory came from the Dean of St. Paul's. But however churchmen felt about his Christian radicalism, Schweitzer was too many-sided to allow for complete excoriation. His book in French on Bach, published ahead of the religious bombshell in 1905, was described by no less a critic than Ernest Newman as taking "a leading place". By others it was termed "an indispensable musical classic". It is interesting to read a contemporary report of his visit to Britain and to gather from it the impression which this complex "rebel" created at that time:

"The most romantic figure in this country at the moment," wrote a reporter on March 3 1922, "is the tall, strongly built, and genial Alsatian professor, Dr. Albert Schweitzer. Here is a man who, ten years ago, had already won his way to one of the foremost positions as a leader of progressive thought in the theological world . . . who was not only the great authority and the standard biographer of Bach . . . but the foremost organist and organ builder in Europe; yet who nevertheless decided to throw everything up and study for a medical degree so that he could offer himself as a hospital doctor to one of the most neglected parts of the world. This most modest of men . . . is only concerned with easing the bodily and spiritual ills of humanity and will not talk about his great achievements. He just says: 'I am . . . a poor, small negro doctor . . .' When asked why such an advanced thinker should devote himself to missionary work, he replied 'that no one touched by the spirit of God could fail to be moved to spread his message'."

Six days later, Schweitzer played to delighted crowds in Westminster Abbey and received an equally moving tribute from another columnist: "How petty the lives of most of us seem, in comparison with the noble labours of a great musician who, giving up culture and ease, lives a desolate and lonely life among the suffering . . ." As Schweitzer collected funds to return to Lambaréné from his recital in the Abbey, and also from a recital in the cathedral at Oxford, such praise must have pleased him well. It was hardly true that he was leading a "desolate and lonely" life, if his own autobiographical books are to be believed. Lambaréné and his hospital there had already grown, under his hand, to a sizable institution with no shortage of human beings in attendance. Mme. Schweitzer was at his side, whenever her constantly recurring bouts of sickness allowed her to spend time in the equatorial climate. Schweitzer was beginning to gather the nucleus of his astonishing team of helpers, the "Schweitzerines". Convention may have been stung by his early scholarship; it rallied now to the cause of the "poor, small negro doctor" who did so much to ease the conscience of an age consumed by self indulgence.

FIVE

BEGINNINGS

A MINOR but curious mystery is Albert Schweitzer's reluctance to communicate in English. Until 1926 he had more than once set himself to learn the language; but in January of that year the news came, unhappily, to his numerous British admirers that he had given up his pursuit of their tongue. An epidemic of dysentery, persistent theft of the timber needed for building by natives (never to be trusted!) and sheer, physical exhaustion in the stultifying heat of Lambaréné had worn down even the Doctor's perseverance. "I have been so tired that for a long time I have had again to abandon my studies in English," he wrote to a friend in Basle. There is no indication that he ever again took them up.

A man of his gifts and achievements can be pardoned this lapse. What is less easy to pass over is the belief that he can and does understand English; can read and write it passably; and is able to speak it well enough for ordinary purposes.

Perhaps something in his eyes as we talked, or more probably the impatience with which he occasionally answered my questions ahead of their translation by Nurse Ali, began this suspicion for me. It grew when one of the staff, an American, told me he felt sure the Doctor could read and write adequately, and understand more than a modicum of English. If this is the case, then it is worth noting that he hides the fact. There are only two likely reasons for this, both of them significant:

1. Dr. Schweitzer does not care for the English tongue, has a reluctance to talk to English and Americans in their language, and is not altogether at ease in their company.

2. He will use no means of communication which puts him at the slightest disadvantage.

The former is so unlikely as to be ludicrous. Dr. Schweitzer received his earliest and most important recognition from both Oxford and Cambridge, to which he pays tribute in his writings. "To my astonishment," he says, "my work (Schweitzer is referring to the publication of his controversial religious study *The Quest of the Historical Jesus*) at once met with recognition in England."* There were also his many English friends and helpers, among them Mrs. C. B. E. Russell, his friend, interpreter and helper, and Miss Margaret Deneke, Honorary Fellow and Choirmaster of Lady Margaret Hall in Oxford. Another was Dr. Agnes Maude Royden, a social worker and preacher who appears to have brought her whole church, the Guild House in London, to his support. Mrs. Clara Urquhart, a South African friend, told me before I went to Lambaréné: "He has a great love of England."

If the second is true, then it is curiously in keeping with the theme of his unorthodox career. It is also important to our analysis. Schweitzer has never sought a secondary position in the world; service, in his eyes, should be to a higher being, not to an individual man. At his most revealing in this connection, the Doctor wrote in his autobiography: "While I was concerned with tramps and discharged prisoners it had become clear to me that they could only be effectively helped by a number of individuals who would devote themselves to them. At the same time, however, I had realized that in many cases these could only accomplish their best work in collaboration with organizations. *But what I wanted was an absolutely personal and independent activity*."* (My italics.)

To work as one of a team, or under someone else's direction, has never appealed to him. He admits, indeed jokes about, this shortcoming. "I am a benign dictator," he says. It is certainly true that his reputation for humility disappears rapidly as one sees him at work in the hospital, booting the behinds of lazy Africans and exercising his control over the discipline of staff and patients. Again, in his life story, Dr. Schweitzer says: "Although I was resolved

* *My Life and Thought*

to put my services at the disposal of some organization, if it should be really necessary, I nevertheless never gave up hope of finding a sphere of activity to which I could devote myself as an individual and as wholly free. That this longing of mine found fulfilment I have always regarded as a signal of the mercy which has again and again been vouchsafed to me."*

Was this, then, the fundamental reason that brought Albert Schweitzer to Africa? Is his mission as much a setting up of a personal despotism as a compulsion to help and to heal poverty-stricken Africans? These are questions which demand close study of those early days before he stepped on to the steamer at Bordeaux to change the lives of so many people.

We know of his birth, at the Alsatian village of Kayersberg on January 14 1875, and of his removal at the age of approximately six months to Günsbach to be brought up, so he says, happily there—an experience which seems to distinguish him from the majority of the world's illuminati—among three sisters and a brother. We know too that his father was a simple village pastor, as was his mother's father; though the latter, Pastor Schillinger, had become better known. As both of Albert Schweitzer's grandfathers and some of his great-uncles were talented organists it was natural for him to inherit a love of playing and building this mournful instrument. Indeed, he was intensely musical and scholarly in his outlook. From the age of three, when most children are learning to say their prayers at their mother's knees, he was a regular worshipper at the local village church, and at least one writer has said that "he looked forward to this all week".**

Religious fascination persisted, and with it grew up a strange delight in self-punishment. Schweitzer notes that: "The strict discipline under which I came in the house of my great-uncle and his wife, who had no children of their own, was very good for me." He had by then entered the Gymnasium—a form of superior grammar school—at Mülhausen in Alsace and the great-uncle he refers to was also his godfather, Louis Schweitzer, who had offered the boy a home during his schooling. The effects of this domestic

* *My Life and Thought*
** *Dr. Schweitzer O.M.* by Nina Langley

austerity on a serious-minded and religiously brought up lad of ten can be imagined. It is no surprise to learn from his journal that he started his major school career "a poor scholar".

Late in his time at this school, as a youth of sixteen, Schweitzer suffered an extraordinary experience. He was allowed to visit a theatre for the first time in order to hear Wagner's militant, bombastic *Tannhauser*. The music that later inspired the Kaiser's and Adolf Hitler's goose-stepping soldiers made a thunderous impact on the young man sitting alone in the stalls. "This music overpowered me to such an extent," he wrote, "that it was days before I was capable of giving proper attention to the lessons in school."*

Soon afterwards, in June 1893, Schweitzer passed his leaving examination with surprisingly poor results. "I did not cut a brilliant figure, not even in the essay," he records of the written papers; though in the *viva voce* or spoken subjects his fluency and charm won top honours. He received an "Excellent" in history and four months later we see him as a student at Strasbourg University, living in the theological College, immersed in the pursuit of Philosophy and Theology. The following April he broke off to serve his one year's national service in the army, taking a Greek Testament with him on manoeuvres in his haversack. The stolen moments of study between mock battles and bivouacs were rewarded when he was awarded a scholarship. In one way, too, the drudgery of military service proved helpful, in that the University reduced the number of papers to be written from three to only one in the case of those students whose studies had been thus interrupted. Schweitzer was able to concentrate exclusively on his Testament, on his research into the Synoptic Gospels, and on the commentary upon them written by his university lecturer and professor, Heinrich Julius Holtzmann. Their study led him to a revelation.

Until then, young Schweitzer had been an obedient follower of established Christian views. Now, abruptly, he felt himself dazzled by a light of inner understanding which left him bewildered. "When I reached home after the manoeuvres," he wrote in his memoirs,

* *My Life and Thought*

"entirely new horizons had opened themselves to me. Of this I was certain: Jesus had announced no kingdom that was to be founded and realized in the natural world by Himself and the believers, but one that was to be expected as coming with the almost immediate dawn of a supernatural age."*

In music, another event of great significance was occurring almost simultaneously in his life. The Parisian organist, Charles Marie Widor, had accepted him as a pupil, a favour usually reserved for the Organ Class at the Conservatoire. Schweitzer, perfectly suited physically to the control of the instrument, impressed the master with his careful playing and obvious dedication. Says Schweitzer: "This instruction was for me an event of decisive importance."

Thus, we see the young scholar rounding two significant corners in his early life; finding himself in controversy with the established theological convictions of his day, and being taken up by a music-teacher of extreme brilliance whose influence on his technique, the "plasticity" of his development, was to be profound.

Germinating at the same time, so he reveals in his autobiographical writings, was a first stirring of conscience. It bothered him that he should be so fortunately blessed with this richness of opportunity. "While at the university and enjoying the happiness of being able to study and even to produce some results in science and art, I could not help thinking continually of others who were denied that happiness by their material circumstances or their health," he recalls.*

But dissatisfaction with the human condition had to wait. For the time, Schweitzer was fully extended in wrestling with his radical theories about the history of Christ and the Bible story. He disagreed fundamentally that St. Mark was the only apostle whose writings could be taken as a true report on the behaviour of Christ; he felt strongly that all contemporary explanations of the Last Supper were "unsatisfactory". He was emerging as a rebel, backed by a humble mien that ably disguised a surprisingly tough and obstinate nature. This was the young man who wrote his first theological examination in 1898: so brilliantly that he was given a

* *My Life and Thought*

scholarship worth sixty pounds a year for six years, on only one proviso: that he should take the degree of Licentiate in Theology at Strasbourg within that period of time or repay the money.

One might think that such an undertaking would be enough to distract a student from continuing any other studies; but Schweitzer decided to, as he says, "take in hand" the achievement of a Doctorate in Philosophy, at the same time moving to Paris so as to attend the Sorbonne University. The subject he chose for his dissertation was wisely connected to the theme of religion, the Religious Philosophy of Kant; a large enough canvas, it might be supposed, but still insufficient for his gigantic academic appetite. He kept at his organ-playing under Widor at the same time.

Ironically, today Schweitzer is a Frenchman, no doubt travelling under a French passport on his visits to the world outside Lambaréné. Ironically, because he detested the Sorbonne; found nothing in the French teaching or examination methods to compare with those of Germany. "I did not attend many lectures in Paris," he wrote. "To begin with, the unceremonious way in which the matriculation ceremony was conducted, put me out of tune. Then the antiquated method of instruction, which made it impossible for the teaching power, that was, much of it, of such outstanding quality, to give out its best, contributed its share towards making the Sorbonne distasteful to me."*

The time, none the less, was not wasted. Widor introduced his pupil to a galaxy of intellectuals and important people; he also saw to it that Schweitzer did not starve on what the Doctor calls "the slenderness of my purse" by dining him regularly at his favourite eating-place, the Restaurant Foyot near the Luxembourg. There were two brothers of Schweitzer's father's in Paris whose families entertained and made him welcome. "Thus," he writes, "I was able to feel myself quite at home in Paris." Nevertheless, he has never been able to recall those years of toil and social contact with anything approaching pleasure.

He did, however, make a remarkable discovery about himself at this time—that he needed practically no sleep. "My good health

* *My Life and Thought*

allowed me to be prodigal with night work," he observed. "It happened sometimes that I played to Widor in the morning without having been to bed at all."* This asset has been of enormous use, giving him the power of working long into the night at Lambaréné while his staff sleep exhausted in their beds. He was once asked if it is wise to burn the candle at both ends in this way. Schweitzer's reply was: "Yes, if the candle is long enough." Thus he was able as he says, to continue his thesis for the Doctorate, keep up his art and still enjoy the pleasures of society. It was a formidable design, but not without pitfalls.

From Paris, Schweitzer moved to Berlin where, as might have been expected, "The intellectual life . . . made a much greater impression on me than did that of Paris. Moreover, the town . . . had an air of healthy self-consciousness and of confident faith in the leaders of its destinies . . ."* Fifteen years later these same leaders were to rend Europe and the world in twain. But there was no hint of this yet. Schweitzer found himself moving easily and freely among the more interesting families of the city and enjoying society life to the full. He has never blamed this distraction for what came after—the near "ploughing" he took in the second examination for his Doctorate of Theology.

Not only that, when he had returned to Strasbourg, with only five months of the nineteenth century still to run, Schweitzer had disappointed his examiners during the *viva voce* for his degree in philosophy. "I fell . . ." he admits, "below the level of what my dissertation had led them to expect from me . . . I had neglected the text books too much."* But it was the theology examination which nearly unseated him, especially as he had followed his own line of research, ignoring the more general aspects of the subject. "It told especially against me," he wrote later, "that I did not know enough about the hymn writers and their lives. My many misfortunes came to a head when I tried to excuse my ignorance as to the authorship of one particular hymn—it was by Spitta, the famous poet of *Psalter and Harp*—by saying I thought the hymn too insignificant for me to notice who had composed it."* Such

* *My Life and Thought*

an arbitrary and high-handed attitude was not wholly welcomed by a board of distinguished academics and theologians (including, it is worth noting, Spitta's son!), even in Berlin at the turn of the century.

However, Schweitzer's unique talents were not even temporarily overlooked and he emerged from these encounters with two doctorates to his name and the post of assistant to the two elderly ministers of the Church of St. Nicholas, where he had been preaching and acting as Deacon during his studies. While in this service, he had time to continue working at both his music and his academic studies, going to Paris each spring to keep up his studies with Widor.

What followed was a direct extension of his complex and individual pattern of scholarship. Schweitzer pressed ahead with his own research into the problems of the life of Jesus and embarked on a far closer inspection of the whole understanding of primitive Christianity. The Last Supper, in its origin and significance as a fundamental rite of the Church, quickly became a watershed for his ideas. He planned a book which would involve three separate studies of the subject: firstly, his attitude to all previous convictions and research; then a portrait of Jesus in relation to the Supper; and finally an analysis of the manner in which the occasion was adapted into the Primitive Church and during the first two centuries of Christianity. But at this point the pressures of his many roles began to take control of his existence.

The first part of the book was completed, and won for its author the degree of Licentiate in Theology before being published as a sixty-two page booklet in 1901. The second was also worked into shape sufficiently to earn him a professorship as *Privat-dozent* in philosophy at the University. This, too, was published as a slender volume and later translated into English to be published in both America and Britain during 1925. The third section, dealing with the growth of the Last Supper and Baptism in the Early Church, was to have been taken into a companion volume to *The Quest of the Historical Jesus*. However, greater events pushed this plan aside. Albert Schweitzer, devoured by equally consuming interests in philosophy, theology and music, put down his pen to study medicine and escape into the jungles of Africa.

It is not surprising that he felt the call of a simpler form of life. In the crowded months which had succeeded his many graduations he had balanced like a circus rider on the backs of at least three galloping horses. The mental departmentalism thus involved was phenomenal. Aside from the theological works already mentioned, he had written a scholarly study of Bach and began what has been called his greatest work (yet how many have read it?) *The Philosophy of Civilization.* There were, not astonishingly, signs that his swift rise to the seats of power would not go unchallenged.

The storm broke in March 1902 when, having given his inaugural lecture to the Theological Faculty at Strasbourg on the Logos doctrine of the Fourth Gospel, Schweitzer found that indignant protests had been lodged against his acceptance as a University Lecturer. Two members of the Faculty said that they disapproved of his method of historical investigation, and were anxious that he should not be allowed "to confuse the students". For the first time in his career, Schweitzer was under fire for holding radical theories; it can be assumed that he did not enjoy the situation.

Nevertheless, his wounds from this attack turned out to be slight, since Professor Holtzmann supported him and silenced the angry critics. When the Principalship of the Theological College fell vacant in the summer of 1903, Schweitzer was appointed to fill it. Writing later about this period of his life, and about the two books on Jesus which were already causing a major stir in theological circles throughout the world, he says: "The satisfaction which I could not help feeling at having solved so many historical riddles about the existence of Jesus was accompanied by the painful consciousness that this new knowledge in the realm of history would mean unrest and difficulty for Christian piety."*

It seems that satisfaction, and not painful consciousness, was more often the fruit of Schweitzer's victories over his contemporaries. Where his ideas triumphed, he felt gratified. Where they met with resistance, as during the examination which had disclosed

* *My Life and Thought*

his lack of knowledge of the hymn author, he was stubbornly put out. His reasons for forsaking the high and dignified positions he had attained have never been argued. It is his own version—that he wanted to repay humanity for his gifts and privileges—that has come to be accepted. Against it should be put the knowledge we get from a close inspection of his early life and the point it was approaching.

Schweitzer, in the first half decade of the twentieth century, was sailing a collision course. He had already crossed the lanes of established thinking with his revolutionary views on Jesus and the birth of Christianity. He might have continued his work and grown into one of the most distinguished leaders of radical thought in the Western world, but it would have been through unremitting struggle against a growing number of opponents. A tolerant man could have seen in this approaching fight a satisfying test of his ideas and convictions; but could Schweitzer? He is arbitrary enough to resent such challenges to his authority.

As a result, there is support for the view that his reason for going to Lambaréné was not wholly positive, a search for a selfless life among the poor jungle primitives of Africa. It may have been an escape from pressures which had begun to make it difficult for the Doctor to continue his dazzling triumphs in the academic world. At first, he says, he planned to go to Africa at most for two years, then to return to his living as a professor and author of learned books. This plan was destroyed by the war of 1914-18. Instead of two years, Schweitzer was away for four and a half. Where he had hoped to return stronger in mind and body, he came home tired and ill. "Moreover," he says, "(I was) deprived of my means of existence."

Such risks might have been known in advance, one thinks. In which case, why did Schweitzer choose Africa—and the most uncongenial part of that continent—for his retreat, rather than some place of work nearer home? He had already measured the value of humane work in Germany, among the tramps and discharged prisoners of his parish. The duty was a torture. He hated to beg, and part of the needs of the service was a bi-annual importuning of some of the richer residents of Strasbourg. Also, Schweitzer soon discovered that here was no regiment in need of a leader, but a group of anonymous, dedicated altruists who worked together, as equals. The lack of efficiency which this involved irked him, and he turned to a search for something more satisfying.

It was, so he says, one autumn morning in 1904 when he happened to notice an article, "The Needs of the Congo Mission", in a magazine put out by the Paris Missionary Society. He had glanced at it almost by chance, in the act of putting the journal to one side. The writer, Alfred Boegner, the President of the Society and an Alsatian, complained that the Mission was short of workers in the Gaboon, then the northern province of the Congo Colony. He particularly stressed that some of those "on whom the Master's eyes have rested" would do well to rally to the cause. He could not have chosen a designation more likely to appeal to the man who was reading his words. Albert Schweitzer recalls: "The article finished, I quietly began my work. My search was over."

SIX

MASTER BUILDER

NINE YEARS before Europe was brought to war by his Kaiser, Dr. Schweitzer astonished the academic world of Germany by resigning his teaching post at the University and his position at St. Nicholas's to prepare himself for medical service in Africa. It was the autumn of 1905. He was thirty years of age, and was to spend seven years becoming a physician and surgeon. In that time, he met the woman he was to marry on June 18 1912, Hélène Bresslau, the daughter of the Strasbourg historian. Yet we hear nothing of their courtship from Schweitzer himself, only a brief bulletin to the effect that "My wife, who had already before our marriage been a valuable collaborator in the completion of manuscripts and correction of proofs, was a great help again with all the literary work which had to be got through before we started for Africa."*

It would be comforting to believe that somewhere inside the superbly efficient skull of philosopher-theologian-musician, and now trainee-doctor, Schweitzer there was love as well as gratitude for the helpful companion who was to share, and endure, so many of the privations, with so few of the prizes, at Lambaréné. In the same spring, however, he spent most of his time in Paris studying tropical medicine and gathering stores for his coming journey. Presumably Hélène stayed at her father's house in Strasbourg, making her own preparations.

Where and how their wedding took place is not explained in Dr. Schweitzer's books. His writings later, as were his thoughts at the time, seem to have been taken up with the importance of his mission, his work and the various tasks he himself had to accomplish,

* *My Life and Thought*

at great personal cost, in order to fit himself for his astonishing self-exile. Walking with his examiner, a surgeon named Madelung, after his finals, Schweitzer recalls with curious emphasis: "I had to assure myself that I was really awake and not dreaming. Madelung's voice seemed to come from some distant sphere when he said more than once, as we walked along together, 'It is only because you have such excellent health that you have got through a job like that.' "*

Schweitzer's health, indeed, was excellent but unfortunately Hélène's was not. From the day in 1913 when they both arrived at Lambaréné until her death on June 1 1957 her story is one of continual breakdowns; of her repeated comings and goings for the sake of her health. When she had nobly helped him to pack and screw down the seventy packing cases which contained the supplies needed to start the Schweitzer hospital, she complained about the weight of gold pieces—2,000 marks—which the Doctor insisted on taking in place of paper money. Schweitzer told her that this was an insurance against the threat of war, about which he had been given warnings by German diplomats he mingled with in the social world of Paris. He proved to have been unusually astute, as both the Doctor and his wife were soon stranded and under guard by French colonial soldiers. This happened just as an exhausted Mme. Schweitzer was planning her return to Europe. Instead, she was faced with inactivity (the Doctor was at first refused permission to operate his hospital) and the dismal prospect of staying in the fierce heat of the tropics for an unforeseeable time.

At the approach of the rainy season in 1916, Mme. Schweitzer became ill. Her husband took her to the coast, out of the damp and stifling air of Lambaréné, and there she temporarily recovered; but the climate was obviously a living terror for her. It came more as a relief than a sentence when the Schweitzers were ordered to be deported as prisoners of war and sent to a camp in Europe. The gold was surreptitiously exchanged for paper money, which they sewed into their clothing, and they were put aboard a ship for France. Now it was Dr. Schweitzer's turn to be ill. He went

* *My Life and Thought*

down with dysentery while his wife was plainly so pleased to be back in a temperate climate that she did not at first appear to be affected.

In Provence, however, where the pair were imprisoned at St. Rémy, Mme. Schweitzer's health again declined due to the chill winds of the neighbourhood. Their release came in time to save her from a breakdown and she was re-united in Switzerland with her parents. Soon afterwards, she rejoined Schweitzer in Günsbach to nurse him—though no word of appreciation for this appears in his books—through a severe and painful aftermath to his illness, subsequently requiring two operations.

Schweitzer recovered from these, but remained strangely tired and depressed. He was given a job as a doctor at the Municipal Hospital, Strasbourg, looking after two wards of women skin-disease sufferers. He was also appointed curate of St. Nicholas's once again. But at Christmas, 1919, when he was invited to lecture at Sweden's University of Uppsala, he was again dejected. "In learned circles," he wrote, "I could have believed myself entirely forgotten but for the affection and kindness shown to me by the theological faculties at Zürich and Berne."* It was fortunate that the lecture invitation came when it did, for the pure air of Uppsala and the welcome he received in Sweden were sufficient to recharge his phenomenal batteries.

It was in Sweden, too, that Schweitzer decided to return to Lambaréné instead of going back to his work as a teacher. Through lectures and organ concerts he was now able to raise funds for his hospital. Yet, in at least one connection, it was a surprising decision. For his wife was nursing a baby daughter, their first and only child, Rhena. The baby had been born on his own birthday, January 14. The first reference Schweitzer makes to her in his autobiographical books is when he describes how, in 1921, he resigned his two posts at Strasbourg to live by his pen and his playing at his father's vicarage at Günsbach. Even then, there is no mention of his feelings as a father, his pride in having a child, or his hopes and fears for its future. He may have regretted that his child was not a son.

The decision to return was certainly more costly for Hélène

* *My Life and Thought*

Schweitzer than for her husband. He wrote later, in somewhat stilted admiration: "When we left Sweden my wife was ready for the great sacrifice of consenting to my plan, although she would be unable to accompany me owing to the state of her health."* This bare epitaph marked the first of many partings.

By lecturing and giving organ recitals in Sweden, Switzerland, Denmark, Prague and England, Schweitzer succeeded in raising sufficient funds to keep himself in Africa and his family in Europe. When, on February 14 1924, the Doctor kissed his wife and daughter good-bye he was not alone. An eighteen year old Oxford student of Chemistry, Noel Gillespie, went with him as a helper; the first of many. If the parting with his baby daughter, now five years old, and his ailing wife caused pangs, we do not hear about them. All that the reticent Doctor allows himself to say in his books is: "My wife could not accompany me this time because of a break-down in her health. For the fact that she so far sacrificed herself as to acquiesce under these circumstances in my resumption of work at Lambaréné, I have never ceased to be grateful to her."** One wonders how many private griefs she kept from the strong-minded man she had married.

Schweitzer came back to a sight that would have spun lesser men on their heels and sent them packing off home again. In seven deserted years, the hospital which he and his wife had struggled to build had been smothered by the jungle. Only one, small, corrugated-iron hut and the skeleton of a large bamboo building remained standing. For the rest, he had to start again, working as a doctor in the mornings and as a "master builder" (his own term) in the afternoons. As the patients, however, increased in numbers, there was nothing for it but to expand. During the first two years of his return, Schweitzer sent to Europe for two doctors and two nurses.

The hospital slowly rose again. By the autumn of 1925 the main work of reconstruction was done. Young Gillespie, the Doctor's English volunteer helper, was of particular, and timely, service.

* *More From the Primeval Forest*
** *My Life and Thought*

Soon after he left, a famine devastated the whole country and an epidemic of dysentery struck with appalling force at the same time.

The dysentery epidemic brought a flood of sick natives to Schweitzer's hospital far larger than he was prepared to expect. At one time he was providing for 150 sick and suffering men, women and children. As the squalor of their over-crowded conditions increased, he realized that a larger site would be needed if the hospital was to be allowed to grow. The prospect of building afresh may not have been pleasant, but there was a compensating satisfaction in knowing that he would now be totally alone, in his own dominion. Also, nothing else could be done, as the present hospital was fast becoming a breeding ground of infection. He finally chose the site of the new hospital some two miles up the river from his original encampment.

Again, it was Schweitzer who took in hand the work of building. His two doctors, an Alsatian and a Swiss, carried on with the healing while for a year and a half the "master builder" struggled with the task of erecting the new hospital. "I was obliged to undertake this job myself," he writes, "because the ever-changing squad of 'volunteers' recruited from the attendants of the patients and from convalescents well enough to work, would acknowledge no authority save that of the 'old' Doctor."* It is noticeable that in referring to himself Schweitzer used a capital initial letter for "Doctor" while the assistants who came to his aid were reduced to humbler type.

Where did the funds come from to keep up the flow of drugs and supplies and equipment to the hospital? Primitive as it was, the consumption of materials was growing. Supplying them was the first duty of the "Schweitzerines", those self-sacrificing persons who have helped Schweitzer's cause from the beginning by working for him in their own lands. The original three were Mrs. Emmy Martin, later Dr. Schweitzer's secretary, the Rev. Hans Bauer, D.D. and Schweitzer's brother-in-law, the Rev. Albert Woytt. "Without the self-denying help of these and other volunteers the undertaking, now so much expanded, could not be carried on," Schweitzer

* *My Life and Thought*

himself wrote in one of his strictly-rationed pats on the back for those around him.

Meanwhile, his wife and daughter were living through the lonely years without him. He had intended to stay in Africa for two years, had no doubt promised Hélène and little Rhena that he would see them at the end of that time. In fact it was nearly three and a half years before he found the strength to leave Lambaréné; two months more before he was re-united with the long-suffering women whose lives belonged to him. It must have been a joyous meeting though Schweitzer, in his books, ignores it completely. Of his parting from Africa, he writes: ". . . there breaks through, time and again, a feeling of pain that I must leave it for a time, and tear myself loose from Africa, which has become for me a second home."*

We see this reluctance to leave Africa, even though his own flesh and blood are eagerly awaiting him in Europe, more clearly than ever when he records his last feelings at the ship's rail as the coast-line is erased by distance. Schweitzer travelled with two of his nurses, Mlle. Kottmann and Mlle. Lauterburg. They stood together on the boat-deck, barely stifling the emotion of sadness at going away. "It seems to me incomprehensible," wrote Schweitzer later, "that I am leaving the natives for months. How fond of them one becomes, in spite of all the trouble they give one! . . . But the far-away green strip, behind which our thoughts would fain see Lambaréné, is getting less and less distinct. Is it still there on the horizon? Or has it at last disappeared below the waves? Ah, now there is no room for doubt . . . There is nothing to be seen but water. So without a word we three press each other's hands and go down to stow away our belongings in our cabins, and so deaden a little the pain of parting."*

Significantly, there had been no mention of such "pain of parting" when he sailed away from his wife and daughter in Europe. The obvious conclusion is that he found a deeper satisfaction in creating his own kingdom of healing among the savages and cannibals of Africa than in his own home. I intend to return to

* *More From the Primeval Forest*

this characteristic of his development later on, but let it be noted at this point that Schweitzer's Reverence for Life and ethical glorification of love were not always able to save those nearest to him from the loneliness of separation.

Now that he was home, however, Schweitzer allowed himself to stay for two, whole years. Did Hélène, and the growing Rhena, persuade him to delay his return to the jungle he missed so deeply? Or did wise counsellors among his friends, and the swelling throng of his European supporters, stress the need to restore himself physically in the lighter climate of Europe? No doubt, there were many and complex reasons for the duration of this visit, not to mention the growing admiration and flattery which greeted him on all sides, making it so much easier to raise money for his cause. In the autumn and winter of 1927 he was lecturing and giving organ recitals in Sweden and Denmark. In the spring and early summer of 1928 a similar programme took him to Holland and England. In London, too, he found his legend already well established.

"There are few more heroic figures in the world today than Albert Schweitzer," wrote a British reporter. "In appearance he is tall, dark and handsome, with the piercing deep-set eyes of the visionary. They say that he has perfect hands. He is a fluent, quick speaker, holding his audiences spellbound by the sheer magnetism of a strong personality." Other journals carried lavish praise for him in their headlines: "Heroic surgeon"; "Organist of the Jungle", etc. On a slightly less flattering note, one story appeared under the title: "Why the natives hate Bach." But this, it was tactfully explained, had nothing to do with the Doctor's skill in playing his pedal organ to the mahogany trees of Lambaréné.

At the hospital, the work of chopping down these soaring trees to enlarge the hospital clearing was going on in Schweitzer's absence. Shortly before his departure he had been joined by a remarkable Englishwoman, Mrs. C. E. B. Russell. She convinced even Schweitzer that she was capable of supervising the arduous de-forestation without his guidance. "Under her leadership," he wrote in open admiration, "a beginning was also made with the laying out of a plantation. Since then it has been my experience on the whole that the authority of a white woman is more readily recognized by our primitives than that of us men."* In the wards, one of his first and most trusted nurses, Miss Emma Haussknecht, carried on the work of healing.

Thus, with an easy conscience, Schweitzer could devote himself to his tour. In London, he was the guest of Dr. Agnes Maude Royden, the social worker who had adopted his crusade into her preachings at Guild House, Eccleston Square. While she interpreted his speech to the audience, translating his French into English, the Doctor told her congregation of his experiences, and appealed to them for money to help banish the scourge of sleeping sickness carried by the tsetse fly. At the same time he explained the problems of dealing with the savages and primitives of his region, with harrowing descriptions of how cruelly the natives treated their own lunatics and mental sufferers. Preaching as he was to Dr. Royden's already converted flock, it is no surprise that he made a considerable impression; far beyond anything that the many hundreds of missionaries and European workers in Africa had been able to establish for themselves over the years.

When not working, Schweitzer enjoyed the luxury of visiting old friends, including the Socialist Prime Minister (and Scottish visionary) Ramsay MacDonald. He also inspected old organs, in which London seemed to be peculiarly rich. It should have been a fine and pleasant holiday, away from the sickly jungles of Lambaréné, but Schweitzer was not really happy. "The Doctor possesses a muscular frame and an engaging smile," wrote a discerning British reporter, "but is not in good health." This was sadly true. Much of the time in Europe, when not travelling on his fund-raising tours, he spent at a mountain health-resort, Königsfeld in the Black Forest, recuperating and recovering his strength. Mme. Schweitzer and the young Rhena were with him. For a brief while, incapacitated by sickness, the great crusader had turned family man; though whether reluctantly or with relief it is impossible to do more than guess.

This European visit marked the acceptance, in European eyes,

* *My Life and Thought*

of Dr. Schweitzer's experiment at Lambaréné as one of the marvels, if not contemporary wonders, of the world. That a man should sacrifice so much when tasting the first, bounteous fruits of extraordinary academic and artistic successes seemed barely conceivable to people who knew little more of the Doctor than what he and his publicists had told them. That he should, as they believed, voluntarily perform humble service to the most primitive of men—living among them in dreadful conditions, exposed perpetually to disease and the threat of attack by gorillas, cannibals and other monsters—all this seemed utterly heroic, magnificent and charitable. The legend of Schweitzer the Jungle Saint was born at this period, with no evidence of any attempt by its host to abort it.

To be fair, Schweitzer was far too busy building his propaganda and fund-raising machine to take much stock of what was being said about him. (He has never shown himself bothered unduly by what is written about him in the popular papers, perhaps feeling that they are beneath his notice.) His main objective was to raise money so as to continue and extend the work of Lambaréné. In this he succeeded.

There were also his serious writings to be given their measure of attention. The last chapter of *The Mysticism of Paul the Apostle* was finally completed during the Christmas of 1929; but by then Schweitzer was on board ship again, heading back to his beloved jungles. His wife, Hélène, this time refusing to be left behind, and no doubt having entrusted her ten year old daughter, Rhena, to grandparents, was with him on the journey. How much she shared his feeling of relief at the finish of his long and tedious theological work can be imagined. For once, apart from a few sackfuls of unanswered correspondence which were the Doctor's habitual travelling companions, she was able to share her husband's lofty world. During the rest of the journey they could find time for each other, for an occasional moment of mutual relaxation. But they were not alone; also on board was a woman doctor, Dr. Anna Schmitz, and a Miss Marie Secretan who had volunteered to work in the hospital laboratory.

Though she felt pride in her husband's achievements and growing recognition, can Mme. Schweitzer have enjoyed sharing him with this exclusive world he seemed to have created? Did she welcome the sight of Africa's dark coastline over the horizon when it appeared? Or did she wish, with all the fervent desire of a dutifully subjugated woman, that she could sail away with her wonderful but eternally occupied man to the end of the earth? There can be little doubt that she found it hard to match her husband's elation at the prospect of return to the savages, the fevers and the humid loneliness of Lambaréné.

Schweitzer, of course, plunged back into it with his usual zeal. His beloved hospital was in severe trouble, resulting from another serious epidemic of dysentery. Wards were overflowing. Mental patients had had to be removed to make room for more infectious cases. The muddle and confusion was frightful. As the Doctor exhausted himself with the building of more and bigger wards, Mme. Schweitzer again repined. Towards the Easter of 1930, less than four months after she had arrived, she had to admit defeat. The jungle had claimed her husband and she sailed, a sick woman, for Europe leaving him to it.

It was two years before he was able to feel free enough to return to his wife and child and his retinue of followers in the world outside Lambaréné. In June 1932, he was in Britain once more, to be honoured with the degree of Doctor of Music by Edinburgh. He was more critically received. He gave a recital in Manchester Cathedral, before an enormous audience, after which critics seemed to be struggling for a way in which to let him down lightly: "A recital which suggested not the concert artist so much as a scholarly love of the art . . ." "(Schweitzer) carried reticence of delivery to extremes . . ." Two years later, when he was again in London, playing at St. Margaret's Westminster, *The Times* was moved to report: "His style is characterized . . . by simplicity and a certain solidity . . ." Elsewhere, these latter visits were paid less attention than before. The novelty of having a living saint in everyone's midst seemed to be wearing thin. Or the trend of the thirties may have been too much against the spiritual and idealistic. Whatever the cause Schweitzer, in the last few years before Hitler unleashed his blitzkrieg, was accepted, enthroned and largely taken for granted in England.

Other fortunes were flowing for him more strongly. In 1928 he had been awarded the Goethe prize for Service to Humanity. It was a sum of money, and he spent it on a small home for his family and visiting members of the hospital staff, at Günsbach, where it remains open for the same purposes today. Aside from the prize, he was beginning to receive large bequests from various philanthropists—something he is today an almost universal target for—and, with these to provide the raw materials he needed, the hospital made big strides towards completion (if anything made by man can ever be considered complete in the jungle).

So rich were the times, by comparison with the early, importunate days, that Schweitzer felt the need to repay what he again saw as his debt to fellow humans. Now, it was a question of money. He set out to work and travel to raise funds for other German charities—simply because his own charity was receiving such magnificent support. In this way he collected through lectures and concerts, 20,000 marks (at that time worth about $2,800) for German missions and German charities.

Meanwhile he and his hospital were receiving many most touching bequests. One of the first came from Britain, through his friend Dr. Royden; a subscription to commemorate a remarkable man, Ambrose Pomeroy-Cragg who, during the blackout and bombing of the First World War, had gone every night to Victoria Station to meet troops coming back from the trenches. With this kind gentleman's help, thousands of shell-shocked and bewildered soldiers had been able to find their families and homes. At his death friends subscribed to a fitting memorial to be placed in Dr. Schweitzer's hospital. With the money the Doctor was able to erect a strong and properly safeguarded building to house his dangerous mental patients. To this day, I am told, it still bears a plaque in Mr. Pomeroy-Cragg's memory.

There were other bequests, equally well intentioned. Three London women paid for a whole building, to be known as "The River House". A rich woman sold her necklace and donated the proceeds to Schweitzer; the building this paid for was named "The Necklace". Another gift commemorated the late Dorothy Mannering; a sum of money, it was used by Schweitzer to supply cement bricks for a well of pure water that he had discovered and which never ran dry. It was at this well that I saw him, during my visit, demonstrate the purity of the water to a visitor while speaking in a peremptory tone to an African woman in the queue.

It is a little surprising, in view of Schweitzer's many German and French connections, that so many of these bequests should have come from England. Even the lamp at his landing stage was placed there by St. Botolph's Church, Bishopsgate. For some reason, the British appear to have adopted Schweitzer's cause in a specially personal way.

Before his sixty-second birthday in 1937 the Doctor made two more visits home, always obeying the same compulsion to travel, to lecture, and to play, and thereby earning money for Lambaréné. Apart from teaching his daughter, Rhena, the rudiments of music these visits were not noticeably family affairs. It is indeed doubtful whether the entire period of domesticity enjoyed by Dr. and Mme. Schweitzer can have amounted to more than a few weeks, or even days, when all other factors were discounted. He went back to Lambaréné each time with impatience to get to grips with his problems there. Sometimes Mme. Schweitzer went with him. On recent occasions Rhena has frequently been out to stay with her father; a married woman now with grown children.

Perhaps the most significant key to the loneliness which Schweitzer's absorption in his jungle hospital has brought to his family came in 1948. A book had been published which bore the title *An Anthology of Albert Schweitzer*, a collection of items from his own works. The publishers had written to ask Schweitzer if they could send copies of it to anyone he knew or was interested in. "Send the first four copies," he wrote in reply, "to my grandchildren whom I have never seen."

SEVEN

WOMEN AND THE LURE

DURING SCHWEITZER'S years of travel and fund-gathering the hospital expanded with the slow insistence of a stalagmite. Buildings rose on the site of giant trees; bush-land was cut back to make paths and clearings; roads were tentatively laid. As the colony increased in size, the patients increased in numbers so that it was hardly known for Lambaréné to be operating at less than twice its maximum capacity. Such a situation could only be coped with if sufficient staff volunteered to give their services, and here the Doctor's legendary appeal proved of value. Doctors, surgeons and a growing number of nurses and general helpers came to Africa with the ideal of Schweitzer's experiment deeply sewn in their minds. They abandoned sterilized and up-to-date hospitals and clinics in Europe, as well as elsewhere in the civilized world, to sweat it out in the primitive wards, caring magnificently for the flowing river of African sick. Their self-sacrifice was an immeasurable tribute to Schweitzer's cause and to human idealism.

When one studies this volunteer group, of which so little has been said or known over the years, a curious factor emerges: Schweitzer's appeal for women far outstrips his attraction for men. There was little shortage of male staff, and male doctors, yet when they had worked for a time under the formidable tutelage of *le grand docteur*, as Schweitzer was becoming labelled, the majority found the situation oppressive. They went on their way, seemingly frustrated by inability to pursue their own paths of healing and helping, or even to succeed in applying methods which they believed superior to those in force.

At its kernel, this ambivalence in Schweitzer's appeal was little different from that exercised in history by a number of spiritual and mystical leaders. Where women found a warm inner satisfaction in serving a man whose ideas were rigidly set, whose attitudes insisted on a profoundly demanding code of discipline and personal austerity, men soon became irritated and repressed in such propinquity.

The psychological explanation of the lure that Schweitzer's solitary hospital, his oasis of healing, had for women is well known. It offered the thrilling challenge of service, on a supremely selfless scale, in conditions of acute and even unnecessary drudgery and squalor. The exact motivation can be left to the experts, for the syndrome in its many forms is well known to students of Freud and other probers of the mind and senses. I can attest, for my part, to the uncanny loyalty and devotion of the women in Schweitzer's service whom I have met, talked to and seen at work in Lambaréné. Their total immolation for his sake and for the sake of his ideal is both touching and awesome.

However, if we are to understand the man behind the fabricated legend of Dr. Schweitzer, some charting of this strange female behaviour pattern must be made. For, though he may not and probably does not realize how clearly the fact emerges from his biography, women have played a phenomenally greater part in his development than men.

Schweitzer's mother died brutally under the galloping hooves of cavalry horses during the First World War in 1916 (her son does not tell us, in his memoirs, which side of the struggle they were on), but long before this the handsome and charming young professor had made a number of lasting ties with women. They had one quality in common: an unswerving belief in Schweitzer and his ideas. Those who doubted were shaken from his bough like errant buds.

Thus, in his early twenties, we see Schweitzer studying Touch in piano-playing with a pupil and friend of Franz Liszt, Marie Jaell-Trautmann. Her interest was such that she used him for experiments in attempting to find a physiological basis for her system; and he rejoiced in the privilege of becoming her guinea pig. "I was the 'corpus' on which she tried her experiments," he recalls, ". . . so I shared in them. How much do I owe to this gifted woman!"*

In Strasbourg, Schweitzer was quickly befriended by Frau Cosima Wagner, a woman of such "artistic ability and queenly bearing", as he records, that he could hardly suppress a feeling of shyness when with her. Yet he seems to have influenced her in his favour enough to gain respect for his ideas on Bach. There were pleasant moments shared between them when Schweitzer illustrated his theme by playing to her some of the composer's choral preludes on a church organ.

Another feminine string which he pulled successfully at this time led through the wife of his father's eldest brother in Paris, Mme. Mathilde Schweitzer. To her Schweitzer owes a considerable debt, as it was at her hospitable home in 1893 that he was able to meet M. Widor, his indulgent music teacher. In grateful memory he dedicated his French book on Bach to Mme. Schweitzer.

The charm of his playing had touched other womanly hearts. Until her death, Carmen Sylva kept up a long and fervent correspondence with him, because "I had made her beloved Bach still dearer to her . . ." as Schweitzer says. That this friendship was unusually warm, he hints in his writings. "I could not accept the Queen's frequently repeated invitation to spend part of my holidays with her under the single obligation of playing the organ to her for two hours daily . . . And when I returned home she was no longer among the living." Marie-Jaell Trautmann, too, died in 1925, but Schweitzer was not left short of female admirers.

Surprisingly, he claims to have been generally shy and somewhat tongue-tied in society. It was obvious that a woman's soft and understanding charm was needed to unlock his ideas and convictions; the gentle, flattering respect of a female soul that kindled in him his greatest sources of inspiration. In Paris, during the time of his medical studies, he met Frau Fanny Reinach, wife of a well-known scholar. With her, he was presented to Countess Melanie de Pourtales, the friend of the Empress Eugenie, and once painted

* *My Life and Thought*

at her side by Winterhalter. Thus Schweitzer was soon being entertained at the Countess's country home near Strasbourg where, he says, "I frequently saw her friend, Princess Metternich-Sander, the wife of the Austrian Ambassador at Paris in Napoleon III's day."

How cosy and titillating these aristocratic associations sound . . . and how hard it is to imagine them culminating in a life of abnegation in the jungle! Yet the two are not lacking ground between them, if we recall Schweitzer's reasons for becoming a negro doctor: a wish, above all, to repay society for the abundant happiness it had given him up to the age of thirty. A major part of this happiness rose directly from the attentions and considerations of these and many other illustrious lady friends.

Paris was particularly sociable for the young Schweitzer, despite his contemptuous aversion to the university and library facilities of the city when compared with the good German, or Alsatian, ones. He made what was obviously a pleasing friendship with an unknown and unmarried teacher, Mlle. Adele Herrenschmidt, who also hailed from Alsace. Together, we can imagine them roaming the student quarter and enjoying the piquant life of the city. Though he makes no excuse or explanation for alluding to her in an exclusive paragraph of his memoirs, except to say that they "saw a good deal" of each other, doubtless Schweitzer's usual reticence about everything private in his life is reflected here.

Schweitzer's greatest attraction for women was his gracious talent for listening to their opinions; oddly at variance with the rugged dogmatism of his later years. Elderly women were completely charmed by this polite attention to their words. In the house of Frederick Curtius, where he stayed for a time as a medical student, he met the aged Countess of Erlach, by birth the Countess de May of Neuchtael. Since she was an invalid, unable to put her nose out of doors, he felt a charitable desire to console her by playing the piano to her for an hour each evening. The old lady saw practically nobody, and sadly missed the concerts which she had attended all her life, so that the recitals given to her by her young admirer were greatly enjoyed. In return she schooled Schweitzer in the ways of the aristocracy. "This distinguished noblewoman gradually acquired a great influence over me," he wrote, "and I owe it to her that I have rounded off many a hard angle in my personality."*

What, one wonders, were these "hard" corners? Schweitzer was stubborn, dictatorial in ideas, a man obsessed by the need to state what he believed to be the truth on as many occasions as possible. Presumably if a girl he was squiring asked his opinion of a hat, or a new dress, he gave it honestly, with occasionally distressing results. Also, the streak of impatience that had brought him into collision with his examiners over the hymn-writer now matured into a disturbingly blunt social weapon. In society, and particularly in dealing with women, a man simply did not *insist*; he might cajole, persuade, even entice, but he did not assert his masculine power without quickly becoming a bore. All this the aged and invalid Countess no doubt told him. The result, as we see it today, is a man whose strong opinions and convictions stay politely chained inside him. Whether his contact is with a sentimental typist or a world sage this patina of politeness remains a part of his equipment.

In fact, we know that Schweitzer has accepted at least one principle of existence from his aristocratic adviser. He has never, since first going to Equatorial Africa, allowed himself to be without his sun-helmet, even in the shadows of evening, when in the open air. It can be imagined what power the old lady must have put into this piece of advice to command such enduring obedience. ". . . for her sake I now renounce the pleasure of letting the evening breeze play upon my head after a hot day on the equator,"* he wrote. In its way, the gesture was rather charming; for Schweitzer can hardly have believed in the scientific wisdom of the Countess's reasoning. She had told him that an uncle of hers had survived a long career in the Dutch Colonial Service without suffering fever solely on account of this practice. Schweitzer boasts that he has never had an attack of malaria himself, and praises the helmet-wearing habit (which he insists on visitors to Lambaréné observing). But he will wryly admit that the disease has never been known to

* *My Life and Thought*

result from going about with an uncovered head in the tropics after sundown.

Wealthy women were becoming increasingly important to Schweitzer at this time, for he was begging funds to start his jungle hospital; using all his reluctant powers of persuasion to extract donations from those whose sympathies could be melted by his tongue. Many were so charmed by the fine-looking and strong-voiced Alsatian that they promised not only to contribute immediately but also to help replenish his coffers in future should he call on them again. In dealing with the bewildering matter of finance, which he says he has no head for, yet another woman came to the Doctor's assistance; a Mrs. Annie Fischer, widow of a Professor of Surgery at Strasbourg University. Her husband died young and the helpful, accomplished widow found a new aim in life when she allied herself to Schweitzer's cause. While he remained in Africa, she took upon herself all the work which needed to be done in Europe.

Soon after the Schweitzers' arrival in Africa, we are given another glimpse of his ability to influence elderly women. He had been invited to preach in native mission churches and was subsequently allowed to share in the examination of candidates for baptism. He preferred to be sent one or two old women so that, as he says, "I might make the trying half-hour as easy for them as possible." There is a pointer, here, to the Doctor's own understanding of where his best powers lie. In several instances during his life he has chosen the association of an older woman rather than a man of his own age, finding in these female friends a readier warmth and sympathy for everything in which he believes.

Since women are romantically inclined to exaggerate the objects of their devotion, and as Schweitzer's saintly legend has largely been created by women, the need is to see the pattern of these associations clearly. Nobody should suggest that anything shabby or reprehensible lies behind them. But the fact that so many more women than men find Schweitzer irresistible is of the deepest importance in assessing his true personality. It has brought praise and flattery. In the case of a powerfully self-willed man like Albert

Schweitzer, these are not likely to have upset the balance of his judgement. Nevertheless, they have flattered his pride and done nothing to encourage a lowly opinion of himself.

On his release from internment during the First World War, it was a woman friend with whom he first sought refuge: Frau Fischer in Strasbourg. When the Germans suffered poverty and privation as a result of defeat, Schweitzer's charity reached out towards Frau Cosima Wagner and Agatha, the sister of painter Hans Thoma whom Schweitzer also helped. He sent supplies and provisions. He was greatly disturbed by their want. And during the time he was writing and playing the organ for a living, before he decided to return to Lambaréné, the Doctor took his wife and family to live in Günsbach while he himself retained "occasional quarters" in Strasbourg at the house of another widow. No doubt she was equally fascinated by the unassuming hero of Lambaréné. Her name was Frau Dietz-Härter, and we know no more of her than that she was Schweitzer's housekeeper shortly before he returned alone to Lambaréné to begin his second stay in the jungle.

Now commenced the flow of women helpers, sacrificing so much more than the comforts of civilization to join Schweitzer in Equatorial Africa. For many of these nurses and helpers service at the hospital was akin to enrolment in a monastery; a dedicated service demanding the essential years of their youth and beauty. In return, they had the spiritual satisfaction of being able to work at the side of the legendary *grand docteur* of Lambaréné. Two women were already at the mission, where the hospital was still to be found on Schweitzer's return, a Mlle. Arnoux, school mistress; and Mme. Hermann, the wife of a Swiss missionary. They did much to make the Doctor feel welcome, so that he was able to record: "By the time we are seated together at table I feel myself quite at home again in Lambaréné."*

Then on July 18 1924 Schweitzer's first nurse and subsequent devoted lieutenant, Mlle. Mathilde Kottmann, came from Strasbourg to join him. "Now the clouds are beginning to lift," he wrote. Mathilde took over the cooking and supervised the linen

* *More From the Primeval Forest*

and stores, turning the confusion of the hospital into something almost approaching order. She filled the lamps and boiled water for drinking. When all these duties were done, she tended the two or three white European patients who were beginning to use the hospital. There were to be many more of these angelic disciples, some of them more suited to nunneries, but Mlle. Kottmann is unique. She is still at Lambaréné, Schweitzer's "left hand" in matters of domestic or administrative routine. She has, in her truly humble way, given almost as much to the hospital as its founder. His "right hand" is the beautiful Dutch nurse and interpreter, Miss Ali Silver, who came after the war, in 1947. I was told during lunch in the hospital that though she looked so pale and fresh-complexioned, Nurse Ali had only once left Lambaréné. On that occasion she flew out a sick nurse who needed urgent treatment which could not be performed on the spot. She was back from the world outside within forty-eight hours and has never since left the hospital.

Mathilde Kottmann's loyalty to Dr. Schweitzer is quite astonishing, and it probably springs from a night on the Ogowe River when the Doctor claims to have saved her from drowning. They were returning together by canoe, in darkness. The native paddlers were hugging the bank to give them a landmark. Suddenly Schweitzer became convinced that they were too close to land and soon would run full tilt into a heavy overhang of foliage, noticed by him on his way down river. The natives disagreed. So strong was the Doctor's presentiment that he jumped to his feet and ordered them to alter course; to steer out towards the middle of the stream. At that moment, he says, the clump of pendant branches and creepers came into view, barely letting the boat scrape by without fouling them and being upset. The river Ogowe seems so gentle and inviting that an English nurse, who shared a canoe with me on one occasion, dangled her hand, innocently, in its surface. Yet I was told that she risked a lot in doing so; according to Dr. Schweitzer the mile-wide stream is swarming with deadly electric fish and bacteria, not to mention hippos, snakes and crocodiles. These were the dangers which the Doctor's act narrowly averted.

For nearly eighteen months Schweitzer had to be satisfied with this single, indefatigable nurse from Europe; but in October 1925 Mlle. Emma Hausknecht joined the hospital. She was a trained teacher from Alsace who had known the Doctor for many years and had given him a promise that she would come to his aid one day. Today, she lies buried outside his bungalow, her promise fulfilled.

The following spring a sister of one of Dr. Schweitzer's two male doctors arrived, raising the number of women to three. And during the same summer it was increased by the arrival of a missionary's widow, herself a missionary, Mme. Rusillon. The group of white faces, white sun-hats and white, cotton skirts was increasing.

Certainly the most formidable recruit was English social worker and writer Mrs. C. E. B. Russell who arrived, literally unable to keep away a moment longer, in March 1927. Not caring what she did, only so long as she helped with the good work, Mrs. Russell quickly showed herself to be a surging power-house of enthusiasm and support. Presumably a strongly-built woman, Schweitzer reports on her with what seems like sly humour, ". . . she at once finds her proper sphere. She takes over the command of the people who are felling in the forest and are working in the plantation . . ."* It was Mrs. Russell, as we have seen earlier in this book, who stayed to work in the jungle when the Doctor finally left for his home and family in Europe.

Such women are universally found in the service of great and inspiring men, irrespective of conditions. They represent the curious female concomitant of man's pioneer spirit; not to take the initiative themselves, but to follow where the most daring men lead. It must be obvious that such nurses as Mathilde and Emma did not need to banish themselves into the jungle of Africa merely to serve mankind. There were many at least equally needy cases at home in their own lands. Mrs. Russell could have stayed with her books and social causes in London and never known the frightful heat and exhaustion of physical work under an equatorial sun.

* *More From the Primeval Forest*

One thing led them all to Lambaréné: a profound, womanly faith in Dr. Albert Schweitzer.

What this faith amounts to has been variously described, but one thing is clear, the name of Schweitzer was already associated with the healing of lepers. Indelibly, his reputation as a leper doctor had spread over the world, ignoring the fact that the disease was comparatively rare among his patients. To women, such healing is a sacred cause. Unfortunately there are also some whom novelist Graham Greene terms "leprophils" in his story of an African leprosarium *A Burnt Out Case*. In the words of Greene's cynical Doctor Colin: "You know very well that leprophils exist, though I dare say they are more often women than men. Schweitzer seems to attract them. They would rather wash the feet with their hair like the woman in the gospel than clean them with something more antiseptic. Sometimes I wonder whether Damien was a leprophil. There was no need for him to become a leper in order to serve them well. A few elementary precautions—I wouldn't be a better doctor without my fingers, would I?"

For those who find satisfaction in flirting with mysterious terror, Lambaréné is a vulnerable target. Schweitzer, wise in diagnosing the thrill-seekers among the applicants, admits few of these perverted martyrs; but inevitably some do find their way into the colony, if only until they are persuaded to go elsewhere. A problem for the Doctor is that his hospital has become a shrine for an uncountable number of simple-minded, no doubt well-intentioned, women who seek only to visit, touch and smell Lambaréné as their incessant and barely comprehensible letters testify. They beg to be allowed to "purify" themselves in its "holy, burning fire"; to bathe their souls in the "fiery blood of Schweitzer's self-sacrifice". They and their outpourings cost the Doctor and his staff long hours of toil and worry when the bags of mail are sorted and answered.

Other women are drawn towards Lambaréné and its father-figure Dr. Schweitzer by a strong though sublimated sexual need. An intelligent woman who has worked and lived in the hospital told me: "Women like to be dominated; they find Schweitzer satisfies them in that way. He is something of a patriarch or, as he calls himself, a benevolent dictator. I suppose the need is Freudian, basically; a deep-seated, unconscious urge to serve a man who is not a physical lover but a spiritual master." This woman has herself served Schweitzer, whom she says "loves me as I love him", since the collapse of her marriage. She leads a sophisticated life in Europe and is a popular figure in society. Yet she goes to the hospital on regular pilgrimages and puts up with the discomfort almost with pleasure. "The softest thing to sit on there," she told me, "is not so comfortable as the hardest bench in Hyde Park." Her feelings for Schweitzer ceased to appear wholly spiritual to me when she described him as ". . . still at this age a deeply attractive man. He is a great persuader and very beautiful. He is the sun and expects everyone to revolve around him." Like other women followers who see Schweitzer as a totem for their love and worship, she plainly enjoys his domination. Indeed, "slave-master" relationships, common in psychology, are hard to avoid in the hospital clearing on the banks of the teaming Ogowe where the legend of Dr. Schweitzer begins.

Of course his detractors find this lure disgusting, depraved and shocking. What did you think of the women working at Lambaréné? I asked a girl journalist who had been there. "Oh!" she laughed unpleasantly, "Oh . . . MONSTERS!" What sort of monsters? Why do they go there? "Well, frustration, I guess," she said this more seriously. "That, and a sort of strange idea of charity." Did she think it was Freudian? "Freudian? Oh *yes*!" she laughed again. "Very much!" Then they are unconsciously in love with Dr. Schweitzer? "Well, I mean . . . yes, any monstrosity possible! Yes. Maybe there is a sort of unhealthy thing there, yes."

A healthy woman with a normal family life or sufficient social engagements to keep her busy and amused may think it strange that women nurses, needed in their own civilized countries, voluntarily join Dr. Schweitzer's primitive kingdom as under-privileged vassals. Yet the act of oblation is no more marked at Lambaréné than in hundreds of convents and holy orders throughout the world. It is the "nun syndrome", possibly linked to the Freudian in some cases, which accounts for a third group of Schweitzer's women followers: the Servants of Higher Causes.

These are not professional nurses, but women who have gone into nursing as a means of serving humanity and their God at the same time. One of their number at Lambaréné showed me a letter she had written to her mother. She had no idea that her mother had been dead for two years because her service had taken her out of touch with temporal affairs such as family relationships. The letter was a perfect expression of the will that drives these women: "This beloved country draws me like a magnet," she had written. "Here, in Dr. Schweitzer's hospital, we are like a big family. It seems we have all followed a master, and in Dr. Schweitzer we see a reflection of Him, pure and selfless, humble and simple, yet a great leader. God has endowed him with the spirits of all great men, such as Lord Nelson, ruling all things with love, Livingstone, and Grenfell, Scott and Raleigh. Yes, all great adventurers who were the instruments of God are reflected in this great man . . . He has learned the great secret of understanding and loving others in preference to being understood and loved."

In an interesting and significant way this declaration differs from an impression given me by the woman to whom Schweitzer was the sun, moon and stars. She had told me, of the Doctor's human relations: "He does not really need anyone; and I believe people like that, people who don't call for any other being's inclusion in their existence, are the only ones who can *really* love. But it does make it difficult for very complete human beings to feel that they are being used to the best advantage at the hospital . . ."

The distinction here is between those who see Dr. Schweitzer as an idol enshrined in Lambaréné, able to receive their sacrifices and their devotion without obviously returning them, and those who think of him as the warm-hearted, all-giving father who can fill the lonely places of the human heart with radiant, out-going love. Between these two we find most of the women who go to serve Albert Schweitzer; the women the local scornful Africans call "Schweitzer's jungle brides".

EIGHT

WHY MEN DON'T STAY

WHAT OF the men? As Schweitzer's hospital grew, and the legend of his work rippled out into the world, little was told of their contribution. In his books the Doctor spares an occasional word or two for his male surgeons, doctors and helpers, but an historian would suffer ulcers of frustration in trying to measure their exact part in Lambaréné's development, and for an odd reason. Nobody at the hospital is ever allowed to feel responsible for what he or she does other than *le grand docteur* himself. At first this strange suppression of the individual can charm the visitor into believing that loyalty and devotion are at the roots of its cause; then the realization comes that the doctors who serve Schweitzer are only obeying an implacable law of the place and, in many cases, are stamping on a rising tide of frustration in themselves. On this account alone many of the younger medical men have left either as soon as their two year period of work was over or before.

In going, they appear to have left no trace. It is a curious quality of Lambaréné under Schweitzer, as remarked before, that those who have departed might as well have died. Their popularity may have been considerable while there but once their canoe disappears round the river headland they cease to be talked or even thought about. Dr Schweitzer is the sole owner of a legend at Lambaréné, nobody else. Even the memory of his most cherished assistant, Dr. Percy, has been veiled in silence since his departure; though this may have been exceptional in that it protected Schweitzer's feelings.

Dr. Percy, so it is said at Lambaréné, was Schweitzer's first serious disappointment. In him, the old Doctor had placed a growing store of confidence and respect, often confiding in the younger man his hope that one day he would take over the running of the place, so laboriously built with the skill and toil of Schweitzer's own hands. A few years ago, however, Percy abruptly left the hospital to marry a local French girl, leaving the Doctor to carry on alone at the head of the staff. His loss was a bitter blow. When the new X-ray equipment had been introduced, it was Dr. Percy who was entrusted with its complicated operation. He had spent several weeks of his overseas leave studying the subject in the works of the Phillips technicians who made the machine. He had taken more than one province of Lambaréné under his special care.

More unfortunately, the defection of this trusted deputy was unlikely to have been for love alone. Schweitzer has never been known as an easy man to work with in male and medical circles. Even his friend Mrs. Clara Urquhart, who admires him in every possible way, admits this: "When I first went out to him sixteen years ago," she said, "we were immediately on the same wave-band; but if I had been a man I wouldn't have lasted a year. Men cannot work easily with Schweitzer; he's such a, what he calls, 'benevolent dictator'. Men can't take it." Yet men have been used unsparingly in the great work Schweitzer has created out of his own desire to repay his personal debt to society; used and rewarded, then left obscurely out of the record.

It is hard to imagine another reason for this than the belief Schweitzer has in his own indispensability as the fulcrum and mainspring of Lambaréné. Where, if this is not true, is the appointed successor, the carefully groomed hierarchy of trained senior men ready to take over in the Chief's absence, or when he can no longer carry on his command? If any plan exists for the continuation of Lambaréné after Schweitzer's death, it is not known to close and intimate friends of his with whom it has been discussed. His trust in the men around him does not apparently extend to the reins. And in the shafts they must do only as he wishes them to do.

Fergus Pope, a young American whose aspirations are covered more fully further on in this book, tells a revealing story of how the great Doctor will stamp on individual prowess in the same way that he obstructs progress. Pope had noticed swarms of wild bees making their homes in the shrubs and trees of the jungle near to the hospital, at heights where it was impossible to reach their honey. To gain such a rich store of nutritious food, he thought, would be a fine advance for the hospital where malnutrition due to inadequate supplies of food is a constant threat, and where five or six hundred people must be catered for each day. Remembering his own youthful bee-keeping experience in America, Pope wrote to a brother there asking him to buy, package and send urgently to Lambaréné some bee-hives.

When these duly arrived, Pope took delivery of the crates and settled down in a corner of the clearing to nail them together. As he did so, he began thinking enthusiastically of the day when he would be able to add to the hospital's larder. His thoughts were disturbed by Dr. Schweitzer, who had walked over to see what was going on. "What are you doing there?" the Doctor asked him. "I'm building some bee-hives so that we can keep bees and use their honey," Pope explained. Dr. Schweitzer walked away, nodding doubtfully.

That evening, over dinner, the Doctor raised the subject again. "Pope," he said, "about those bee-hives; well, I wouldn't bother to put them up if I were you." Pope was astonished. "Why not?" he asked later. "They're mine, and I'll be glad to let the hospital have them and benefit from them." Schweitzer looked wisely at him. "Ah yes," he said, "but who will look after the bees when you are no longer here? You are the only accomplished bee-keeper we have, and once we have trained the bees to live in your hives they will need skilled attention, won't they?"

Schweitzer has regularly suppressed all such attempts to introduce methods or machinery over which he is not to have complete authority. Even in the case of his most valuable unfinished writings he has been hard to convince that they should be microfilmed by somebody else in order to protect and preserve them, simply because he would then have to surrender his exclusive hold on them if only for a few days. Norman Cousins, the American magazine editor and author, managed to cajole him into accepting this service during a visit he made to Lambaréné in 1957; but he had Schweitzer's persuasive woman friend, Mrs. Urquhart, acting as his advocate and interpreter. And when I was in Lambaréné I was told that the photographing of two manuscripts, Schweitzer's *Kingdom of God* and the unpublished part of his still unfinished *The Philosophy of Civilization*, had been interrupted by the Doctor's indecision. Only the former of the two manuscripts was put on film, as Cousins has described in his book.*

A young English doctor, Frank Catchpool, says of Schweitzer: "His one weakness, or greatness, is that he does things his way—the right way. He resembles de Gaulle in that respect." Catchpool was at the hospital between October 1956 and December 1959 when there were only some 3 doctors, 6 nurses and 8 girl helpers working there. He is now an instructor in biology at the California Institute of Technology where he teaches about two classes a week.

His opinions of the hospital where only one man gets credit for what is done are worth noting. Catchpool, now a man of thirty-five, looks back on his experience in the jungle with quiet detachment. "It was a fantastic experience," he says. "It should be recommended to every young doctor. There is, it's true, a lot of responsibility for one so young in his career; perhaps too young. However, whether this is a good thing or a bad thing that one has this responsibility so young, I couldn't say. Personally, I learnt a lot."

How near Catchpool got to leaving Lambaréné without ever practising medicine came out in conversation. "When I arrived, I just made furniture for two months," he explained, "I had been fully qualified for two years and had finished my house job in Britain so that I really wasn't in the mood to spend my time nailing pieces of wood together indefinitely. Then, in one step, I was promoted from assistant carpenter to senior physician. Schweitzer may have done that on purpose, I think he probably did; he has a mania for contrasting things. Maybe he just wanted to see if I was willing to do the most humble job there, as a sort of test of my personality, my character. I was not very happy being a car-

* *Dr. Schweitzer of Lambaréné*

penter and if he had read the signs right he would have held up my promotion for a few more days, because by then I would have been ready to quit. I was already thinking about it."

Catchpool first went to Lambaréné because his father was a great admirer of the jungle Doctor. He left for personal reasons, to marry an American girl, but also because he felt that the native Africans were being treated unfairly. "I had a strange objection," he says, "to the general political atmosphere there, with regard to the Africans. As far as the staff were concerned, I got on with them pretty well. There were the usual little difficulties, of course. You know, people would say: 'I'm the only one who can interpret Schweitzer correctly' when he wasn't there to argue or consult. Somebody would always say, in his absence, 'this is the way the Doctor would have done it'. That usually led to a bit of a squabble."

Among the men forced to accept Schweitzer's repressive authority, his disinclination to move with the times beyond a point where he can remain master, there is a noticeable air of tension. The visitor is quickly aware of it. Young doctors are tired when they sit down together to dinner in the late evening, yet they act nervously and sometimes abruptly. Their conversations with one another, or with the nurses at the table, progress in staccato murmurs. They crumble their bread impatiently, almost neurotically. When, at the end of the meal, the Doctor rises with some difficulty to his feet and slowly makes his way round the long table towards the piano (mysteriously kept on the far side of the room) several of the young doctors, perhaps with good medical excuses, hurry away before Schweitzer's regular evening "service" of hymns and prayers and Bible reading begins.

It seems that Dr. Schweitzer's applied Reverence for Life has upset more than one of these practical and scientific colleagues. Daily, they have to make their way among wards infested by pets—dogs and goats with sore and fly-ridden ears among them—to carry out their ward inspections. They are constantly being reminded by the Doctor that the life of an ant or a cockroach is as precious as their own, or that of their patients, with irritating effect. In the privacy of his room, a doctor can drop his mask, provided that he feels safe from the eagerly poised ears of Dr. Schweitzer's chief female lieutenants. Then he may give vent to his own feelings about this curious creed. More often than not, they differ from the Doctor's.

In an otherwise balanced and highly respectful book* telling of his months at work in the hospital the distinguished Danish surgeon L. Østergaard-Christensen wrote: "It is not easy at first for a foreign surgeon to fit himself into the new surroundings. He is unknown in the hospital, one of the many birds of passage whom the more senior nurses have seen come and go. They know the ways of the place and are reluctant to deviate from the accustomed pattern . . . a man must make his own reputation. A newcomer has to understand that he does not bring recognition and respect with him from home as a matter of course. He must shed his official rank and be plain Dr. X. His reputation must be built up from the bottom. This is quite a healthy system." But the criticism of Lambaréné is that it is *not* always a healthy system for men of proven professional ability to be made to accept methods of less medical advancement than elsewhere. Dr. Christensen is charitable.

He recounts how Dr. Schweitzer surprised his wife, Mrs. Christensen, when she was conducting a furious beetle hunt in their room. The Doctor put in a plea for the insects, saying that they had a right to their lives; but Mrs. Christensen was sufficiently incensed by their attacks on her clothing and possessions—she had brought a small rake with her from Denmark to deal with spiders—that Schweitzer made a bargain with her. She could destroy those she found in her room provided she respected those outside the door.

If this seems no more than a charming eccentricity, it must be remembered that Dr. Schweitzer's whole philosophy is built on a colossal respect for all forms of life, even those of microbes and vegetation. He virtually cocoons himself in the creed's protective folds, making it difficult for more practical persons to uphold contrary views without appearing savage and unfeeling. How a doctor of medicine can follow his professional and ethical concept of healing while trembling at the thought of destroying dangerous

* *At Work With Albert Schweitzer*

insects and even bacilli, is hard to understand. It certainly forms an important block in his association with other medical men who work with him.

Another man who found room for reflection at Lambaréné was the American dentist, Frederick Franck, whose visit in 1956 when he set up the now barely used dental room had ended by the time the Christensens arrived. Franck subsequently wrote in his book:* "The mythical Albert Schweitzer does not exist. It is high time that someone should publish an authoritative, definitive condensation of all the nonsense published about him and Lambaréné . . ." Franck was able to treat a number of sufferers who had never before had proper dental treatment. He managed to persuade Schweitzer to give him a room in the main pharmacy building, "the tape worm", where he could install a dentist's chair and other equipment donated to the jungle hospital. When last seen this room had the air of a museum-piece, standing isolated and silent; though I was assured that it is used from time to time. A doctor who left Lambaréné last year insisted that the services of a good dentist were urgently required.

Schweitzer has said that his most arduous periods at Lambaréné have been those when he has been short of capable medical assistance. While he remains intolerant of such advances in medical science as other, younger doctors wish to import, while he stresses the value of an insect poisonous to human life, and while he allows such fields of healing as dentistry to go untended there will surely be many such periods. With all his world reputation as a saintly hero, it seems unlikely that many brilliant doctors will be persuaded to join him in the jungle for indefinite stays. Christensen says that it had been ten years, in the old Doctor's reckoning, since he had had the services of a fully trained surgeon, prior to the Danish surgeon's arrival.

One disadvantage of this is that a constant turnover of doctors and others persists. Christensen notes it in his book, remarking on the number of different instruments in the operating theatre, brought there by surgeons with a number of differing skills and

* *Days With Albert Schweitzer*

techniques. Doctors may serve a term of two or three years at Lambaréné, after which they receive a generous grant of money and travel tickets to enable them to rest, or study, for six months in another part of the world. Few stay longer. Fewer still return. While at work they may be paid about two pounds a week "cigarette money", on a par with the nurses and other assistants. The irony is that smoking is frowned on by Schweitzer, except in the privacy of the bedrooms.

During one of these evening coffee-and-cigarette parties, which take the place of more sophisticated entertainment since Dr. Schweitzer does not believe in advancing the inroads of electricity or employing the cinematograph projector, the visitor can learn a number of curious facts about the staff who appear during the daytime, and in public, to be so loyal to *le grand docteur*. Firstly, there are a surprising number of cross-currents of feeling expressed about the Doctor and his works; newer arrivals showing open doubt, if not disgust, at the primitive conditions while some of the older staff try to explain these away. Then, the Doctor's Reverence for Life may be debated with reference to a particular case. After an exhausting day in the sticky heat of Lambaréné it is not always easy to be diplomatically guarded in criticism, so that things are said which are a good deal more heartfelt than the chorus of sycophantic writings by spell-bound visitors would suggest. Finally there is likely to be a certain amount of harmless gossip, no more destructive than in other communities but seeming odd in the holier-than-thou setting of Schweitzer's hospital.

For women, these rivalries and confidences are no doubt stimulating and psychologically necessary, within bounds; but men, especially men confined in an isolated and narrow colony, find them upsetting if not unbearable. If fortunate, they may strike up a romantic friendship with one of the more nubile of the young nurses, a fate which has overtaken at least one of Schweitzer's doctors and will certainly fall to several more. But if they become involved, if they are sucked into the tight little group-play of the off-duty hospital, then they may suffer morally as well as physically from Lambaréné's wretched condition.

Six years ago a beautiful young Dutch woman doctor, Margaret van der Kreek, was working at Lambaréné alongside a male colleague, Dr. Friedmann, who was said to be in love with her. The temptation for both of them to leave the hospital and marry must have been considerable, but they talked of other plans to a visitor whom they befriended. They admitted that they felt involved with Lambaréné, where Dr. Margaret had already spent two and a half years. They hinted at hopes that one day they would be ready to step into Schweitzer's shoes.

It could not and it did not happen. Schweitzer seems to sense the aims of his would-be successors and wither them. Dr. Margaret was as popular at the hospital as anyone could be. But when she finally left it, not to marry Dr. Friedmann but to become the wife of a French journalist who paid a chance visit to Lambaréné, there was no suggestion that she would ever return. She had come, she once told a friend, in answer to mystic voices which she heard telling her to go out into the jungles and help the stricken natives. She stayed long enough to become almost as legendary, with her astonishing beauty and good humour, as Dr. Schweitzer. The African patients called her "*la doctoresse*".

The interesting thing was that here was a woman doctor who, aside from the Joan of Arc quality of her inspiring inner voices, had little medical experience; yet she became senior surgeon at Lambaréné. The daughter of parents who were both painters, she had intended at one time to become an artist herself. When she discarded this pursuit in favour of medicine she quickly dedicated herself to its cause. But her only experience when she came to Lambaréné at the age of twenty-seven had been at a small Dutch hospital. Whenever a visiting specialist operated in the theatre she tried to learn from his work. Before performing an operation in which her skill was, according to an eye-witness, both neat and unflurried, she read up notes relating to it in her text book.

The rise of such an inexperienced, if brilliant, surgeon poses a serious question about the efficiency of Lambaréné, where many complicated operations are performed each week. Christensen more than once laments the lack of an adequate blood-transfusion service (largely due to lack of adequate supplies from the natives who, even when their blood is strong and healthy enough, resent giving it as donors) in his book. Combined with the reluctance of men doctors and surgeons to come to work for Schweitzer, and the average shortness of the stay of those who do, this creates a situation in which mistakes can and do occur where they could be avoided in a modern European hospital.

During the past twenty or so years, the Doctor has practised the minimum of medicine or surgery himself, giving most of his time to writing and thinking about theology, philosophy and his latest cause, the prevention of nuclear disaster. And in the last few years the number of bed, or in-patients, has nearly doubled. Today there are five large wards with some twenty-five beds in each, and a good many smaller wards. With the population of the leper village —about 120—this brings the total number of people at Lamberéné, when full to capacity, to about 600. For such a large community of sick and needy, there should be no shortage in a world driving itself to provide funds and help for underdeveloped areas. Yet Schweitzer finds it hard to attract men of the right skills and experience.

While a medical student at St. Bartholomew's Hospital in London, Fergus Pope warned in an article published in the hospital *Journal*: "Today the Gabonese have a choice of several hospitals to which they may go. The urban and city population usually attend the big hospital in the capital Libreville or one of the outlying regional government hospitals. The village people usually come to Lambaréné. But many people, Gabonese and foreign, find conditions at Lambaréné too primitive for their taste."

Pope also added an interesting note about the surgical conditions: "Emergency cases requiring surgery are dealt with on arrival," he wrote. "Routine surgery is put on the waiting list for operation on Tuesdays, Thursdays or Saturdays . . . Though the wards are far from clean, post operative sepsis is not a major problem." Furthermore, Pope claimed: "To call the community at Lambaréné a hospital is slightly misleading, it is nearer the truth to regard the community as a nursing home with surgical facilities and three (the number present at that time) doctors living in. But it is impossible to say where the nursing home ends and the community which supports it begins, for they are one. The goats at Lambaréné seem no more out of place than the doctors . . ."

To be as much in keeping with the atmosphere of his hospital (or nursing home) as a goat is not the ambition of every young man who has spent many gruelling years obtaining his medical degree. Nor does he necessarily fit easily into a community where the single guiding light is pitched at the intensity and, in terms of medical progress the period, of oil lamps. To be constantly frustrated in trying to better conditions found uncongenial and professionally dubious can also prove distressing. Thus it seems clear that Schweitzer could more easily attract young assistants if he cared to bring his hospital—for such it is, however Mr. Pope chooses to regard it—up to date, and to use for that purpose more of the now enormous funds subscribed for the purpose. His persistent failure to do so forces the conclusion that he does not wish to see his experiment in Christ-like living drift out of his own control. Nor, perhaps, does he wish to encourage too many agile young medical men to stay and put their own roots in his adopted, indeed conquered and colonized, soil.

Revealingly, editor Norman Cousins asked Schweitzer whether he was glad he had come to Lambaréné, and the old Doctor replied that, without hesitation, he could answer yes. Because without denying Cousins' suggestion that he had come in imitation of Christ, the important thing was the pursuit of the Christian ideal, a worthwhile aim for any man. Lambaréné, he said, had made it possible for him to make his life "an argument". In such frankness there is little to question for it gives the whole reason for Lambaréné's deliberately squalid conditions. Here is an experiment in which only one man must be paramount, or he will lose his argument. Only one man can pursue the Christian ideal in imitation of the Christ he has denuded of the divinity ascribed to him. At Lambaréné that man is Albert Schweitzer.

NINE

BEAUTY IN THE JUNGLE

EVEN MORE curious than Schweitzer's impression on his male helpers is his strongly magnetic attraction for young and beautiful women. To say that some of his nurses and girl assistants would fit well into a Hollywood film of the jungle hospital is not an exaggeration. There has been a succession of comely and attractive maidens through the hospital, each as refreshing in her clean white gown, white sun hat and stockings as any film actress cast in a similar role. Why these girls sacrifice themselves to an austere and sexually frustrating existence under the fiery African sun is a problem for the analysts, but it is not the only mystery associated with the women of Lambaréné. Even more strange is the lure Schweitzer's ascetic kingdom offers to women with large personal fortunes.

Olga Deterding's service at the hospital has caused world curiosity in this phenomenon, and a number of varying explanations have been attempted by writers and journalists. Miss Deterding herself has not been silent on the subject, but more often than not her alleged statements have later been ridiculed by her as palpably absurd and misreported. She is, as is well known, an exceedingly rich young woman who has never married and who divides her time between travel and what appears to be a search for the more exotic form of adventure. Yet the three visits and subsequent periods of service she has given to the Schweitzer hospital stand out as remarkably distinct from her worldly way of living.

Another wealthy visitor is Mrs. Marion Mayer who is better known by the name of her previous husband, the film producer Otto Preminger. As Marion Mill Preminger she became something of a legend at Lambaréné when she took to arriving in time to join the celebrations for the Doctor's birthday each January. Marion, who dots the "i" of her christian name with a tiny heart, is anxious to be known as the "Mother of all Lepers", not only at Lambaréné but throughout the world; a far-reaching ambition.

Aside from their own motivation in going to the hospital, there is the far more pertinent question of Schweitzer's reasons for letting such women join his company. Neither Miss Deterding nor Mrs. Mayer is a qualified nurse. While Mrs. Mayer is a doctor of philosophy, this hardly seems to fit her for the type of service most needed at Lambaréné. Olga Deterding has little knowledge of any of the more important duties performed at the hospital, other than an understanding of journalism and history, both of which she once studied. She has so far been unable to put these to use and, when I was there, seemed to have been given only menial work to do such as painting or cleaning, rather than any job calling for the use of her expensively educated brains. In fact one of her last duties before she again left the hosptal in February 1963 was painting a door. She also worked in the bandage room, a more responsible duty, but only for two weeks while a nurse was sick. This may have explained her sudden decision to leave. I am told she felt "disappointed by the many changes".

What changes? And what did this restless multi-millionairess seek at the equatorial hospital that, in 1963, she no longer found? The answer to these questions throws light on Dr. Schweitzer's tolerance of such visitors; rich women who see his hospital as a shrine of self-denial. For Miss Deterding has frequently complained that her wealth has been a persistent handicap in her life, and that at Lambaréné nobody knows or cares who her father was (he was Sir Henri Deterding, an oil tycoon) and how big was her fortune. There, she has told reporters, they do not even understand the meaning of money. They judge you by the service you perform to mankind, and that is the only worth-while gauge in life. Thus, she has said, she is happy at Lambaréné and unhappy away from it.

Regrettably, Miss Deterding has not always been able to find her niche at Dr. Schweitzer's hospital, and it is hard to believe that she has always been a satisfied and happy guest there. Her first visit occurred in 1957 when, following a friendship in London with the then Mr. Antony Armstrong-Jones, now the Earl of Snowdon and Princess Margaret's husband, she joined a party of young friends on a highly daring journey through Africa by jeep. There was talk at the time that she was hoping to bump into Group-Captain Peter Townsend, who was also in Africa, but even if true this only suggests that her initial reason for making the voyage was more social and romantic than self-sacrificing. She has admitted that she went for no "do-gooding" reason, and that her first visit to Lambaréné was partially an accident.

One story of this is that she came down with malaria fever in Kenya and the rest of the party—an ex-débutante named Miss Lavinia Lambton and some young Hussar officer friends—had to continue without her. While in hospital she decided to pay a call at Lambaréné instead of catching up with them. When they reached Stanleyville there was supposedly a telegram awaiting the party in which Miss Deterding informed them: "Bitten by snake. Gone to Lambaréné. Not to worry. Love. Olga." Another version of how the visit came about was published by *Sunday Express* reporter Angela Huth after an interview with Miss Deterding in October 1961. Miss Huth wrote: "She explained a bit about Lambaréné, the place in Africa where she spent three years helping Dr. Albert Schweitzer . . . 'I had six days with nothing to do, waiting for the connection to Nairobi. So I took the plane which takes provisions to the jungle, just for the fun of the trip. When I got there, I was very impressed with Dr. Schweitzer and casually said how wonderful I thought it would be to work for him. He said: "Why not?"—and, well, I stayed . . .' "

Since Miss Deterding once told me that she quite often takes an airplane trip on a whim, and once flew round the world to reach England from North Africa because she was impatient at being unable to get a direct flight immediately, this story seems the more credible; though both could be separate parts of a whole. She may have had fever, then left her friends and taken the freight-plane to Lambaréné. Her mother, Lady Deterding, has said: "Olga had read books by Dr. Schweitzer and set her heart on doing some sort of charity work. She had tired of society life." Her daughter confirmed this to a reporter. "It was marvellous to find something worth while to do," she said. "I'd spent seven years of seasons in the South of France, Switzerland, places like that, and I was pretty browned off with that sort of life. So when I found this opportunity for something better in Africa, I took it."

Jaded socialites with a charitable urge are not, perhaps, what one associates with the hard and skilled work of healing sick patients in the jungle. But Dr. Schweitzer had found something in Miss Deterding which persuaded him to offer her a post as a menial helper, a job where she rarely did anything more exciting than scrubbing floors, disinfecting ward-rooms and peeling potatoes. The fact that the multi-millionairess stuck this sort of privation for two years was not, however, entirely due to her pleasure at having found a spiritual and physical solution to her boredom. It had a great deal to do with the companionship of the young and handsome English doctor, Dr. Frank Catchpool.

On this subject I have the word of friends who saw both Miss Deterding and Dr. Catchpool during the time of their stay in Lambaréné. There was no doubt that the rich socialite was in love with the doctor. They spent much of their spare time together.

Catchpool was unfortunately far too poor and proud to hope for marriage to the fabulously rich Miss Deterding. He told a friend who visited the hospital that she had suggested they should get married, but he felt that the difference in their financial positions made it impossible, even if desirable. He was, as everyone in Lambaréné knew, deeply fond of his rich friend and kept a photograph of her in his room among his medical books. There was even talk between them, so he said, of setting up a similar hospital in another part of Africa, backed by some of Miss Deterding's fortune.

This, as well as their romance, came to nothing. In California where he is now working Dr. Catchpool recently recalled his friendship with Miss Deterding in these words: "I was very fond of Olga, but I met my wife in Lambaréné when she came out there as interpreter for a famous American film star. She stayed to work in the hospital and after that I suppose I didn't see so much of Olga as I had before. When my fiancée left, I left too. Today we rarely get a letter from Olga." Privately, Dr. Catchpool added: "I always felt that Olga needed taking care of, though she's not the kind of person you'd think would do so."

This is not a new impression of the restless multi-millionairess, and it is a key to Dr. Schweitzer's kindness and perception in taking her into his already crowded hospital. Miss Deterding has been a shiftless wanderer during most of her adult life, rarely staying more than a few weeks in any place of rest. Her mother has told friends that she is deeply worried about her. More than once she has been seriously ill and may even have contracted a chronic disease at Lambaréné, where amoebic ailments are common among the staff and patients and extremely hard to cure. In November 1961 she underwent a course of psycho-analysis in London, suggested by friends who hoped thereby to prevent her returning to the jungle. In Paris her close friend, Mrs. Cynthia Sainsbury, told me during Miss Deterding's third visit to Schweitzer: "Her mother is dead against her being there. Her friends don't know what to think. She had been in hospital in England again before she left this time, with this same tropical bug, I think. But she is unhappy anywhere else, and Dr. Schweitzer is always inviting her to go back, writing her letters and so forth. I don't know what is the matter with her . . . I think she wants to prove something. I am sure she's not well."

When I saw Olga Deterding, in the same cockroach-ridden aircraft which was taking me to Lambaréné, she seemed tired and unhappy. Her face, without a trace of make-up in the fierce heat, was sallow and greasy. Her clothes looked very far removed from the garments I had seen her wearing at the Ritz Hotel in London on an earlier occasion. We talked as we strolled across the blazing-hot tarmac, but her voice was listless and she showed no animation. As to how long she was planning to stay, she told me she had no idea. But that night she took a plane to Brazzaville and did not return to Lambaréné. The woman who finds wealth such a hardship, but who cannot fit easily into the austere life of Lambaréné, had gone as she had come: on an abrupt and unexplained impulse. At the hospital a woman visitor said: "Nobody is wanted in Lambaréné who does not help the work here. Olga means well but she is not trained to do a job that could be of much use. The question bothering me is why does she come?" Dr. Schweitzer, however, remained loyally silent about his departed rich helper, perhaps out of sympathy for a woman he regards more as a patient than some of his inmates.

The question is asked, can Schweitzer be influenced by a clever and pretty woman? It may be that the Doctor's lack of sophistication in the world makes him more vulnerable than most men of his age, but he is also shrewd. Marion Preminger, now Mrs. Mayer, has influenced him as much as anyone in the past years. Mrs. Clara Urquhart, his South African friend, is able to reach his inner self on occasion. And an American woman photographer, Miss Erica Anderson, achieved an unusual position in his affections; she persuaded the Doctor to let her make a film of him and his hospital after a friendship which people at the hospital say was closer than any they had seen with Schweitzer.

These women are certainly not without their charms. Marion Preminger is now a portly blonde; but in her youth, according to photographs, she was voluptuously attractive. Her belief in Dr. Schweitzer's creed and way of life began at university when she wrote a thesis for her doctorate on Dr. Schweitzer and Lambaréné. "He had always been a child love of mine," she told me. It pleases her to say, today, that next to Schweitzer's dog, Tsu-Tsu, she is his closest follower, and this humility may be characteristic. She once said: "I may be the only woman alive whose reputation is better than she is herself."

Marion has a special reason for being welcomed at the jungle hospital, apart from her devotion to the Doctor. She comes loaded with gifts of the most unlikely, and expensive sort. These are donated in response to her pressing appeals throughout the United States and include silk ties from smart shops in New York, socks, shirts, dresses, and even baseball caps. "Both Doris Duke and

Barbara Hutton give me $10,000 a year each," she told me. "I ask all the rich people to help my hospital. They know how important it is to me."

To distribute these bundles of donated finery Marion sets up shop in the hospital clearing. There is then a great handing out of goods, and explanations of what they are. Primitive natives whose acquaintance with civilized comforts has previously been slight may suddenly find themselves the possessor of a necktie marked, in a language they would not understand even if they could read, "Countess Mara tie. Hand painted, Pure silk". Small and semi-naked children wearing plaited belts of leaves against evil spirits parade joyously in peaked "Dodgers" caps. The air is one of mystified carnival.

For much of the rest of the year, when she is not in Lambaréné, Marion involves herself in lengthy and well-paid lecture tours of America. In embracing Schweitzer and his hospital she has given herself a career which co-exists happily with her work as a writer of travel and auto-biographical books. The title of her best-known volume, dealing with her adventurous life, which began in Hungarian opulence and has included residence in a palace in Hollywood, is *All I Want Is Everything*. She told me that it would better explain her motives if she could add ". . . that money cannot buy." Yet, seeing the queue of African children at her door and watching the delight with which they accepted her novel hand-outs, I wondered if she would feel able to do so much for Lambaréné without the power of other people's money.

Marion's inclusion in the community was certainly not accidental. She had read and studied Schweitzer at the University of Vienna in the days when she was a student there before the war. As a twenty-two year old girl, in 1937 she wrote the thesis which gave her a degree of Doctor of Philosophy and fifteen years later she met Dr. Schweitzer and his wife in Paris. They were charmed to hear about her studies, flattered by the admiration of such a personable and attractive young woman. An invitation to visit them in Lambaréné followed quite naturally.

At that time, Marion shared the distinction of being among the ten best-dressed women in the world, according to an American magazine. In Paris she may have seemed less sensational, but when Dr. Schweitzer saw her arrive in his plainly decorated hospital among the starched whiteness of his staff, her magnificence dazzled him. "You look like a bird of paradise in a nest of sparrows!" he exclaimed. Marion was not in the least put out. She continued to wear her low-cut, figure-hugging dresses and gowns. Even in white, with which her wardrobe was well stocked, the expensive cloth and cut of her clothes stood out from the rest. Clara Urquhart remembers a night when the old Doctor, with a slightly shocked look in his eye, sent an attendant to the American visitor with a white sheet and a word of advice that she should "cover her *décolleté* against the mosquitoes". On another occasion, the story goes that he asked one of the nurses to take Mrs. Preminger, as she then was, a "Christian nightdress".

Such sartorial reproofs did nothing to quench Marion's growing ardour for the hospital and its ways. She says that she came in 1952 because "Reverence for Life seemed a good philosophy". She has no false estimation of Schweitzer's rating as a doctor of medicine. "I think he is a simple country doctor with world authority on human kindness," she has said. The saga of his arrival in the jungle ("He came with thirty cases of medicines and started to operate in a chicken coop . . . The miracle of Lambaréné is that he is alive") has stirred her deeply. Against the critics she is apt to say, "I admit it as a qualified doctor (of philosophy?), we have no light, no water . . . still, I ask you, why are we a lighthouse to all other hospitals in the world?"

One reason might be that no other hospital in the world has the attentions of such a purposeful and all-providing "bird of paradise". Marion's hand-outs are marvelled over in primitive villages hundreds of miles from the hospital site. As Østergaard-Christensen, the Danish surgeon, wrote in his finely-drawn portrait of Lambaréné previously referred to, the natives want to possess some of the white man's magic. In their belief, things that have belonged to a man acquire some of his strength, which can be transferred to others. "When I left," the surgeon explained, "I presented a pair of old shoes to my faithful black assistant in the ward for post-operative patients. They were certainly much better than the shabby ones he was wearing, but even so his joy was disproportionately great. Now he was getting a share in the white doctor's strength . . ."* When Marion unloads her baggage in the hospital clearing, distributing garments such as are rarely if ever seen in the home villages of the patients, she is beating a big propaganda drum for Schweitzer. Outside the hospital, I was told by educated natives that one reason why a number of Africans will walk miles to reach the Doctor's primitive colony, yet will trudge past more modern and better-equipped hospitals on the way, is that they have heard stories of the marvellous "hand-outs". The Mother of All the Lepers has many children on this score alone.

And Marion insists that they shall regard her as their mother. She gives the gifts and goodies she has brought with her to children on the understanding that they thank her *as* their mother: "*Oui, ma mére*," they must recite in French. It is a confusing moment for some of the little ones who have always believed, until this moment, that they have only one mother. However, with the help of a native interpreter-assistant assigned by Dr. Schweitzer for the purpose, the child is invariably persuaded to murmur the words sufficiently audibly to satisfy its donor.

Marion sits at a table dressed in shimmering white, her fair-skinned well-manicured hands protected from anything unseemly by white gloves, her gifts bulging out of stout polythene bags. The native children whom she has adopted stand goggle-eyed round her table, no doubt seeing her as a white goddess with golden hair and blood-red lips (Marion's make-up would cause no comment on Park Avenue, but is almost unique in Lambaréné). They come prepared to wait hours for the least chance of her favours. Not one of them has the slightest idea that his self-appointed Mother is providing him with goods which have been subscribed to by a number of charitable Americans. They all think her magic absolutely splendid.

What is more questionable is Dr. Schweitzer's feeling about

* *At Work With Albert Schweitzer*

Marion's munificence. In discussion with others, he excuses any incongruity by saying that "Marion has a big heart". He has never tried to shrink it by dissuading her from bringing her gifts to the hospital. Indeed, he may well recognize their value as an attraction to the patients; one he accepts as morally if not wholly justifiable. How he privately regards her more lavish behaviour in the hospital (she annually carves her name, complete with symbolic heart, on a bench beside the path leading to the leper village), is something he has never confided to anyone.

So for thirteen years the plump, blonde, philanthropic American-Hungarian has flown into the jungles of Africa, put on her expensively low-cut white gowns, white sun helmet, and gloves, and unpacked the gifts for her "children". At meals in the cement-walled dining hut she is given an honoured place opposite to the Doctor, from which she enjoys long conversations with him in throaty German. Her voice is as large as her gestures and, in Dr. Schweitzer's opinion, her heart.

But how would the Doctor feel if he knew how muddled some of Marion's generosity has become? Before she left, during the time when I was staying at the hospital, she kindly insisted that I should take six new pairs of woollen socks from her collection for my own use. When I demurred, saying that they were obviously intended for the sick and poor natives, she told me they were surplus to her requirements. At the time, I felt that such generosity was questionable. Discussing it later with one of the staff doctors I was told that it was not uncommon. He had received an equal number of socks from her.

In her New York apartment, Mrs. Mayer keeps a roomful of African curios as mementoes of her charitable stays among the lepers. She spends much of her time expanding and disseminating the legend of Lambaréné, her dedication to the ideals of Dr. Schweitzer, and her own part in the pattern of his work. Thus the Doctor can see rewards from her allegiance; a rich fountain of material benefits pouring towards Lambaréné from the U.S.A., for which he is grateful. The inclusion of such an unusual hospital-visitor among his disciples may well be worth any small embarrassments to his modesty. Marion is only one of a number of devoted "Schweitzerines" in different parts of the world, and they are mainly women. His tolerance towards them all suggests that he enjoys their adulation.

In London, Mrs. Clara Urquhart calls herself "something of a mother to the hospital". She holds an equally high place in his esteem, and claims that the Doctor knows her as one of his few intimate friends. This claim is not uncommon among the women who know Schweitzer well, but is truer in Mrs. Urquhart's case in that she actively serves the hospital in Europe. During her visits to Lambaréné which began seventeen years ago, there have been times when the Doctor has found her presence relaxing as well as comforting. "Sometimes," she told me, "he will ask me to join him in the leper village. He may have been particularly moved by some terrible case of suffering. He may be tired. Whatever the reason, he doesn't tell me, but beckons me to sit beside him in almost complete silence. For perhaps an hour we will sit so, he holding my hand as much as to say 'Don't talk . . . let us just be together.' "

South African Mrs. Urquhart gives no impression of being under the Doctor's spell despite the warmth of her affection for him. She describes him as the most wonderful friend in the world, but certainly no saint. As an example of this, she recalls how her wealthy brother once offered to pay to have showers and proper lavatories installed, with main drainage, at Lambaréné, only to have his offer firmly turned down by Schweitzer. As a rich woman herself—her income from an inheritance is believed to approach fifty thousand pounds annually—she could do much for the hospital, were it permitted. Instead, she handles a number of small concerns for the Doctor in London, among them the recruitment of an occasional nurse and the sending of supplies. "Even if Dr. Schweitzer wants a new pen," she has said, "I am only too pleased to get it for him."

Mrs. Urquhart is an attractive and well-preserved woman who has twice been married. She is not by any means fully employed in helping the hospital. Her books are published regularly and they show a keen and energetic mind. In addition, she is an ardent worker for other causes which seek to help the semi-nourished and under-privileged. It may be that her knowledge of such works has given her a particular insight into Dr. Schweitzer's colony, especially his followers and adoring disciples about whom she expresses mixed feelings. "I'll tell you one thing," she said. "The people round him really have no idea about his philosophy, or what he's all about." There are, of course, exceptions as Mrs. Urquhart is quick to point out. She names a woman called Lotte Gerhold in Salzburg, Austria, as among them: "A very cultured person who really understands the Doctor."

But some of the protective cocoon spun round Schweitzer by his closest disciples, by such devoted women as Mathilde Kottmann and Ali Silver, strikes the more sophisticated Mrs. Urquhart as well-intentioned but excessive. "If the world were about to blow up, and Mathilde had to pass on the cable announcing it to the Doctor, she wouldn't be able to do so if she thought it would disturb him," Mrs. Urquhart once said. "Sometimes I wonder what it is all about." She added that in her opinion Mathilde and Ali and another senior nurse, Toni van Leer, "would all be nuns if they didn't have Schweitzer".

For herself, Mrs. Urquhart says she does not have "this complete abnegation". She prefers to regard the Doctor as a perfectly normal and very dear friend, a position that allows her to disagree with him and, occasionally, to ignore his commands. "He gets furious with me when I go out to see the sunset at 6 o'clock in the evening (on the equator, sunrises and sunsets do not vary from season to season) without a hat," she said, laughing. "But, actually, if you see Schweitzer's philosophy as both Reverence for Life and responsibility for all around him, then it is not distasteful."

For Mrs. Urquhart, with her sense of humour and her love of the great man of Lambaréné, it may not be. Any more than it is offensive to the huge and universal club of people who revere in the legend of Schweitzer their idol's insistence on commanding the lives of everyone around him with a military zeal more in keeping with a Calvinist priest. But the question more likely to prove disturbing, even to the most credulous, is why Albert Schweitzer deprives those who come to serve him of so many comforts and consolations while allowing himself to be flattered and made much of by so many charming, warm-hearted and wealthy women.

TEN

ECCENTRICS' GOAL

SO THE wealthy come to Lambaréné with Schweitzer's blessing, to be helped if not healed of their golden guilt complexes, their insatiable desires to philanthropize, to succour the poor and needy. Some, like Marion Preminger and Clara Urquhart, achieve a certain influence over the old Doctor. Others, those oddly sad cases such as the onerously rich Miss Deterding, merely fit into the loose pattern of the hospital. If the therapy they seek is of little value to Schweitzer, at least they are made the more content by scrubbing an occasional floor or peeling a sack of potatoes. Perhaps in the Doctor's scheme of things there is as fierce a sympathy for the rich as for the poor. In Lambaréné he may try to widen a little the eye of that needle through which the camel can pass more easily than the rich man.

Many another sort of woman, unburdened by great fortunes and inheritances, is also to be found among the workers of this curious hospital and widely different compulsions mark them out. Few have come for conventional reasons. The eccentrics are by far the most colourful. These are women who have been driven towards Lambaréné by the most urgent and extraordinary personal motives, following a path similar to that trodden by countless worshippers of the great prophets, mystics and preachers of history. An evangelical fervour possesses them, urging their feet in the direction of The One they have singled out as a fitting object for their devotion. It is no good turning them away or spurning them, since the very act would be translated into an even more evident need for their help and support. They are well-meaning, industrious, even noble.

Were we concerned only with a pretty picture of Schweitzer's hospital, it would be kinder to pass over this group of spiritual camp followers; but, in assessing the fundamental values of his experiment in Christ-like living, they must take their place on the scales, if only as witnesses to the power of Schweitzer's legend. A man who knows Lambaréné well vouches for the fact that they are regular applicants for posts among the nursing staff. Schweitzer, according to this informant, does his best to weed them out and dissuade them before they arrive. Yet not a few find their way to the jungle hospital and have to be taken in.

While there, they may do useful work. No pride or pretension stands in their way and they are satisfied with the most unpleasant of chores. The woman seen bandaging a goat's ear or scrubbing bloody bandages is probably a devoted eccentric who finds complete joy in this menial service. Ask her what she feels about the hospital, and about Dr. Schweitzer, and she will reply with radiant face and shining eyes that here is the nearest thing on earth to the Kingdom of God. To such as she the Doctor is "a living miracle", "the most marvellous man on earth", "a pure saint".

In the early part of last year one such woman was making an unusually favourable impression in Lambaréné among even the most grudging of the long-serving staff veterans, normally aloof and reserved towards the eccentric worshippers. She was an Englishwoman, a twice-married mother of two grown-up children, who rejoiced in the belief that she had been directed by God to come to Africa and serve Him and Dr. Schweitzer at the same time. No better example of the eccentric fringe among Schweitzer's helpers exists.

Mrs. Joan Clent was forty-five when she arrived in Lambaréné dressed in ragged, travel-stained clothing with one leg bandaged and cruelly molested by flies and insects. She had completed an incredible 1,000 mile journey on a bicycle to reach the hospital, yet that was not the whole of her story. When he heard it from her lips, Dr. Schweitzer was so moved that he invited her to stay and join his band for as long as she wished.

The saga of this extraordinary Englishwoman is worth serious study as an example of the power of Dr. Schweitzer's appeal, and the magnetic attraction of the legend of Lambaréné. So far as I have been able to substantiate it, the facts which follow are true. Mrs. Joan E. C. Clent began life in an atmosphere of discipline and conformity such as one would expect to find in the family of a British naval commander, which her father was. He was stationed then in Portsmouth, where she was born. Nobody need doubt that her early days at home and at school were normal and formal to a point of conventional satisfaction.

Either at that time or later, Mrs. Clent read about the lives of great adventurers, naval heroes and explorers. In all of these she found a common link; the breaking of fresh ground, of moving outward from their island home to discover fresh lands where strange souls flourished. These illustrious men of history seemed to her to have spread lofty ideals and the word of God among the savages they encountered. Her imagination was particularly caught by their religious strength.

In time, she married a Mr. Harry Shiston, a draughtsman, who no doubt persuaded her to put away her dreams for a while. Mr. Shiston now lives in Weymouth, Dorset. So far as is known, they lived quietly and pleasantly together there, though the marriage did not last. Today, Mrs. Clent has two good-looking, grown-up children; twenty-one year old Andrew, a merchant seaman, and Ann, twenty-three, a slim and attractive brunette. Neither knew in advance of their mother's plans to dedicate herself to Dr. Schweitzer. During her travels in Africa and before they helplessly awaited news of her, at home in England.

Mrs. Clent's second marriage was to a Mr. Richard Clent, now a sixty-three year old man also living in Weymouth. According to his wife, Mr. Clent was in favour of her disappearance into Africa once they had both taken their vows to serve God wherever he might direct them to go. Three years before I met her in Lambaréné in January 1963, Mrs. Clent told him she had "given herself to God". Her husband, she said, had decided on a similar life of devotion, but in another direction. She had no compunction about leaving her husband (she made no mention of a family) since she had looked in her Bible and found advice that: "He that loveth father or mother more than me is not worthy of me . . ." (Matthew 10:37). This being so, she set out on the journey that led, finally, to Lambaréné.

Apparently Mrs. Clent continued to look in her Bible, or to be guided more directly by some form of spiritual and mental command from God, so that nothing she did from that moment represented her own will. She came to London at God's instruction, took a job as a saleswoman in a firm where she was able to meet and study many Jewish people, living meanwhile on a diet of oranges and honey, without even water to drink.

Mrs. Clent's diet, which she says she kept to for the three years before she arrived in Lambaréné, was the cause of some confusion in the mind of a distinguished Swiss dietician, Dr. Nussbaum. The silver-haired and gentle scientist was visiting Lambaréné at the same time as myself. He overheard Mrs. Clent telling me of her frugal fruit-diet and questioned her keenly about it. She insisted that she had eaten nothing other than these two foods during the three years, at which Dr. Nussbaum looked even more disturbed. He took me aside later, to ask if I believed the Englishwoman's story. I told him I had no reason to disbelieve it. The reason he asked, he said, was that it tended to upset a lifetime of calculations. The body, as we know, cannot sustain energy without a certain number of necessary proteins. In the doctor's experience these could not be provided by Mrs. Clent's professed diet.

When she heard of Dr. Nussbaum's confusion, the eccentric Mrs. Clent gave the following explanation, which must stand as one of the most remarkable acts of human subjugation and self-denial since the early martyrs. As it bears directly on the attraction of Dr. Schweitzer's "totem" for the more eccentric of his followers, I propose to repeat it here.

Quite simply, without any hint of distaste in her rather staring grey-blue eyes, Mrs. Clent said: "I don't want to shock you, but my diet was lacking in certain properties for a very special reason. Through it, I was able to lose the stigmata of womanhood, if you know what I mean by that. And I succeeded, so that my travels and service to God are easier to carry out."

It is a little hard to imagine a more extraordinary wish in a mother of two healthy children, especially as Mrs. Clent was approaching fifty years old when I met her, an age at which most women are naturally relieved of the "stigmata of womanhood" by menopause. Dr. Nussbaum might have found her explanation revealing, but I was unable to tell him what she had said as he had already left the hospital. His final words on the subject had expressed the gravest doubts whether a human being could live for a year, let alone three years, on a diet of honey and oranges alone. It is doubtful whether he would have appreciated Mrs. Clent's peculiar reasons, or believed her assertion that she did live as she claimed. All his records, he told me woefully, would have to be revised if this actually had taken place.

To continue her story as she told it to me, when not selling goods Mrs. Clent took a course in psychiatry ("so that I could understand the Jews and their problems more readily"). She told me that at one time she had qualified as a doctor at St. Thomas's Hospital, London but had "sickened of treating effects, pushing drugs into people . . . I wanted to get down to the causes, as Dr. Schweitzer is doing". A check made at St. Thomas's brought nothing to light as the hospital could find no record of anyone under the name of Joan Clent having qualified in medicine there. She may, of course, have used her maiden name. In Lambaréné she was addressed by everyone as "Dr. Clent". Her psychiatry may have been useful in tending the African natives who speak as many as sixteen different dialects; but she was employed while I was there not as a doctor but as a nurse.

She wanted, so she told me, to "influence" the Jews, feeling that in many ways their poverty and problems stemmed from a lack of understanding of the true God. "I did not try to convert them," she said, "but some did change over to Christianity while I was working with them." Mrs. Clent made many Jewish friends. She felt a great compassion for their race and attended their synagogues, learning their ways of life. For a year, she devoted herself to their service, helping where she could in cases of poverty and suffering. All the while, she continued to observe her stringent diet

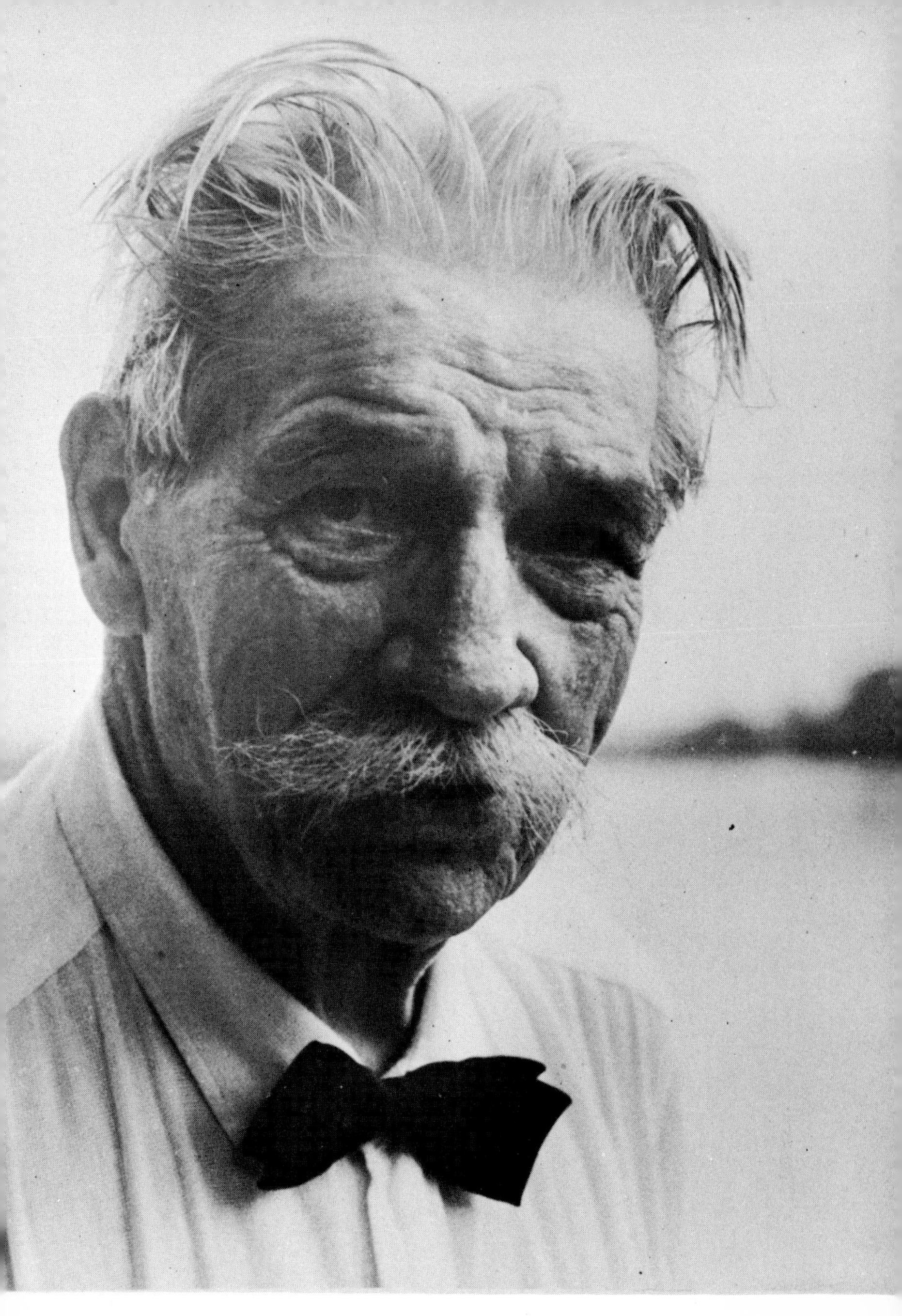

Doctor Albert Schweitzer

A view of Lambaréné hospital from the river Ogowe

Left, remains of the old operating theatre. Below, children play on the site of the proposed new theatre

A nurse holds Parsifal the pelican, a favourite pet of Doctor Schweitzer's and the hospital "watch-dog"

Some of the nurses at Lambaréné: left, Trudi Boschler; below, Christine Lloyd, left, Joan Clent, second from left, and a Dutch nurse examining a "tum-tum" drum

Patients queueing for medicine

Treatment tables being scrubbed

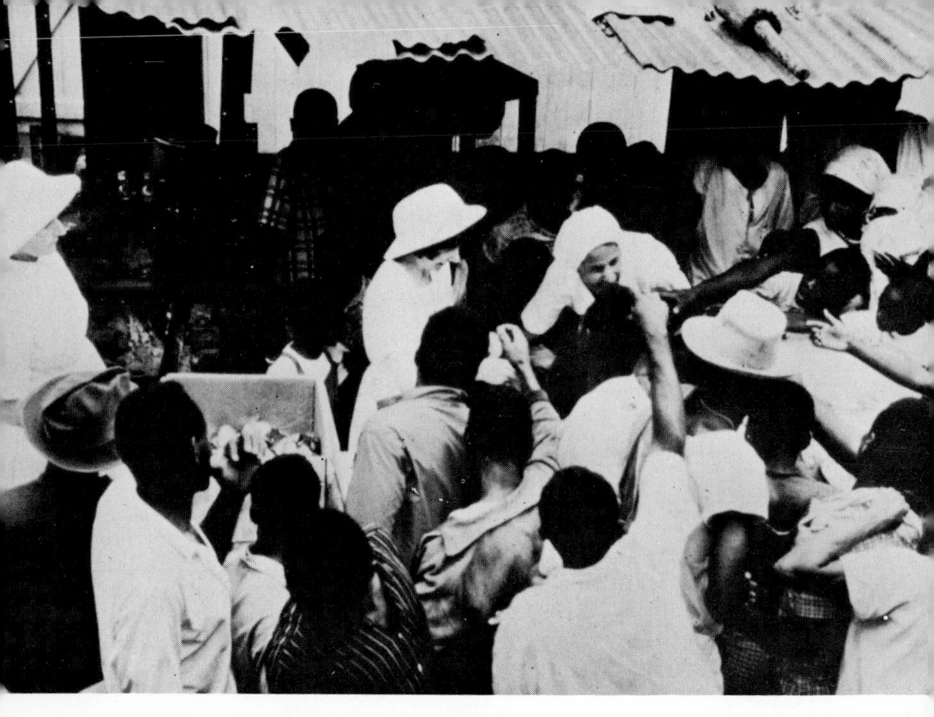

Nurses Ali Silver, left, Christine Lloyd, centre, and Olga Deterding distribute gifts at Christmas

As part of a "therapy" treatment, patients unable to work are given rocks which they have to break into stones for use on the new road

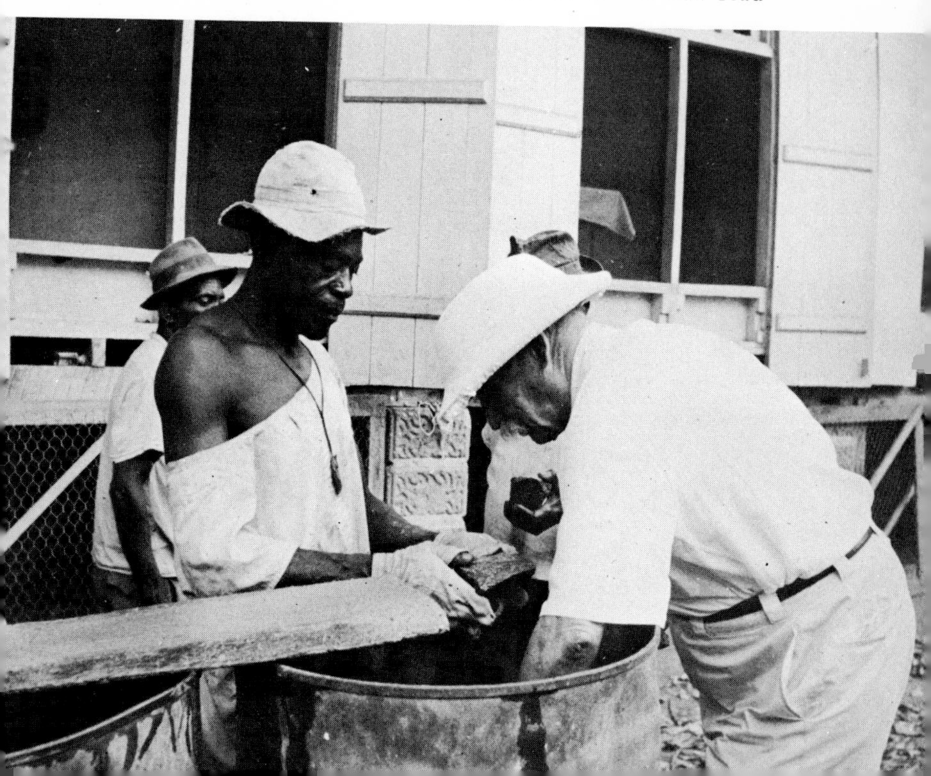

An open-air sterilizer outside the "tape worm" pharmacy building

Living quarters for some of the patients

Doctor Schweitzer visits one of the hospital wards

Animals roam freely among patients and nurses

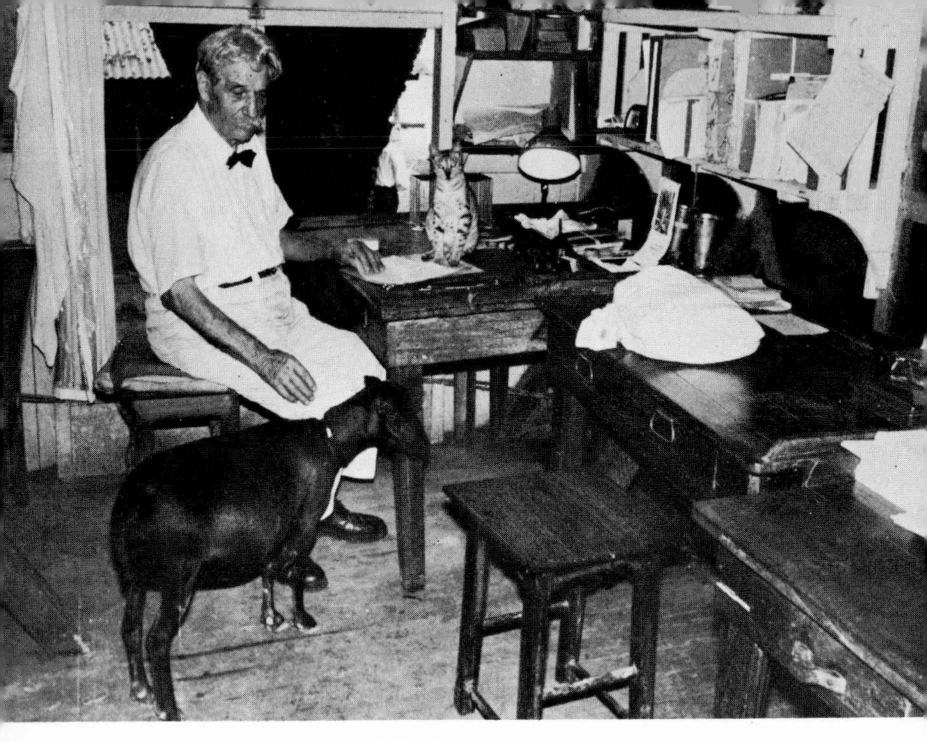

Above, animals are part of the furniture in Doctor Schweitzer's office

Below, Parsifal and master pass the time of day

with the result that her weight fell alarmingly. A tall, strong-shouldered woman of five foot seven and a half inches, her loss of flesh became increasingly noticeable to her friends, many of whom advised her to eat more or accept medical supervision. She had one reply for them all: God will look after me. To eat meat, she said, "would be like eating myself".

However, after a surge of particularly anxious persuasion, Joan Clent did take herself off to a Jewish woman doctor who, not surprisingly, pronounced her far too thin. At that time she weighed only seven stone. The doctor had to admit that she was quite fit and asked why she was punishing herself in this manner, denying herself normal food. Mrs. Clent told of her decision to serve God, adding that He had directed her to reach Dr. Albert Schweitzer and enter his service in due course. The woman doctor confessed that she, too, had been trying for three years to get to Lambaréné, but Schweitzer had refused to let her come. She told Mrs. Clent: "I feel you will get there."

The time came when Mrs. Clent was "told by God" to go to Africa via France. She had been working with and for the Jews for about a year. She was to spend two years serving the cause of Vietnamese refugees in France before continuing her journey. Very soon after this batch of orders, Mrs. Clent was at work among the refugees, making new friends among her French colleagues and the wretched displaced native families in her care. It was the latter, the poor Vietnamese, who clubbed together at the end of her stay among them to buy her a bicycle so that she could reach her jungle goal. When she accepted it as a perfectly sensible vehicle for reaching Dr. Schweitzer in the Gabon, Marco Polo might well have admired her.

Friends also paid her fare to Dakar, handing her a return ticket to be on the safe side. After touching farewells Joan Clent set forth. She landed in Africa, elated at the nearness of her target, enjoyed a meal of honey and oranges, and sought out the High Commissioner who promptly told her that on *no* account could she cross Guinea. She would, he said, certainly be cut into small pieces, and possibly eaten, by the panga-carrying savages if she did so. He had no wish to have her blood on his hands.

Mrs. Clent had a large-scale map, also given to her by the kindly Vietnamese whom she had left in France. A study of it convinced her that there were other ways to reach Schweitzer, though none of them started from where she was in Dakar. All she possessed was her bicycle, on which she was forbidden to leave the country, and her return ticket to France. By good fortune she happened to meet a woman who was returning to Marseilles and who did not have a ticket. When the two had exchanged confidences, Mrs. Clent's no doubt the more exciting of the two, this good soul insisted on paying her fare to Abidjan on the Ivory Coast, in exchange for the return half of her French ticket. The deal done, Joan Clent found a ship to take her on, now carrying only a one-way ticket to the heart of Africa.

She had no money with her. Food was given to her by natives she encountered *en route* and, with a smattering of French and native words she picked up, chatted to. Whenever she saw a native mother with a small baby, she opened her arms towards it and pleased the mother by fondling and teasing the child. Her clothing was confined to the garments she had on her back, the only pair of shoes belonging to her were on her feet. She had deliberately taken nothing, believing that God would provide while she obeyed His will. There is evidence that the provision was often slight, but she survived.

When the ship reached her port of destination, Mrs. Clent trundled her bicycle down the gangplank, mounted it, and rode towards the jungle. Her path to Schweitzer lay across nearly 1,000 miles of jungle, bush, scrub, wild-land, bad-land, swamp, river, tundra, forest, lake, and plain. The tribes she would pass among contained many with savage reputations. Cannibalism is not extinct, by any means. (While I was in Lambaréné, there were seven convictions for it in Sierra Leone, farther up the coast.) A few miles east of Abidjan Mrs. Clent crossed the border into Ghana. Farther in the same direction she entered Togo; then Dahomey, Nigeria and the Cameroons. Here she turned south, though by now she had parted with her map and went only in the directions given her by friendly natives. Having cycled her way across the huge Cameroon and skirted tiny Spanish Guinea, she entered Gabon. The end of her journey was unbelievably in sight.

By now Joan Clent was travel-stained and worn to the point of filthy raggedness. She admits that she had rarely bathed and "smelt horrible". She had taken her food and shelter where it was offered, sometimes staying in missions, at others sleeping with primitive natives in their *kraals*. When they offered her their food, she swallowed it down though sometimes it was so disgusting that she had to force herself to bring it back up again in the privacy of the jungle afterwards. The impression this contact with native cooking left on her was that something must urgently be done to teach the Africans how to use food. "They give their small children hot peppers!" she reported. "No wonder the poor things are so often seedy."

In other ways, Mrs. Clent found her journey satisfying. "It was the most wonderful experience," she told me. "I went from village to village, town to town, and staying in missions of every denomination, having a fellowship with them all that was binding for ever. Sleeping in tiny villages in their little houses with them, living as they live, eating their food and learning from them many wonderful things." She also wrote home to say: "I cannot tell you the great love that flows from my heart for these people, and they in their turn send out that great transmuting power called *love*. They are the most wonderful people in the whole world. Right in the heart of the bush, when they had never seen a white woman before, their first reaction was to disappear. But when they got used to me, they were simply wonderful. They are not called Christians, but their actions would put any European Christians to shame. They beckon you into their homes, they have no furniture only the mud floor to sit on but all they have is yours. Yes, perhaps you would say they are dirty. But by the time I reached them I was very dirty and I know I smelt pretty awful. You realize many of them are pretty far from water . . . But the first thing they always gave me was a bucket of water."

One night when she was putting up a small tent she carried on the back of her cycle, and used frequently in the jungle, Mrs. Clent felt something cold and moist on her arm and looked down to see a dangerous snake coiled round it. At first she was terrified; but the moment she remembered that the snake as well as she belonged to God's kingdom, the fear passed. As she relaxed, so the snake seemed to sense that she was no longer an enemy. It slithered harmlessly away. "But when I told the natives whose village I was in, they said I had been in the most terrible danger," she said. "I told them 'not at all. We are all God's creatures.' "

Mrs. Clent completed her journey convinced that there is nothing to fear in Africa. In a letter to her mother, she wrote: "The minds of these people are clean, wholly pure and completely unspoilt. God grant that they will remain that way. I am sure that with a little more confidence in themselves they can lead the world." She told me she had come across young African terrorists while they were ambushing soldiers. They fired shots from their rifles, then when their quarry fled "they flung down their arms and laughed and shouted like boys". What the same terrorists might have done to her had she appeared in front of their ambush instead of behind it she does not think about. But she will admit that Africa can be dangerous to the unwary. In a letter, she wrote revealingly from Lambaréné: "And so, after my stay here and learning all I can I may go forward in God's service. How long shall I be here? I do not know, I am not a law unto myself, but God will make it quite plain. It may be this time to die, but it is in dying that we are born into the eternal life, and to live in hearts we leave behind is not to die . . ."

Those who know Africa well would say that Mrs. Clent has been almost miraculously spared so far. If she intends to continue her journey through the wild jungle lands, the hope of her return to the husband and family she left in Weymouth is not great. For this reason, her son and daughter were anxiously planning to visit Dr. Schweitzer's hospital so that they might persuade her to come home with them (this was in 1963, when I brought them the first news of their mother's whereabouts). Both Mrs. Clent's husbands have joined forces to try to stop the young couple from following their mother, but they are equally anxious. Her present husband, Mr. Clent, told a reporter who visited him in March 1963: "I love her still, but I could never persuade her to come back." The first husband, Mr. Harry Shiston, added: "It takes a superman to hold her admiration."

Dr. Schweitzer was not only holding her admiration when I met Mrs. Clent in the hospital, it seemed to me that he was expanding it. She had been given clean white clothes. Her greying, sandy hair was tied in a neat bun. Her strongly-boned face shone with a release of reverent joy at the mention of the Doctor's name. Furthermore, her skinniness and wounds had all but vanished. For some reason, now that she had reached her goal Mrs. Clent felt free to eat normally, or as normally as the mainly vegetarian diet of Lambaréné will allow.

How close she came to disaster when almost at the hospital she told me herself. She had ridden her bicycle into a village late in the afternoon. Even under normal circumstances it was not a good time to travel through the bush. For a lone white woman, exhausted and emaciated, it seemed sheer folly to the Headman from whom she asked the way. Also, as he pointed out, the track had been partially washed away by heavy rains. "He was so upset when I told him I must press on that he asked me to take some money he had and hire a car to take me the last few miles," she told me. "I was grateful for his kindness, but I pointed out that I was in God's service and I had nothing to fear."

As she rode away from the astonished chief, Mrs. Clent said that she felt a slight twinge of anxiety. And when she found her bicycle skidding and bumping down a steep hill in the dusk, running away with her over the flood-destroyed pathway, she suddenly wondered whether God had not sent the kind native to give her assistance. It was too late to do more than wonder because in the next few yards she felt the cycle wrench away from her and she fell heavily on her left side, paralysing the arm. One leg was badly cut, and soon buzzing with jungle flies. She had to pick up her damaged machine and walk fourteen miles before a passing jeep, with a European couple aboard, picked her up,put her bicycle in the back and drove her to a near-by mission. "A good night's rest and I continued my journey," she told me. "I couldn't wait to get here and meet Dr. Schweitzer."

She came across the Ogowe River weighing little more than six stone. She had no money, a broken bicycle and only the tattered clothes she wore. Dr. Schweitzer made her welcome. Having heard her story, he asked her to stay on as one of the nursing staff. The goal that had taken her three years, that had removed her from her family in England, was won. Mrs. Joan Clent had joined the worshippers at the shrine of Dr. Schweitzer to demonstrate to the whole world what an astonishing strength lies in the lure of his legend.

I saw a good deal of Mrs. Clent while I was in the hospital. She always looked to me like a communicant who had just received the sacrament, so light and joyful was her tread. We walked to the leper village, along the mile-long, beaten pathway. As we passed the hospital's strange little cemetery of graves, some with obscure *fetichist* headstones, she talked openly of the need she still feels to travel on through Africa, risking death if necessary. Then we came across a long, dirty and blood-soaked bandage lying in our road, and Mrs. Clent said: "That is one of the problems we have here. It is so hard to get the Africans to take their surgical dressings seriously." From her tone of voice, expressing almost proprietory interest, it seemed that Mrs. Clent would remain at Lambaréné for a long while, both in the service of God and Dr. Schweitzer.

The lesson of Mrs. Clent is that Lambaréné is a better healing-place for some of those sick of materialism and civilization than for all those sick of more bodily ailments. The Doctor may not prefer this sort of volunteer helper. He cannot turn her away and continue to preach his philosophy. In Reverence for Life there is always a danger of giving more reverence to one life than to another, and Dr. Schweitzer knows this and guards against it. What it costs him to have to recognize his position as a beacon in the world for spiritually hungry souls such as Mrs. Joan Clent, is hard to estimate. He may delight in the adoration he sees shining from their eyes.

More probably, he finds their worship flattering but more than a little disturbing to his ethical mind. The answer would seem to be simple, if that is the case; he could use the funds which are pouring hourly into the coffers of his many U.S. Fellowships to create a strictly clinical hospital in which the work of healing the sick in body would be paramount. He could then, no sooner than he richly deserves, retire to develop and expand his philosophies and theological beliefs and writings.

Would he, or the hospital, lose greatly? It is no longer possible for the Doctor to add much to the medical bank balance of his experiment, if he ever did so. Most of his time is now taken up with other work. He would be greatly missed as a presence, as a leader, but surely other distinguished medical men would cover his omission in time? And in peace and comfort in Europe, or near by in Africa if he so chose, Albert Schweitzer could give the whole of his remaining time and energy to the work he believes is more important even than healing. Until he does so, or until his death, Lambaréné will remain the universal target for the Mrs. Joan Clents of this world.

ELEVEN

THE NOVICE

BUT IF Schweitzer is as much concerned with the needs of his flock of helpers as with those of his suffering patients, does this excuse his strange choice of helpers? No doubt it does, if one accepts that Lambaréné is an intellectually-conceived retort for a rare and dangerous experiment in human and spiritual chemistry. If one believes that a Christ-like form of living can be a useful example to a world where many such may be found in the straggling ranks of nuclear disarmers, anti-vivisectionists, opposers of veal and *paté* production, and the League against Cruel Sports, to single out only the best-scorned of the dedicated and pitifully vain societies for human improvement, then it must be so. We may go a long way towards accepting Dr. Schweitzer as a living prophet (though of doom, if his incomplete Philosophy is a guide). We may say that his attraction for people who seek to bathe their impressionable souls in his reflected light is wholesome and pure. Nevertheless, we must not overlook the extravagant claims of his legend.

Schweitzer is not only renowned as a jungle saint, or prophet, but as a force for healing in the underdeveloped regions of emergent Africa. When administrators and public-spirited beings seek to put up hospitals, to send out mobile clinics and teams of trained, equipped medical workers, what is the thought in people's minds? Let them do as Schweitzer does . . . But such a yard-stick is good only if what Schweitzer is doing contains the ingredients of a solution to the problem of sickness among primitive Africans. If it is an end in itself, a mere means by which the Doctor can experiment with his theological and philosophical beliefs, then it should be known to have these limitations, not disguised as a shining example to all who must follow him.

In the Gabonese Republic there are nearly half a million people, free and independently able to provide for themselves through their sizable exportation of plywood and other raw materials. A number of Americans now working there for oil-prospecting firms in the States believe that oil and other rich minerals will soon be located and mined in this area of 103,000 square miles. As a former member state of French Equatorial Africa the country still receives help and technical advice from France. But these facts can be left on one side since they relate only to the potential of the Gabon, while Schweitzer stands against the tide of present expansion. Already officials say that his hospital is a distressing example to the world of local backwardness, while they are striving to convey an impression of what progress has been achieved. They point to their large and modern hospital in Libreville, to their many smaller medical centres and maternity clinics, and to their thorough vaccination and pest-elimination programme; but the world tends to ignore these excellent improvements while Schweitzer and the crumbling hospital of Lambaréné remain the picture which fantasy paints in universal minds. The leader writer of *The Times* in London can say with assurance that "The insistent demand of the African masses for modern health services is one of the forces that should modernize African society and foster the growth of disciplined professions." This can only apply to the Gabon once the legend of Lambaréné has been put in perspective.

The striking fact is that Dr. Schweitzer's appeal for women has been and still is the keel on which the whole fabric of Lambaréné is laid, the basis from which he has been able to rule in god-like mastery over his kingdom. Men could never have given such obedience. It is in using female loyalty and support that Schweitzer has allowed his work to become sentimentalized and sanctified by women all over the world. His position is now so revered that he can demand acts of heroism, long periods of self-denial and a loyalty and affection that are wholly enduring. There are always more young women clamouring to be allowed into Lambaréné to work than there are positions for them.

Yet if the casual observer were to ask who these heroines of Lambaréné are, and have been, the query would be tactfully ignored. It is not Schweitzer's policy to add to anyone's legend but his own, and his closest and most experienced staff know and observe this with scrupulous care. In civilized countries it is usually the hardened criminal who "forgets" when faced with his crimes, but in Lambaréné it is paradoxically the virtuous Doctor and his angelic assistants who suffer a lapse of memory when questioned about their wealth as a hospital ("When I need money, I ask my Fellowship for it") their intake of patients ("We do not keep records") or their more remarkable colleagues. One of the strictest of many "taboos" is the need to mind only one's own business in Lambaréné; indeed, to talk of nobody else there, past, present or future.

Thus I frequently found myself chatting in near-whispers with nurses and doctors, in the privacy of their curtained, screen-walled rooms, while they unburdened themselves about their fellow workers. For the most part, these accounts reflected nothing but the highest credit on the subjects, so that there seemed no sensible reason for obscuring them. Yet time and again I was asked not to mention that I had heard such-and-such, or been told about so-and-so. More than once, a careful watch was kept by those I talked with to be sure that we were not overheard.

From what they told me, and from a number of other sources, I have pieced together an inadequate portrait of the women (other than the rich and eccentric ones whom we have already discussed) who have given their services to Lambaréné over the years. I have been helped by eye-witness accounts and impressions given to me by other visitors. I present the sketchy picture because it seems to me to be the first attempt made, other than a slight pen-study once published by Dr. Schweitzer's South African writer friend Mrs. Clara Urquhart, to pay tribute to a band of exceptional and heroic women.

These women have contributed solidly to the Schweitzer hospital, not through their money or the driving force of some inner compulsion, but because they responded to what they believed was a real and tragic need. For the most part they came to work humbly and anonymously at a task which had upset their sense of pride in the human race; to attempt a form of slum-clearance of the jungle. It was none the less an act of great valour and distinction. Mostly, they worked until ill-health or climate forced them to retire, but a few adapted themselves to the mystique of Lambaréné as a permanent, life-long crusade.

Those first volunteer nurses, the redoubtable Emma Haussknecht and Mathilde Kottmann, surely had no idea when they came to Lambaréné soon after the First World War that they were emigrating, body and soul, to this tortured country. Yet Mlle. Haussknecht died in 1956 after thirty-one years of service. A plain white cross marks her grave between Dr. Schweitzer's room and the river. She lies beside the ashes of Mrs. Schweitzer in a position of almost unique honour, under the Doctor's constant gaze. When looking out from his desk, or walking down the path to the staff quarters of the hospital, the Doctor has a constant reminder of two women brought closer together by death than they ever were by life.

Mathilde Kottmann's length of service puts everyone else's to shame, including Nurse Haussknecht's. This serene Alsatian woman, her face pale and soft as *crêpe de Chine*, her eyes expressing an infinite knowledge of suffering, has spent forty years at the Doctor's side. Her silver hair is drawn into a tight bun over the tall column of her graceful neck. At the long table in the staff dining-room she sits next to Schweitzer, speaking quietly and seldom, but pervading the room with an unmistakable air of authority which seems almost to extend to the jungle outside. She is the Doctor's most loyal helper.

Then there is the beautiful Dutch nurse, Ali Silver, who came in 1947, only comparatively recently. She first heard of Dr. Schweitzer in her church in the north of Holland. Then, as the idea of what he was doing took root in her imagination, she began to consider joining him. "I thought . . . well, you are strong, you have an all round training; why don't you do something about it?"

she explains. After three months in Günsbach with Mme. Martin, Schweitzer's secretary and manager of affairs in his absence, Miss Silver came to Lambaréné to serve without question the man she sees as a god-like master. "There is still much work for us to do here," she says simply. "Who would show so much pity to the very poor?"

Ali Silver is plumper, smaller and more cheerful than Mathilde. She has fine grey hair and bright, eager eyes. Unlike Mathilde, her knowledge of English makes her a useful interpreter for visitors, and a ready informant for Schweitzer on all that passes between them that he does not hear himself.

A doctor from Lambaréné has said that Ali and Mathilde run the establishment between them on Schweitzer's behalf, but that neither has complete control. Rather cunningly, the old Doctor has divided the power he delegates so that no one person can effectively take control. As his two lieutenants are said to guard their provinces with the tenacity of nesting sparrows, there is small danger that they will ever unite against him. Yet, though they keep a firm check on each other, these two women do virtually run the hospital and, it is increasingly said, Schweitzer. They sleep and do most of their work in rooms adjoining his, cut off from the other staff quarters. They are in charge not only of administration but of the nursing staff as well. They are the main guardians of the thick veil between Dr. Schweitzer and the outside world. "With their devoted hard work and their gentleness," wrote one visitor to Lambaréné, "goes an iron determination." It is certainly true that younger women on the staff are uncomfortable under their censuring gaze, especially when they have received some small favour from *le grand docteur* himself.

Younger women predominate among these lesser orders of the staff and, since it is widely known how rough and primitive conditions at Lambaréné are, it is hard to find a satisfactory general answer to the question of why they come. Big money cannot be the lure, since they get only a pittance of about two pounds a week and their keep. Does a desire for social importance play a part? On the contrary, most of the girls come from good and some from high-born families in the social upper brackets. Are they then ugly ducklings seeking a sphere where they will be more appreciated than heretofore? This also falls far short of the mark. Most of the girl nurses of Lambaréné are nice-looking, not a few dazzlingly attractive.

No, the magnetic pull which draws these young women to the jungles of Africa is unquestionably the Image of an old man with a graven, kindly face, strong white hair and the eyes of an Old Testament prophet: Albert Schweitzer. They come to serve at his altar, to worship at his shrine and to share something of the glamour of his kingdom if only by an act of dedication and service. On arrival, when they step out of the canoe after an exciting journey by sea or plane, the jungle closes round them, and the reality of their mission meets them face to face. It is worth considering for the effect it has on them.

The coming of a new nurse is an event at Lambaréné. Dr. Schweitzer comes down to the jetty to greet her—as one day he will come to join in the opera-chorus farewell on her departure. Never in her life will she forget her first sight of that legendary figure, probably accompanied by a small dog or some pet animal. A little disillusionment may be felt as her senses react to the first sights, sounds and smells of the hospital colony, with its apparent squalor and disorder; but this is soon explained as necessary for making the natives feel at home. She is also told that nothing more modern and hygenic would woo them from the *fetichman*, or witch doctor (an explanation which was true fifty years ago, but is scarcely valid today).

When she has been shown her room and introduced to some of her colleagues, the new nurse is escorted by an older hand—each novice being put in the charge of an older-experienced nurse or worker who speaks her language—to her lowly place in the hierarchy of the dining-room. There, as she waits amid the hushed assembly of white-clad nurses and doctors for the arrival of the Doctor, she may feel a little nervous. The sensation passes as Dr. Schweitzer enters the room, moving quietly to his seat in the centre of the table, his back to the jungle. After his grace, she sits in her chair, opens her linen napkin bag and wonders what food this strange meal will bring forth. To her surprise it is neither unpleasant nor austere. True, there is butter only three days a week, and the diet is limited in meats and fish and eggs; but otherwise it is palatable and adequate, if not plentiful. Food is the besetting problem of a colony where marketing is done by foray into near-by villages, and by hard bargaining with native fishermen who bring their catch to the hospital clearing.

Now the new arrival has time for a few moment's reflection. She sees the atmosphere as not unlike that of a convent, with nurses Mathilde Kottmann and Ali Silver as "Abbess" and "Mother Superior". Schweitzer is more in the nature of a divinity, so that if her religious education has not been neglected she may see in his appearance at the table a striking similarity to the Last Supper of Jesus. Here, as there, the host sits in the middle of the table, his disciples declining outwards from him on either side. Here, too, the ones nearest at hand press dishes upon him, watching his every move and trying to gratify his wishes before he can even hint at them. Neither Ali nor Mathilde would dream of eating her own food until she is sure that Dr. Schweitzer has been properly catered for. All the communal dishes, which at Lambaréné are served family-style on to the table in duplicate, one set to the Doctor's left and another to his right, are marshalled for his attention. Delicacies prepared exclusively for him the two nurses guard so that no one else will get them. The Doctor, however, may indulge a momentary impulse of generosity or esteem by offering a part of one of these to some favoured guest or member of the staff. He once kindly offered me a small piece of a cooked banana so that I might try it. When nurses receive these titbits they look as elated as though they had been absolved by a confessor. The effect is electric.

Should this first baptism into the communal life of Lambaréné occur at dinner, seven large oil lamps will be burning on the long table. The aura of darkness veiling the corners of the room will give a feeling of closeness to her neighbour. Our novice may find herself talking gently to the person beside her, probably the more experienced nurse who speaks her language. Her voice, she finds, is unusually soft, as though she were speaking in church or in a hospital ward. She is constantly aware of the Doctor's presence, though he may never look in her direction. So much seems to be going on around him, so many dishes and actions flowing either to or from his vicinity, that all attention is unconsciously drawn to him. Yet it is only after the coffee that Dr. Schweitzer rises a little stiffly to his feet and begins his slow, ceremonious walk round the table to the piano set against the opposite wall, on the river side of the hut. There, with his back to the room from which a number of workers have mysteriously disappeared, the great expert on Bach and the church organ plays a hymn (two on Saturdays and Sundays) with everyone singing the words in German. This is made easier for the new nurse by the number of German hymnals which are in the room, and are handed out by one of the doctors each evening.

She will not know that each of the hymns may be to honour the memory of one of his earliest nurses, perhaps of the late Mlle. Haussknecht, or of his dead wife. Emma's favourite, No. 124, is played every Saturday night in her memory. A tradition in the hospital exists for all these choices, but it would require patient study to explain it. Suffice that Dr. Schweitzer is not without this rather touchingly sentimental side to his nature.

The hymn is accompanied on a piano which has astonished more than one musically-knowledgeable visitor. His American admirer Norman Cousins was shocked by it. It is an old, black upright with a stained, chipped and yellowed keyboard in which some of the notes stick. Schweitzer makes it sound adequate, but it is something of a mystery why he keeps a brand new-looking piano standing closed against the end wall of the room by the door. Perhaps the great showman knows that he produces twice the effect on his humble instrument.

After the hymn-singing ritual, Schweitzer walks heavily back to his seat at the table and opens the Bible carefully provided for him by one or the other of his acolytes, Ali or Mathilde. In a strong and rasping Alsatian voice he reads through a passage. He will then, if the occasion demands it, repeat the performance on the piano, playing a further hymn and walking all the way over to the old instrument and back, before giving his sermon on the Biblical message which he has read.

Provided that the new nurse understands German, she may be fascinated by this sermon. For those of his visitors who do not, it is a chance to study the old Doctor at his most theatrical. He levels his gaze and delivers his sentences like an ancient orator (Evtuchenko, the young Russian poet, has a remarkably similar, though more vital, delivery). He is, or appears to be, transported by the weight and beauty of what he is saying. As a preacher, Schweitzer must have left few people unmoved among his flock.

It is now getting late. With the insistence of all tropical nights, langour begins to steal over the company in the oil-lit dining-room. Dr. Schweitzer relaxes, chatting to one or two people near at hand. He soon leaves for his room, helped and accompanied by the faithful Mathilde Kottmann. The new nurse can perhaps stay to listen to a concert on an old, cracked and battery-operated gramophone kept in the dining-room for these recreations.* She can go visiting. Or she can retire to bed. In any case, she is not advised to stay out for too long in the night air, as mosquitoes carrying malaria will certainly menace her if she does, and her health is now her most vital consideration. She will probably be persuaded, on this first night, to take her burning paraffin-lantern from the hallway of the dining-room and go straight back to her room. There, if she wants to read, she can light her own oil lamp; though this may bring a swarm of flying insects, despite the screens. (I solved the problem with insect-repellant candles, which kept the bugs away but nearly burnt off my hair!) She will soon be asleep. If lucky, she will not be disturbed by cries of pain, howls of animal distress, screaming babies, thunder, rain drumming on the iron roof or any of the other mournful and frightening jungle night noises. She will sleep, restlessly in the humid heat, until the cocks begin their dawn chorus at approximately 4 a.m. the following morning.

* Since my visit, a new stereo model has been presented by a donor in California, U.S. The first night that it was played, Schweitzer abruptly rose and urged everyone to leave as "it is going to rain". No rain fell, but the stereo was silenced.

Then she will learn that the sternest discipline prevails in the hospital. As soon as the first gong sounds, there must be a scamper to reach the dining-room. Everyone, including the new arrival, must be in her place by the time *le grand docteur* strides in, putting his sun helmet in its accustomed place on top of the piano. Again, as on the night before, he will probably sit down without a glance or a word to left or right.

Breakfast is as simple as other meals. There is bread and usually some imported jam; also some locally-made mango jam which tastes good to those who like mangoes. The tea, served in large pots, is fresh and strong; ideal, after an equatorial night followed by a cold wash in an enamel basin. Where supper produced cheese and salami, or other imported foods, breakfast is usually based on local produce where possible. All bread is baked in the hospital ovens.

Should our nurse have been particularly anxious to freshen herself after her journey, she may have been introduced to the bucket-shower. Perhaps she will get at least semi-wet before the contents run out. A supply of jugs then completes the job, which leaves a lot to be desired as a form of actual cleansing.

But on days when the temperature is sure to be in the nineties, with a wet-blanket humidity that makes this feel even higher, there may be gratitude for this crude comfort. The nurse will soon realize how little else she can obtain at Lambaréné that is pleasant or comforting. Her days will be gruelling, sometimes sickening, as she has to tend vile sores and post-operative wounds in her patients. She will see conditions of the human body that nothing in her nursing training has prepared her for. Hernias would be trifling in primitive Africa if they were treated early; but women consider the condition an adornment, not to be removed on any account, until the time when it becomes strangulated. It is possible for natives to suffer their steadily expanding growths until they weigh too much for comfort; a scrotal hernia hanging two-thirds of the way to a man's knees is not uncommon.

From such frightful conditions the new nurse may suffer a number of shocked reactions, until she grows used to her environment. Jungle sores will need the most delicate treatment. Patients dying of poison must be fed by hand to avoid contact with food provided by other patients, or by the witch doctor. Surgical operations of the most complicated and difficult sort will need her attention. As if that is not sufficient, the heat will be clammy enough to make the earth perspire and blot out the sky, so that the sun is rarely seen. The whole climate is so enervating that all movement becomes an effort. Water and air are infested with disease, as she will discover if she does not take rigorous precautions against amoebic pests, and almost certainly she will soon go down with at least a mild attack of dysentery. In spite of all these trials, she is expected when fit to be on her feet from morning till night ministering to the hundreds of patients afflicted with every kind of infectious and contagious ailment from tuberculosis to leprosy and sleeping sickness (these cases are sent to a State hospital when discovered, but they are not always traced out in the early stages). She will find that she is not only a nurse, but a maid of all work.

And though she survives this experience of physical hardship even without distress, the newcomer is soon bound to find that the barriers of Lambaréné are not confined to the dense vegetation that surrounds her. There are worse barriers, emotional ones, from which she will find little chance of escape. Facing her is a wall of emotional repression brought about by lack of normal companionship. Only a few male doctors, mostly exhausted at the end of their day's work, are available as partners for the more than twenty young girls on the staff. It has been suggested as probable that Dr. Schweitzer deliberately imposes his crushing programme of work and discipline on his women helpers in order to leave them too tired by evening to bother about any social activities. Yet, as a previous visitor has noted, there is a strong and pathetic tendency for the girls of Lambaréné to dote on small pet animals, offering them a love and affection that seems far beyond the normal ration. Native babies also are cuddled with an extraordinary warmth and tenderness.

This, then, is the reality which the newcomer discovers. Why does she not only stay her term but often far beyond it? Unlike the men, who are not so easily impressed by the spiritual value of physical discomfort, a woman seems to accept the harshness and squalor of life in the hospital without question. The petty controls, obstruction and inefficiency are also tolerated far more easily by most of the female nursing staff. While the Schweitzer Image in close-up tends to lose its charm for men, for most women it merely changes. Schweitzer becomes the Father Figure; strong, kindly, strict, good. For them, there is a pleasure in obedience and in the knowledge that they are in the paternal care of a man hallowed by the outside world. When one day our newcomer finds herself being passed one of the favoured titbits from her hero's plate at meal-time, her flush of pleasure will show that even suffering on this scale can have its moments of exquisite reward.

TWELVE

UNSUNG HEROINES

EVEN IF it is true that most women stay with Schweitzer out o
hero-worship, the justification is that by this means the Westerne
brings to Africa something other than liquor, a restless desire fo
shiny motor-cars and blaring radio sets, and a fear of the H-bomb
Some of the more discerning and dispassionate among the wome
helpers know this as a more important cause than the saving o
an occasional ant colony or the healing of natives to the strains o
Bach in the jungle. Such women may secretly own to a certai
disenchantment with the Image, but they stay on in Lambarén
to do work which they believe transcends the aims of the ma
behind it. These are the heroines of a community that is neve
short of self-sacrificing idealists. Their quiet and little-praised act
of service have been vital to the establishment of Schweitzer'
legend.

The beautiful, green-eyed, titian-haired Dutchwoman Albertin
van Beeck-Vollenhoven was such a heroine. She came to Lambarén
nearly ten years ago to stay two years nursing, with infinite tender
ness and patience, the hospital's mental patients. She was culture
and sophisticated, with a worldly poise usually lacking in th
"simplicity" found (and encouraged) among most of Schweitzer'
staff. Mrs. Clara Urquhart noticed her during one of her visits a
"a vital personality and deep intelligence". She liked to talk in he
spare time about music, the theatre and books she read and enjoye
in the outside world. Yet the one memento she brought with he
to the jungle was an ancient stringed lyre, on which she woul
sometimes play madrigal music in a pathetic attempt to find beaut
and relaxation.

Her work, her daily routine, can hardly be imagined. To say hat her crazed and tormented patients were brutal and violent is o understate the case. They were often so bestial in their habits, o menacing in their attitudes, that men preferred to visit them n pairs. Albertina walked alone among these human monsters and howed none of the fear that must have been her constant, daily ompanion. A man who visited Lambaréné while she was there old me: "I have seen her confront menacing creatures more animal han human as they crouched in the darkness of their pens. She ould calm them by her sheer lack of fear."

Caring for these mental sufferers is one of the hospital's heaviest nd most doleful chores. Schweitzer soon discovered, when he first ame to Africa, that anyone who professes to heal the sick in the ungle must accept responsibility for a number of such disordered ndividuals. The causes of their madness are not always known. They may have committed atrocious crimes before being brought, hained, to the hospital by policemen. Once handed over, they nust be cared for, fed and as far as possible treated and healed by he Doctor and his co-workers. Albertina undertook their nursing.

For the most part, her expression of selflessness and service has een forgotten; but we catch a glimpse of her during an evening n January 1957 when Norman Cousins was at the hospital, intent n persuading Dr. Schweitzer to let him micro-film his unfinished nanuscripts. It is the American writer, in his book *Dr. Schweitzer f Lambaréné*, who briefly lifts the curtain of darkness veiling this xtraordinary girl. The hospital has never attempted to do so.

A visitor had brought each of the women staff a brightly coloured lress, something rarely seen in their uniform life. A fervour seized he younger and prettier girls as they held the gay colours and soft naterials against their figures. Before long they were dancing and wirling joyfully along the verandas. Albertina's tiredness left her nd suddenly she was transformed into a young and beautiful voman with flushed and excited face. It was she who called for a arty at which the finery could be worn before the (for once) ndulgent Schweitzer. Albertina of the madhouse became for that ne evening a lovely and lively person, able to forget her terrible

and compassionate work. The next morning she was back amon
the violent sufferers in her care.

If this work took its toll, she did not admit to it until she lef
Lambaréné. Since then reports reaching friends in England hav
hinted at after-effects which anyone who has seen the condition
she worked in would understand. The heroine of the mental patient
is said to have been broken in health and almost deranged by he
ordeal. When last heard of, she was reportedly a restless passenge
in Europe, trying to recuperate from the physical hardship she ha
undergone in Lambaréné; also, no doubt, striving to obliterate th
spectre of a haunting and terrifying experience.

For the heroines of Lambaréné such tragic conclusions are no
an altogether uncommon fate. Dr. Schweitzer, with his daily egg
and boiled water, may survive. The legacy of his nurses' exhaustin
work in this sickly and inhuman climate is seldom less than
permanent disfigurement of some kind, though the scars do no
always show on the surface. There have been lucky ones who hav
actually gained and been made happier by their experiences, bu
few, very few, have managed to return unmarked. Even fewer ca
claim the happiness which fell to Trudi Boschler, Lambaréné'
dedicated leper nurse.

She was a young and attractive Swiss when she came to th
hospital, a girl with fair, red-golden hair and wide-set, large, gre
eyes. Everything about her suggested sympathy, authority an
dedication. She looked beautiful in her white uniform, her su
topi tilted back on her softly curling hair. It was hard to imagin
her doing any of the disgusting, indeed nauseating, work necessar
to the running of the leper colony. Dr. Schweitzer, however, sav
the vein of steel running behind her eyes and knew she could b
trusted with this important area of the hospital.

So Trudi Boschler became Lambaréné's "lady with the lamp"
The bobbing twinkle of her storm-lantern along the path to th
leper village at night was seen whenever her patients were in pai
or need. She trained them to work at arts and crafts, giving to man
the first happiness they had known in their lives. From her the
learnt how to perform a touching and simple Nativity Play whic

gave everyone in the hospital great joy one Christmas. Behind the Doctor's back, she coached teenage African girls in her care to become nurses. They loved her and she loved them. She was among the happiest women in Lambaréné.

Seeing her at work, Norman Cousins recorded: "This young white goddess looked the part. She was twenty-four or twenty-five, flaxen-haired, slender, attractive, intense, inexhaustible. It was clear that her work was giving her the kind of fulfilment she sought in life . . ."* Trudi Boschler had been orphaned at an early age. In the lepers, whom she nursed for seven years, she had found the first family of her life.

What others felt or thought did not matter to her, provided that it was for the ultimate good of her patients. When Olga Deterding offered to become her assistant, she accepted readily; but when Dr. Schweitzer disagreed with her over an administrative matter she resigned and went home to Switzerland. For six months she studied every possible aspect of the care and nursing of lepers before writing to Schweitzer to ask if she could return and run the leper village as she wanted to run it. Schweitzer agreed and Trudi came back to the people, many of them prisoners for life, whom she loved and trusted. All day she worked among them, as mother, nurse, guardian, magistrate, teacher and friend. When a witch doctor threatened them with frightening consequences if they accepted the white woman's treatment she sought him out in the jungle, faced him, and ordered him to take off his spells or she would apply her own, far more potent, "magic" to him. Convinced that she meant business, he promptly ordered the patients to accept the white woman's instructions.

Trudi earned her patients' respect and love in many other ways. She refused, despite Schweitzer's almost pathological mistrust of the Africans, to lock things up in her colony. Nothing was ever stolen or tampered with. Her name is still a legend among the black-skinned people she nursed with such complete devotion; though at Dr. Schweitzer's all-white table it is rarely, if ever, mentioned.

* *Dr. Schweitzer of Lambaréné*

Often at night Trudi would be called out of an exhausted sleep by the anxious tap on her door of a relative of one of her patients who had become suddenly ill. She would light her feeble lamp and walk off into the jungle crackling with weird noises, alive with menace. A mile walk brought her to the small village built by Schweitzer to house these pathetic, disfigured sufferers. There her work of comforting and healing began; and rarely was she back in bed before the first light of dawn had softened the ebony silhouettes of the jungle trees.

It may seem strange that her name is now unknown in a world that heaps honours, even the Nobel Peace Prize and the Order of Merit, on Dr. Schweitzer. Such lack of recognition does not disturb her, since she sought none of it. She was happy with her tragic "family" and her story has a suitably happy ending. For she married the son of an English shipping magnate, who was also a doctor. When he visited the hospital and saw her at work he fell deeply in love with this very wonderful orphan of Lambaréné.

There have been many other, if less vivid, acts of heroism by Schweitzer's women nurses, whether or not they have become disillusioned with the aims of the Doctor and the strict methods by which he sought to attain them. As one writer who had been on a visit to Lambaréné put it: "All women go to Lambaréné in search of something. Some find it in adoration of Schweitzer; some in serving the African; and a few find nothing but a bitter taste in their mouths." When I was at the hospital I counted thirty-three people around me at table, only seven or eight of them men. In the atmosphere of reserve and secrecy it was not possible to ask each one of these women why they personally had come to the jungles of Africa, and what they had got out of coming. But where it was discreet to do so, and where we could understand each other's language, these were the questions I put to them. The answers were illuminating.

In the strange, cathedral-close atmosphere of Lambaréné, a rigid discipline lies too near the surface to allow easy associations. A number of the younger, prettier nurses did their best to keep themselves to themselves. Some were as shy as novice nuns. None was easy to talk to, and I had to make the best of my opportunities. For example, one day I found Christine Lloyd, a pretty young Welsh redhead, dressing sores and infections in what seemed to be the hospital's Casualty hut. She had a pert, humorous face and kittenish eyes; but at depth Christine is a serious and strongly determined girl.

Christine was at work on her father's farm near Abergavenny when she first heard of Dr. Schweitzer. That was some five or six years ago. Since then she had been thinking of little else, though she had only been on the staff of the hospital—recruited in London by Mrs. Clara Urquhart—for some four weeks when I met her. Her story began when Christine's father brought some books home from the local lending library, among them one written by the Doctor in which he set out some of his experiences in the jungle. She read this book and immediately began to feel a strong urge to give up her farming life and take to nursing so that she, too, could be of use to many lesser-privileged people in a world of which she was just becoming aware.

Why she did not seek to nurse and heal the sufferers in her own land, or in other more civilized parts of the world, is something she does not fully understand, though it certainly had much to do with the lure of Dr. Schweitzer. In his books, the Doctor's appeal is solitary, valorous and tragic. A young girl reading one of them, with no experience of jungle conditions and little of life, is sure to be stirred with an answering pity. In Christine's case it grew into a firm desire to train as a nurse, so that she might go to Lambaréné as the Doctor's servant.

More worldly-wise, her mother tried to dissuade her, even arguing that she would do no good and only contract some dreadful disease. The call of the lonely, kindly Doctor in the jungle was too strong to be silenced by such opposition. Christine had quietly made up her mind, and was not to be put off. She enrolled as a trainee nurse at Hereford Hospital and duly qualified as nurse and midwife. By now the family, a sister included, were resigned to her course of action, knowing her well enough to understand that her decision was basic and binding. Good, religious, Methodist people they prayed instead for her safety and support in the jungle.

They had asked her to let them into her thoughts, to tell them what it was about this far-away healer that had suddenly and dynamically charged her with longing to be at his side. Christine tried, but she is a girl to whom long words and serious sentiments do not come easily. All she could say was: "I just feel I'd like to do something like this; I think Dr. Schweitzer is marvellous, and what he is doing is *right*."

To a close friend she confided that she had no great wish to marry and settle down in Wales, working on a farm and raising a family as her mother had done. "I want to try to do some good in the world first," she said. She found her way to Mrs. Urquhart's London home for an interview that was completely successful. "My job in recruiting staff is to make sure that they are serious about going, not just goofy about Dr. Schweitzer, and that they have the necessary training," Mrs. Urquhart explained. "Of course it helps if they have enough French to be able to make themselves understood in the wards. Then I tell them something of what they are going to have to do and the conditions they will be living under. If they are still keen, and I think they are the right sort of people, there is nothing to stop them going, provided the Doctor wants a nurse at that time."

For Christine Lloyd, twenty-three years old and dedicated to the ideal of Schweitzer's crusade against poverty and disease in the jungle of Africa, the opportunity ripened in time with her wishes. Soon after Christmas, 1962, which she spent with her still wondering family, she packed her new white dresses, stockings and shoes, tried on a green-shaded white sun-helmet to an accompaniment of giggles from her sister, and left home for Lambaréné. A few weeks later she was standing in the oven-hot Casualty hut unwrapping pus-soaked bandages from a nine-inch wound in a tall African's leg as though she had been at this sort of duty all her life. A quiet, helpful native orderly handed her drugs and dressings as she asked for them. She was not only at home in her surroundings, she seemed to radiate that air of authority which only professionals in complete command of their environment have.

That night she sat on an iron bed in one of the younger doctor's rooms while his wife made coffee and offered the guests biscuits from food parcels sent her from the United States. Dr. and Mrs. Joel Mattison, from Florida, were known in Lambaréné for their hospitality whenever supplies reached them. Mrs. Jean Mattison, a pretty young scientist, did laboratory work and was fully acquainted with the many forms of virulent bacilli encountered there. As a result she and her husband ate sparingly in the communal dining-room. They made up their diet with food sent from home, using carefully sterilized dishes and plates. These "snacks" were served in the double-room which they shared, and which they had made pleasantly attractive with works of native art and small touches of decoration. The Mattisons and Christine Lloyd had become good friends.

As she sipped American coffee, Christine talked of her decision to leave the Welsh farm for Schweitzer's jungle. She discussed it simply and unemotionally, as though it were an everyday excursion. "Sometimes, now, I wonder if I am really English," she said. "I know I have only been here a month but in this part of the world a month is a long time." She put down her cup and looked gravely into the softly-burning light of the oil lamp on the table. "You see," she said slowly, "I hope to stay about two and a half years. And if I like it still, at the end of that time, I will come back. This is the sort of life I have always dreamed of living."

Christine's seriousness had shown for a moment, though normally she was a vital girl who liked fun and amusement, and was playful enough to ignore some of Dr. Schweitzer's more arbitrary commands despite her admiration for him. During her first days in the tropics she suffered slight sunstroke, due to walking about the hospital without her helmet. Now she always kept it on her head, earning an approving smile from the Doctor as he saw her. In the weeks that she had worked for him, her adoration had increased to the point where she could say with absolute sincerity: "I think he is a most wonderful man. I'd do almost anything for him." It is such total and absolute dedication that Albert Schweitzer depends on to continue his life-work. Without it, he would be forced to cede at least part of his manifold authority to others, an unthinkable alternative to the man who will never build a larger hospital than he can run himself. In brave, self-sacrificing young girls like Christine Lloyd the key principle of Lambaréné is securely reflected; an unquestioning faith in the power and the glory of Dr Schweitzer.

Yet not all the women who go to work for the autocratic jungle Doctor will admit to such slavish devotion. Margaret Bernhard, an attractive twenty-one year old helper from Zürich, Switzerland refused to allow that her feelings for Dr. Schweitzer had anything to do with her reason for volunteering to join the staff of Lambaréné. Insisting that she had come only to tend those in need, only to serve others and to give back something in return for what she had received from life, this dark-haired, plump and comely girl would not accept the statement, made by a Lambaréné doctor to Norman Cousins: "Some of us may have come here because we were in good circumstances and didn't feel quite right about it; others because they were in difficult circumstances yet managed somehow to survive, and they wanted to find some way of acknowledging their debt. But always it is the debt. And always you will find that somewhere we happened to read something by Albert Schweitzer that opened up a big door in our mind and made us know we had to come."*

Margaret's desire to come to Africa began when she was in England working and living as an *au pair* girl with a Rugby School housemaster and his family. It grew because: "I thought I was young enough to give two years to serve others. I'm not a very religious person, but I did feel a need to give rather than to take all the time. But this really had nothing to do with Dr. Schweitzer; he just represented exactly the sort of thing I wanted to do. Now I want to go back to Switzerland and do social work, because I feel that there is much that I can do in my own country." From her colleagues I learnt that Margaret, whose large brown eyes were always darkly ringed, had suffered severely from the strain of her work in the humid heat of the equator. Few of those who mentioned

* *Dr. Schweitzer of Lambaréné* by Norman Cousins

ıer to me believed that she would remain at Lambaréné long.

The truly dedicated disciple is another sort of woman; a soul vith deep emotional responses and probably a hint of confusion ınd tragedy in her ego. When the heroic and beautiful Dr. Margaret 'an der Kreek decided to seek entry into the colony, she was young ınd untrained. She had read one of the Doctor's persuasive books ınd fallen under its spell. Living in Holland with her father and nother, she knew of other girls and women who had left her ;ountry to work for Dr. Schweitzer (many of the nurses have been, ınd are, Dutch), but she realized that she would stand little chance ɔf winning Schweitzer's invitation to join him while she lacked nedical experience.

So Margaret went doggedly to medical school, qualified, and ɔractised surgery sufficiently to ensure even Dr. Schweitzer's lofty espect for her talents, at which time she persuaded a friend to vrite a letter of introduction. She followed this with her own .pplication to join the Lambaréné medical staff. The Doctor, in eply, welcomed her and warned of the many problems she would ind in the hospital. She arrived in 1955.

To be top surgeon in a hospital where a remarkable number of ntricate and unusual operations are performed in the one tiny heatre was an extraordinary privilege for so young a woman. For ɔne whose facial bone-structure gives her a photographic re-emblance to Ingrid Bergman, it was astonishing. Fatalities on the ɔperating table at Lambaréné, due in part to the way in which ɔrimitive Africans behave, often delaying their surrender to surgery ıntil too late, were higher as she knew than in any European ıospital. Yet the challenge was immense, and she welcomed it.

A visitor who saw her shortly after she had performed an intricate, ınsuccessful operation on a native women testifies to the fortitude ɔf this Dutch woman surgeon. Dr. Margaret—*la doctoresse* as she vas nick-named—had been forced to operate against her pro-essional judgement by a sudden collapse in the condition of her ɔatient. When the woman died, any surgeon could have been ɔardoned for doubting whether his diagnosis had been correct; ɔut Dr. Margaret showed no outward sign of being unsure of

herself. She chose the following morning to work in the little garde
of jungle flowers which she had sown outside her hut, but in n
other way did she give a sign that she had passed through a terrify
ing ordeal. Yet, in failing to save her patient's life, Dr. Margare
knew she had inflamed the superstitious doubts of a tribe wh
backed by their jealous witch-doctor, might have sought deadl
vengeance against her.

How is it that so little is known of these heroic women c
Lambaréné? When people think of the hospital they generally se
a mental picture of one man, Dr. Schweitzer, tending his legendar
lepers with the support only of a few vague and elderly wome
assistants or missionaries. Yet many skilled and courageous wome
have sacrificed themselves to the jungle beside him, to be rewarde
only with anonymity. Maria Langendyck, a senior nurse, wa
another angel of mercy described by all who know her as a mos
loving and lovable person. Who has heard her name? Toni va
Leer was as dedicated and selfless as any nun on a battlefield
beloved too for her sense of humour and infectious sparkling gaiety
Is she buried in Schweitzer's heart, or is the testament to he
courage and service written in some fading manuscript of th
Doctor's, incomplete and subject to the invasions of insects tha
must not be killed, and animals that may walk where they will?

What became of Verena Schmidt whom Mrs. Urquhart onc
called "One of the veritable pillars of this establishment"? A Swis
girl, she was an active assistant to Dr. Schweitzer in building th
new leper village a few years ago. What of his English voluntee
helper, Miss Margaret Deneke, the Oxford Choirmaster who wa
allowed to name the road she had supervised the building c
"Oxford Street"? Where is Sonya Muller, the young and prett
girl from Alsace who cared for expectant mothers and the newly
arrived babies? And Elsje Boes from South Africa? The list of th
heroines who have come and gone from Lambaréné is longer tha
anyone remembers. It casts a disturbing shadow.

THIRTEEN

THE TRAGEDY OF MME. SCHWEITZER

IN THE mists of secrecy and reticence that wreathe about Albert Schweitzer, the histories of his wife and daughter are almost totally obscured. There is an occasional, fleeting tribute to them in his memoirs; an enigmatic dedication of Part II of *The Philosophy of Civilization* "To my wife, the most loyal of comrades" (Part I had been offered to Annie Fischer "in deepest gratitude"); and some references of a more fulsome kind in the reports and writings of visitors. We can be grateful for these, Mme. Hélène and Mlle. Rhena (before her marriage) Schweitzer would hardly appear as real people. What there is of them to know, we learn from these outside observers, at least one of whom knew Mme. Schweitzer well before her death in Zürich, Switzerland, on June 1 1957. But the picture they create is diplomatically veiled, if one is to believe the private reports of eye-witnesses; a pretty smoke-screen to hide the odd fact that Dr. Schweitzer, for all his charm towards women other than those in his own family, was not by any means a triumphantly successful family man. His marriage was certainly a severe test for the simple, charitable soul he married.

What do we know of Hélène Schweitzer, *née* Bresslau, the long-suffering mortal who allied herself to the man variously regarded as the world's noblest, and the world's most bigoted leader? We are told that she was a Jewess who suffered from tuberculosis—a result, perhaps, of privations—in her early years of marriage. We learn that her father was a famed historian in Strasbourg and that she was scholarly and patient, able to help unravel the complexities of Albert Schweitzer's research and to collaborate with him in the completion of manuscripts and the correction of proofs.

For a writer, these virtues sound ample enough attraction, but Schweitzer was not only a writer. As he assumed the role of doctor of medicine and jungle surgeon, it became increasingly necessary for him to lean on a qualified nurse, which the resourceful Hélène had become.

Thus she appears to have possessed all the qualities most called for by the extraordinary man who was setting out into the savage wildness of Africa; a fit mate for his lonely sojourn on the bank of the Ogowe; a handy comrade and companion in the work he was preparing to do. Indeed, so gifted a partner might be expected to have called forth some answering enthusiasm from the man fortunate enough to have found her. What we get is a bare and parenthetic announcement recording, no more, the seemingly unimportant fact that "... Last of all I left my residence on the St. Thomas Embankment, in order that with my wife—Hélène Bresslau, the daughter of the Strasbourg historian, whom I had married on June 18 1912—I might spend the last months, so far as I was not obliged to be travelling, in my father's parsonage at Günsbach ..."* Hardly a statement gushing with the sentimental fervour which the Doctor was to be capable of later in lamenting his parting from Africa.

In the first book he wrote of his struggles as a doctor in Equatorial Africa (more a diary of events than a narrative: *On the Edge of the Primeval Forest*) Schweitzer deliberately avoided mentioning Hélène whenever possible. This could have been and is believed by his admirers to have been, proud and praiseworthy reticence. Perhaps in the old-world Germanic school of *kultur* in which the Doctor had been brought up it was considered bad form to discuss one's wife. Nevertheless the rigorous skirting of Mme. Schweitzer's role in events he was describing gives an altogether different impression from chivalry. And where she is mentioned the reader can be pardoned for wondering what special reason lay in the Doctor's mind for choosing to reveal her.

Twenty-nine closely printed pages of one English edition of the book leave Hélène Schweitzer strictly out of the story, other than

* *My Life and Thought*

a necessary reference to the fact that ". . . I started with my wife, who had qualified as a nurse, for the River Ogowe in Equatorial Africa, there to begin my active work . . ." Not, let it be noted, "our" active work, though Mme. Schweitzer was to work long and hard beside him, giving anaesthetics and supervising the washing and cleansing of blood and pus-soaked bandages and linen. She was to keep house under conditions likely to unhinge a lesser woman, to prepare the operating theatre at any hour of day, or night in an emergency, and to do all this without complaining to the zealous man at her side. He, when not working in his hospital, was often away, visiting local Europeans, risking his neck and skin travelling long distances through country preyed on by savage animals. These social unions must have been pleasant and relaxing as a stimulus for the great Doctor's mind. But of their reaction on the woman who, presumably, was left alone in the fowl-house hospital with the noises of the jungle tautening her nerves, the heat suffocating her, there is no mention. Did she not fear for his safety—and her own—as he hazardously journeyed home in the darkness along miles of river and canal infested with dangerous creatures? Is it in the least likely that she shared his exaltation when, though he had been warned not to take a certain route, he took it and came up against a pair of deadly hippos which could have upset his canoe and drowned the inmates in seconds?

Fourteen per cent of the white population of Libreville died annually at the time when Mme. Schweitzer was first taken to the Gaboon, as the country then called itself. She was not sturdy. Her chest was weak and she complained of pains and difficulty in breathing. Whether she contracted in Africa the tubercular condition which later afflicted her is not known, but certainly this disease remains today one of the most virulent pests of the area, so that it is not unlikely that Mme. Schweitzer succumbed to its infection while working as her husband's "assistant". He was immersing himself in his work, enjoying each conquest made over superstition, ignorance and death. There was perhaps little occasion to study the needs of the nurse who was also, when he had time to appreciate the fact, his wife.

No doubt Albert Schweitzer admired his wife deeply, but his urgent requirement at the time was for a nurse, a hand-maiden of all work, a housekeeper-provider. Hélène had to be these things without expecting more of her husband than he was able to give as a professional companion during most of the shared moments of their life together. It can be asked whether such devotion to an ideal embracing Christian beliefs and culminating in a creed of Reverence for (all) Life was not unduly self-centred. If it is true, as Mrs. Clara Urquhart has told me she believes, that Dr. Schweitzer chose marriage to Hélène Bresslau partially as a means of taking a trained and able nurse with him to the jungle without raising scandalized eyebrows in those easily-affronted days, then it might be possible to believe that Hélène had no right to expect more of her husband's companionship and attention than he was giving her. Yet stories of her sad life do not seem to bear this out.

There was the occasion when, late in their married life, Mme. Schweitzer was riding in the back of a motor-car near Günsbach while the Doctor sat in front with the driver (he has never driven an automobile). A gust of wind blew Schweitzer's hat off his head and into the back, where Hélène caught hold of it. For some time she continued to clasp it, I was told, "fondling its brim like a beloved doll".

In Lambaréné, she cut a pathetic figure, coldly eclipsed by the phenomenal man she had married, whose stature appeared to shut out the warmth and light of her life. They did not always seem to visitors to be getting on well together, but in such circumstances who can imagine that they would. Whenever Dr. Schweitzer noticed that his wife was upset by his habitual, if courteous, interest in a new arrival at their table, he would do his best to favour her, perhaps passing her a titbit from his plate. Once when a visitor received this bounty before it had been offered to Mme. Schweitzer, she appeared so upset that the Doctor told her in a kindly voice: "You know that you have first choice of everything."

There was little chance of her exercising this choice, even if she had it. The time and pursuits of her husband belonged to him and to his work. In a revealing moment with a woman friend, Mme. Schweitzer sat one night on the veranda of her room after a particularly festive dinner for some important visitors, a dinner at which she had been more than usually shut out of her husband's presence. She fumbled in a holdall and produced a crumpled and faded letter. It was dated some twenty years before, and the writing was hard to read, but she pressed her friend to study what the letter said. In the light of a paraffin lamp the friend tried to decipher its message. What she discovered was a perfectly formal, polite note of thanks for hospitality, but the point was that it had been addressed to Mme. Schweitzer, and not to the Doctor; and it had been written by a man who had sat at her side during dinner. Now, he wrote to thank her, and to say what a charming and interesting companion she had been. Mme. Schweitzer took back her faded trophy and replaced it fondly in her reticule. "You see," she said, "I have had *my* admirers, too."

These are not stories that cast a strong light of sympathy on Dr. Schweitzer's role as a husband and father, but they are necessary to the understanding of a facet of the great Doctor's most diligently hidden failing: his inability to sustain and foster close personal relations. With "people" he is immediately at ease, the preacher and public figure to his finger tips. In public he can sway multitudes and project the perfect image. But in dear and intimate associations with individual persons there is no sign of the same ready ability. His closest doctor assistants have found it preferable, ultimately, to admire him from a distance. His wife and daughter have shared relatively little of his life. With nurses and helpers he can preserve the most lasting and satisfactory relationships, because these run on the established tracks of professional reserve and respect; but the respect is of the assistant for the master, not of equals. It is when he finds himself forced to meet someone on the level of the kind of equality demanded by friendship and intimacy that the Doctor finds it hard to adapt himself.

There have been, of course, exceptions to this. One such was the heroic woman surgeon, Dr. Margaret van der Kreek, who told Norman Cousins: "People know the Doctor as a great philosopher and theologian. I am lucky to know him as a human being . . ."*

* *Dr. Schweitzer of Lambaréné*

Dr. Margaret was serene and gracious enough to support an association which rose above mere professional limitations, yet she left the hospital after saying that she would return. Another woman who is believed to have nursed warm feelings of friendship for the Doctor was the American photographer, Miss Erica Anderson, who persuaded Schweitzer to let her make a film of him and his hospital. Today she is a fairly regular visitor to the colony.

There are, too, such admiring friends as Mrs. Marion (Preminger) Mayer and Mrs. Urquhart. But these are birds of passage who come and go in the Doctor's life. It is possible that the basis of their affectionate friendships with the Doctor lies in this; that if they were to stay permanently and work at Lambaréné they would, like the others, have to take their place among those who serve as well as love the great Doctor.

For Mme. Schweitzer, the difficulty which her husband plainly had in making warm and sentimental associations was a cross she bore only too willingly. This dutiful woman told a visitor shortly before her death: "I have done much hoping in my life, and some of the hopes have come true. In recent years for me there has been not much to do except to hope—and to look at pictures and think back." She seemed to accept the role of helper to a phenomenal, an amazing, man even though it cost her such a harsh price. When asked to describe herself during the war, she said proudly, "I am the oldest nurse at Lambaréné." This tragic woman could have said that she was the wife of a great and celebrated man. She could have claimed a status which the German officials would readily have understood. Instead, she chose to see herself in the character which was hers from the outset: a simple nurse in a great cause. "It makes me feel so foolish," she told Norman Cousins, the visitor referred to above, "this being so helpless. I ought to be working with the Doctor." Less than six months before her death, Mme. Schweitzer was still clinging to this ideal of service to which she had dedicated herself.

The question remains whether another, less driven, man would have subjected an ailing companion to quite so rigorous a lifetime in order to work out his experiment in Christ-like living. Mme.

Schweitzer has said that she contracted tuberculosis, from which she was later cured, during her early years of marriage; in other words, after she had spent some time in Lambaréné. Schweitzer makes no mention of this, referring to their recuperative visits to the mountains of Germany as though he and not she were the sufferer. Time and again he allows readers of his autobiography to learn of his own exhaustion and sickness, but never is the serious illness of his wife more than hinted at. In an otherwise candid and objective narrative, one wonders why this reticence exists.

Chronologically, the record tells a tragic story of Mme. Schweitzer's attempts to remain at her husband's side, when nothing but enforced returns to Europe allowed him to remain at hers. We read from his books, and from others, that:

1916 "My wife's health had suffered from the sultry air . . ." (Schweitzer)

March 1918 "The bleak winds of Provence did not suit my wife, who in the mountain air of Garaison had improved considerably in health . . ." (Schweitzer)

July 1918 "For my wife's sake, who suffered much from the confinement and from home sickness, I was glad indeed when, about the middle of July, it was disclosed to me that we were all . . . going to be exchanged." (Schweitzer)

February 1924 "I left Strasbourg. My wife could not accompany me this time because of a breakdown in her health . . ." (Schweitzer)

December 1929 ". . . on board the river-steamer which was taking to Lambaréné myself, my wife . . ." (Schweitzer)

Towards Easter, 1930 ". . . my wife had unfortunately to return to Europe, since she felt the climate telling on her . . ." (Schweitzer)

1933 "Mme. Schweitzer left Königsfeld with their daughter to settle in Lausanne where, as much as his travels and work permitted, the Doctor spent his time when he was in Europe . . ." (Everett Skillings)

May 1939 "Mme. Schweitzer and her daughter had set sail

for Lambaréné. This was Rhena's first visit to Africa." (George Seaver)

1940 "Mme. Schweitzer, who had been spending some time in Lausanne, was visiting the Eckerts (her daughter and husband) in Paris." (George Seaver)

Summer, 1941 "My wife arrived at Lambaréné; as if by a miracle she succeeded in getting from France . . . She has stood the strain of the exacting climate better than I had expected. She keeps going all day long and her help is very precious." (Schweitzer)

September 1945 "My wife who had been at Lambaréné since August 1941, returned to Europe. Since then she had been at Lambaréné only when better weather prevails, that is from May to September (of the years 1946 and 1947)." (Schweitzer)

April 1956 "Nowadays indifferent health has made it impossible for her (Mme. Schweitzer) to play an active part in the work of the hospital . . . She is frail to look at but has an indomitable will." (Mrs. Clara Urquhart)

January 1957 "The first time I saw Mme. Schweitzer I could see she was not well. The blue veins stood out in her forehead and seemed stark against the pure whiteness of her skin . . . When she spoke it was with considerable effort. Her breathing was laboured . . . Once I saw Mme. Schweitzer start out across the compound, her weight bent forward on her stick and her whole being struggling for breath. I rushed to her side and took her arm. She looked up at me, somewhat puzzled, as though I did not know the rules of the game at Lambaréné." (Norman Cousins in *Dr. Schweitzer of Lambaréné*)

June 1 1957 Mme. Schweitzer died at Zürich, Switzerland, aged seventy-five.

Essentially, Mme. Schweitzer's life had been honoured by contact with the great Doctor of Lambaréné. She had been allowed to share, while her health and strength permitted, the work and adventures that built up the figure of one of the world's most exceptional contemporary men. But in all other ways it seems to have been an existence which few women would choose, a form of living in the shadows as consort and helper rather than as wife and mother. That she nobly professed to nothing but satisfaction is greatly to her credit. Writing to Dr. Schweitzer's admiring, industrious biographer, Dr. George Seaver, in March 1945, she said: "It is now forty-three years since we became friends and started to work together. We met with a mutual feeling of responsibility for all the good that we had received in our lives, and a sense of our duty to pay for it by helping others. It has been the joy and the pride of my life to follow and assist him in all his activities, and my one regret that failing strength prevented me from keeping pace with him . . ."* A noble sentiment that seems strangely at odds with those stories of her tragic behaviour at Lambaréné, but a great tribute to her loyalty.

Mme. Schweitzer's only child Rhena is perhaps less tragic but even more removed from Schweitzer's orbit than her mother. "You see," Mme. Schweitzer told Norman Cousins, "when Rhena was small, the Doctor did not feel that Lambaréné was a good place in which to bring up a child. And so we sent her to boarding school. In later years, when she was grown up, she came here for a visit—for a few weeks."** Cut off from her father, the little girl had grown to maturity in another sphere, a separate culture, and a younger generation from that of the distant man who was her father. Consequently she was a stranger in his world; a Swiss-thinking, modern young woman who could never imagine Lambaréné as even partially her home.

On Albert Schweitzer's eighty-third birthday, January 14 1958, Rhena sat at his table in Lambaréné surrounded by his devoted staff—an outsider. The moment is worth noting; fortunately a shorthand transcription was taken privately. Her father was in festive mood, wearing his ceremonial black bow-tie to signify the importance of the occasion. Wine and an unusual variety of delicacies lay on the board before them making their contribution to the party atmosphere. But as the Doctor rose to make his speech his bold, grey eyes were sad. "I am an old man," he said, "whose life did

* *Albert Schweitzer, the Man and His Mind*
** *Dr. Schweitzer of Lambaréné*

not quite go as he had wished it to go . . ." He talked of his work in the hospital, speaking more candidly and intimately to his staff, and to the daughter he hardly knew, than anyone present had heard him speak before. Then he turned to the dark, well-built young woman at his side. ". . . And now I have to add what I always add," he said, "that the Light of the World has looked today on me, and not only on me but on my daughter too." He bent towards her. For a moment he seemed to be talking only to her. "I thank you for coming to celebrate this birthday with me on your own initiative (Rhena, one gathers, had not been invited). I do not know your life story well, and I am not much of a psychologist, so I cannot guess whether your life has fulfilled your wishes. However, I think that, having me for a father, and having good children and a good husband, one might well feel rather contented. Here in Lambaréné you cannot, as you used to do as a child in Königsfeld when the admirers arrived, take the photo from the piano and say 'this is my father . . . he's so like me, don't you think?' There will only be a few admirers coming here today . . ."

There were, in fact, many admirers both at Lambaréné and all through the world who rejoiced at Schweitzer's miraculous survival to such an age. Among them, how many knew that the birthday they celebrated was also that of his daughter Rhena? Who knew that *le grand docteur* of Lambaréné *had* a daughter, then thirty-nine years old? The coincidence of their shared birthday is striking enough, but it is even more astonishing that the Doctor made no attempt in his speech to honour it with more than a passing reference.

Rhena had been born in 1919, three years after her father's mother was killed in the war, but apart from filling the vacant place in the female establishment of the family the little girl with the large dark eyes had no special setting in her family's grand design. For her ailing mother she was doubtless a delightful and beloved companion; yet a burden which more than before prevented her from being with the man she worshipped. To Albert Schweitzer, her father, she may well have seemed an entrancing adornment of family life, but sadly out of touch with the realities he embraced more urgently. To bring such a tender infant to the jungle was unthinkable. To spend his time with her was to turn aside from his chosen path. The dilemma was solved by Mme. Schweitzer's ill-health, which made it impossible for her to accompany her husband to Lambaréné on his second visit in 1924, and by her tolerance in agreeing to stay in Europe alone to bring up the child herself, excepting those necessarily rare occasions when Dr. Schweitzer could be with them. Perhaps it is not surprising that he wrote so heartily in his autobiography: "I have never ceased to be grateful to her . . . unceasingly I thank her in my heart."

Not only did he thank her, but he named his hospital after her, "The Albert Schweitzer-Bresslau Hospital". All equipment, instruments, cutlery, towels, etc. at Lambaréné are branded with the three initials "A.S.B.". The mark of his gratitude will continue as long as the hospital remains.

The story of Rhena's development, or rather the lack of this story, might astonish any researcher into the many biographical studies of *le grand docteur*. When Dr. George Seaver compiled his 346 page biography for publication in 1947, he borrowed copiously from nearly every book, pamphlet and available piece of correspondence about the Doctor, his life and thought. Yet Rhena emerged only once from the shadows, to be granted notice on the day of her birth. With this bald statement, the biographer exhausted his supply of information. She was not to be found in the book's index. Neither Albert Schweitzer nor writers about him have been able to add much more to Rhena's dim portrait.

Norman Cousins perhaps goes nearer to elucidation of this twilight figure than any other observer. He records a talk with her mother in which Rhena was discussed. "She is now married, to Jean Eckert of Zürich, an organ builder, and she of course has her own home," Mme. Schweitzer told him. Then, together, they looked at photographs in the family album which Mme. Schweitzer treasured in her bedroom at Lambaréné. There was one print, an early one, showing Schweitzer as a sturdy young man with thick, black hair, heavy moustache and clear, un-graven face. Hélène, his wife, looked young and vivacious with thin, sensitive features and a strength of character showing in her face. Rhena had large dark eyes. She was holding her mother's hand, and wore an expression familiar to all parents of little girls—part shyness, part curiosity, part uncertainty, part feminine delight in being asked to pose. Then there was a picture of Rhena and her husband, taken soon after they had married. In this, Cousins recalls, M. Eckert looked alert and well-groomed. The photograph was followed by several others of the growing Eckert family, their daughters and a sixteen year old boy, Philippe, who had been seriously ill but was then on his way to recovery.

For Mme. Schweitzer these photographs were living treasures from a world she had voluntarily sacrificed to her husband's austere design for living. She turned to them whenever the burden of her life and illness became insupportable. With infinite wistfulness she told her visitor: "Now, we do not take pictures any more . . . And now I have very little to do except to look at these pictures, and old letters, and think back upon our life together."* It is to be hoped that her daughter was with her when she died in Zürich, tragically unable to be at the side of the man she had struggled so long to keep pace with.

For, though Rhena may not have shared much of her father's life in Africa, she was well aware of the toll which it had taken from her mother. She had only to recall her own loneliness. As a perceptive visitor to Lambaréné wrote after a meeting with her: "The most touching figure in this sad story is the daughter, Rhena. Her mother absorbed herself in books. She was kind to Rhena, and scrupulous in her maternal attention; but the impression she left was of solicitude dictated by the mind rather than the heart. The girl grew up without the warmth and relaxed atmosphere with which a united family surrounds its young. Small wonder that she sought to fill the gap in her emotional life by marrying as soon as she could. She was eighteen when she became Mrs. Eckert, wife of an organ builder. She met him through her father, whose attainments include a specialist knowledge of organs. But Schweitzer and his daughter have been all but strangers. She was the mother

* *Dr. Schweitzer of Lambaréné* by Norman Cousins

of three children when, for the first time for twenty years, they celebrated their birthdays together in 1958. Rhena travelled to Lambaréné specially for the event."

She had heard her father's remarkable speech in silence, as impassively as she had so often heard that he would not be coming home this year, again. At the end of the speech, the visitor noted: "The Doctor joked, and his remarks were not without tenderness. But to some who listened to him in that wire-netted room where such infinite solicitude was expended on the well-being of an insect, it seemed strange that he should not himself have invited his daughter to join him for their birthday; and stranger still that he should confess to knowing her so little." The explanation is that the places closest to Albert Schweitzer have all his life been reserved for others than his wife and daughter. They have been, are, for women who work in the cause of the Schweitzer hospital and the Schweitzer Image.

FOURTEEN

THE IMAGE MAKERS

THERE IS a strong feeling among Schweitzer's followers that no writer should describe Lambaréné or the Doctor without having spent several weeks, even months, at the hospital. This may in part be responsible for the chorus of flattery and adulation rising from most books on the subject, with few but praiseworthy exceptions. The greater number of writers seem to have fallen under a spell, or persuasion, during their sojourn in the colony. They have left works which bear little evidence of truth and objectivity. These confections have seriously distorted the legend of Albert Schweitzer.

The dictionary says that a legend is a traditional story popularly regarded as historical. Thus, how it has been sugared is important. If future scholars are to embark on a quest of the historical Schweitzer, as he once essayed a quest of the historical Jesus, they will need an unusually sweet tooth to escape nausea. The Doctor's biographers have garnished his traditional story, doubtless with the most innocent and praiseworthy intentions, to a point of unreality.

To analyse them all would be both wearisome and redundant, since their reflections differ little. But, to take the work of Mrs. Clara Urquhart, Schweitzer's wealthy and twice-married South African admirer, *With Doctor Schweitzer in Lambaréné*, as an example, her tiny book of only sixty-three pages, of which a mere twenty-seven contain text, mirrors nothing but the purest and most glamorous goodness of the hospital. Schweitzer is seen as a noble, handsome appearance blending with a purer-than-pure simplicity and humility of soul into a personality as warm and precious as molten gold. On page after page Mrs. Urquhart explains her own rationalization of the principles of Lambaréné, though it is implicit that some of the more repugnant aspects of the hospital had at first surprised her. "Schweitzer says of himself that in Africa he has no opportunity of being the saintlike person which his European admirers imagine him to be," she writes. But, in making this admission, the author has gone as far as she is prepared to go. Elsewhere, the reader is treated to a confetti-shower of epithets describing the Doctor she loves . . . "that rock-like man", "the great European", ". . . the man has such radiance; he emanates such vitality, such creativity, such spirituality, that all who meet him face to face are moved—often beyond words." The final sentence can hardly be said to be true of Mrs. Urquhart, or of many of her contemporary "Schweitzerines".

This is not to say that Mrs. Urquhart's book, or any other that I have tried to digest in re-assessing the Doctor of Lambaréné, is anything but an honest reflection of its author's view and vision. But is anything of value, of lasting worth, capable of standing up to public appraisal unless it is humanized by blemish as well as beatitude? I remember how R. C. Trevelyan answered the question, in a moving foreword in verse to his translation of Virgil's *The Eclogues and The Georgics* which closed with these lines:

> . . . So, when he lay dying,
> From time to time he asked his friends to bring him
> The book-boxes wherein his Aeneid lay—
> With all its blemishes and incompletions,
> Its ambiguities and sublime defects—
> That he might burn it: but they shook their heads
> Weeping, though he besought them earnestly.
> Thus, like a lover still unsatisfied,
> Heart-broken, did death take him; but his book,
> That for so long he had loved and laboured for,
> Death has no power to touch.

It is defect that an imperfect world demands, as well as magnificence, in any immortal greatness whether of man or work. And only when it receives both is it possible to say of such a legend that "death has no power to touch" it. Left to his flatterers, the legend of Albert Schweitzer would perish in a swamp of sentimentality.

When Mrs. Urquhart writes: "He is a conservative in the best sense of that much misused word. He believes that progress can only come at the gradual pace at which all creation takes place. But he does believe in progress . . ." she is testing the elasticity of her readers' credulity well past breaking point. The "gradual pace" of creation is nonsense, as any botanist knows. And would it be "conservative in the best sense" to deny the use of twentieth-century drugs to primitive Africans until they have served their apprenticeship in modern living? This sort of false flattery does the Doctor's cause no service. Nor does it help to eulogize Schweitzer's undoubtedly beautiful hands with such tributes as "They have also planted many of the trees which, together with the indigenous ones, have made of that unhealthy corner of the earth *a veritable Garden Of Eden*" (my italics). In a colony doing constant battle with malnutrition, disease, loneliness, frustration and death, it is a wild over-statement, and the kind of misrepresentation that coats the lenses of outside viewers with the deepest rose.

"If ever a man has lived up to his knightly heritage it is Albert Schweitzer . . . in his own way of life there gleams a gold thread of hope for the unity and brotherhood of all the creatures who share in the glorious phenomenon called life." That, too, is the view of Mrs. Urquhart, as expressed in her book, and perhaps we need go no further than to state it. Though how a highly intelligent observer who has read, and discussed with Dr. Schweitzer, his fatalistic philosophy of civilization's inevitably approaching doom can imagine such gilded day-dreams may be worth consideration.

The author must have been aware of the anomaly when she wrote, a little farther on in the same volume: "Laughter . . . plays a big part in the life of Doctor Schweitzer. How heartily his silvery laugh will ring out when—as they never fail to do—members of his staff recount the amusing incidents of their heavy day. It seems to me that Schweitzer's spontaneous sense of fun and his great and ready sense of humour have balanced the pessimism which his prophetic insight might have brought in its wake . . ." The needs of rationalization being what they are, Mrs. Urquhart has allowed herself to be carried away towards this ingenious conclusion. In doing so, she misleads her readers. For Dr. Schweitzer has little time to listen to, let alone to laugh at, the anecdotes of the majority of his staff. On the contrary, he is apt to join in discussions, sometimes jocular or hilarious but more often intensely serious and weighty, with only the chosen hierarchy of his table (the sole communal meeting point, other than by his express wish, in the hospital). The amount of laughter that he gives vent to, and the outward presence of his "spontaneous sense of fun", are unlikely to balance the pessimism which Mrs. Urquhart has thus dismissed. The man who wrote, in one of his lesser-known but most profoundly characteristic utterances, "We are at the beginning of the end of the human race",* needs no such apologists.

Nor, I think, does the Doctor require tributes of the sort expressed by the United States dentist Frederick Franck in his account of the time he spent at Lambaréné. Franck's book *Days With Albert Schweitzer* was published in New York in 1957. It confessed that "as a boy, he (the Doctor) was one of my idols". But it was not primarily a work of idolatry. "The ward, at first sight, looks like an inferno of smoke, suffering and stench . . ." wrote Franck in a descriptive passage hardly likely to endear it to the coterie of Schweitzer's closest admirers. He also quoted a young African as saying: "*Eh bien*, the treatment (at Lambaréné) could not be finer and the doctors are better than in any other place, but of course the accommodation is terrible . . ."

Where Dr. Franck's appreciation of the mystic purpose of the hospital shows through, he inclines to be incomprehensible. At one point he asserts: "Schweitzer rejects modern man's belief in the Redemption of the World by Things . . ." but what is this belief, if it exists? And how many "modern men" really accept

* An epilogue to *The Theology of Albert Schweitzer for Christian Inquirers* by E. N. Mozley

any such philosophy? "The mythical Albert Schweitzer," says Franck with finality, "does not exist . . ."

Far greater as a work of observation and delineation is the book written by another medical helper, the Danish surgeon L. Østergaard-Christensen, and published in this country by the Beacon Press in 1962 under the title *At Work With Albert Schweitzer*. If all studies of the hospital and its creator were as concise and unsentimental the legend would be well served. The author was entering the second half of his sixties when he made the journey to the African Equatorial jungle to work at Schweitzer's side. He went as the result of a brief and half-forgotten discussion at a party which turned on a general longing to get out into the world and expand the personal universe. A friend at the party had taken him seriously when he had said that he would "go tomorrow" to work for Schweitzer; had written to the Doctor, and had finally persuaded the surgeon to act according to his alleged word. The result was a visit which must have been as helpful to Dr. Schweitzer and his hospital as any made in its history. Mr. Christensen performed several operations and has written a book that will ring truer in the future as an expression of feeling than a library of more flattering pamphlets.

"His (Schweitzer's) hospital is a little State within the State, like the Vatican," he wrote, and later told the amusing story of the Doctor's chamber pots. Apparently these, marked with the customary hospital cypher "A.S.B." were regularly stolen by African patients, to be discovered later in remote jungle villages being used as cooking pots. "What do you do?" Schweitzer was once asked in Europe. "I supply Africa with chamber pots," he replied. On this theme of Schweitzer's notorious distrust of the African, Christensen also quotes the Doctor as having warned him with great sincerity: "Whatever you do, never get into a car with a native at the wheel."

These comic details aside, Mr. Christensen paints a full and objective portrait of Lambaréné. Though Dr. Schweitzer's white female assistants impressed him, he did not fall into the drooling and sentimental pattern of thinking which their existence stirs in more impressionable observers. He wrote: "Most, I think, come for idealistic reasons, led by the same motive that brought Schweitzer himself. Others are drawn by longing for adventure and by the world-famous name. In most cases there is probably a mingling of all three motives, but it also happens that luckless individuals, bearing the marks of many reverses in life, are washed up on the shore of the hospital and find an asylum there, far from the world into which they could not fit.

"One cannot help admiring the young women who use up their time and strength in hard work far from the comforts of civilization . . . Some are fascinated by the strange black world and find their pleasure in continued nursing among the natives, whose childlike gratitude and confidence they have won. A few are so charmed by Schweitzer's personality that their lives are bound up with his for ever . . ."

This is a refreshing and true understanding of the motives inspiring Schweitzer's many women helpers, but it is rare to find such an example of dispassionate accuracy among writings on Schweitzer's kingdom. With equal fairness, the surgeon assessed the value of Lambaréné as a hospital: "When, as sometimes happens, critical comparisons are drawn between modern European hospitals and Albert Schweitzer's work at Lambaréné, directly in favour of the former, it must not be forgotten that our hospitals at home are monumental expressions of a civilized welfare state's contribution to the fight against disease. The hospital at Lambaréné is purely one man's work in a country which knows neither civilization nor welfare. It is founded on one man's almost superhuman endurance and strength of will in the most difficult circumstances imaginable."

As Schweitzer has said that Lambaréné is for him the fulfilment of an ambition to make his life an argument, so Christensen recognizes that questions are, and must always be, asked about the man Albert Schweitzer. "Are his life and his teachings really at one;" he asks, "or is there disharmony? For this reason he is a symbol of controversy." Yet other writers, notably the prolific researcher and inexhaustible biographer George Seaver, prefer to regard the Doctor as a monochrome of virtuous hues; a saintly paragon. Seaver divides his elaborate portrait, *Albert Schweitzer—The Man and His Mind*, published by Adam & Charles Black in 1949, into the two sections reflected in the title. He begins with the less than modest assertion that "Albert Schweitzer is probably the most gifted genius of our age, as well as its most prophetic thinker." If the Doctor's gifts can be taken to include the single-minded absorption which kept him in Lambaréné while his family grew up without him, they are not above reproach. If his prophetic vision sees nothing but the doom of man, there are those whose lives, though less an emulation of Christ's than the Doctor's, are given to an opposite conviction. Dr. Seaver turns a Nelsonic blindness towards such issues. While presenting relevant criticism of his subject, he allows them little freedom. Of Schweitzer's spartan family relations, he remarks only, and with a touching faith, that Schweitzer is: "Reticent as always about his deepest personal feelings . . ." This out-does the most phlegmatic understatement of literature.

Still, Seaver writes a nice and useful book which does, so to speak, throw under one roof all the various jottings and pamphlets, newspaper reports and correspondence, of both Dr. Schweitzer and his many publicists. The trouble, not unique among such scholarly biographies, is that it creates an impression of dealing with someone already dead, while Schweitzer is the most alive phenomenon of the age. His ideas and arguments will continue to be heard for many years after his death.

The serious question is whether his legend can survive the adulation and flattery of many of his biographers. His own autobiographical writings incline to be pedantic and egocentric, so that few people in Britain today (unlike Germany, where they are set-books for study in schools; and where schoolchildren, at least in the West, are taught to think of Albert Schweitzer as a "great German") read them as they deserve to be read. It would seem that we must wait for the years beyond his lifetime to see in print the final volumes of his *Philosophy of Civilization* and his theological *Kingdom of God*. Meanwhile, the misrepresentation goes on.

But such expanded essays as Norman Cousins' "personal appreciation", his book entitled *Dr. Schweitzer of Lambaréné*, published by Harper & Brothers in 1960, do provide helpful glimpses of the Doctor and his world. In Lambaréné, and among Schweitzer's admirers elsewhere, I heard scant praise for this work on the grounds that it is poorly researched and superficial. Certainly it is digressive, as the author freely admits. But unless the main reason for its rejection in the Schweitzer colony is disappointment—since Mr. Cousins is such an eminent writer and editor in the United States—I cannot understand their feelings. Cousins spoke more closely with Schweitzer, and reported more candidly what the Doctor said, than anyone has yet dared, or been skilled enough, to do. Some of his descriptive passages strike the recent visitor to Lambaréné as brilliantly observed. His sympathy and admiration for the Doctor and his work is cleanly expressed, and some of his conclusions seem profoundly considered. The defect of the book is that it lacks form; as such a narrative, coined from notes taken on a general voyage through Africa, must do.

It is part of the mystique of Lambaréné that nearly everybody there, the "insiders" of Schweitzer's tight little colony, regard themselves as bound somehow into the Doctor's personal legend. They do nothing to usurp his limelight, but they jealously protect the plinth on which he is shown to the world. So they watch each utterance and publication referring to their subject with the zeal of bodyguards. Journalists who have reported their meetings with the Doctor have received long and declamatory letters from his admirers and supporters, here and abroad, often being drawn into controversy with many of the Doctor's protectors who are only too willing to rush to his defence. The universal camp of the "Schweitzerines" bristles with sharp weapons of attack as well as defence, as though the legendary figure they enclose is above criticism. It is probably this pattern of resistance to any outspokenness on the part of a privileged visitor—himself an "insider"—that provoked the feeling of dissatisfaction with Cousins's book.

Yet this author has offered hard facts, strong sympathy, and a rousing conclusion to his book. I take the liberty of quoting an abridged passage from this conclusion because, in any verdict on

Albert Schweitzer, it is worth noting: "History," says Norman Cousins, "is willing to overlook almost anything—errors, paradoxes, personal weaknesses or faults—if only a man will give enough of himself to others. The greater the ability to identify and serve, the more genuine the response. In the case of Schweitzer, later generations will not clutter their minds with petty reflections about his possible faults or inconsistencies. In his life and work will be found energy for moral imagination. This is all that will matter.

"Albert Schweitzer will not be immune from attack. There may be a period of carping and intended exposure, much of it with an air of fresh discovery and all of it in a mood of disillusion. But in the long run the inconsistencies and paradoxes will be as nothing alongside the real meaning of Albert Schweitzer and his place in history. For Albert Schweitzer has done more to dramatize the reach of the moral man than anyone in contemporary Western civilization. No one in our times has taught us more about the potentiality of a human being. No one in our times has done more to liberate men of darkened skin. No one in our times has provided more inspiration.

"If Albert Schweitzer is a myth, the myth is more important than the reality. For mankind needs such an image in order to exist. People need to believe that man will sacrifice for man, that he is willing to walk the wide earth in the service of man. Long after the hospital is forgotten, the symbol of Albert Schweitzer will be known and held high . . .

". . . Albert Schweitzer is a spiritual immortal. We can be glad that this is so. Each age has need of its saints. A saint becomes a saint when he is claimed by many men as their own, when he awakens in them a desire to know the best that is in them, and the desire to soar morally . . .

". . . It matters not to Schweitzer or to history that he will be dismissed by some as a do-gooder or as a sentimentalist who frittered his life away on Africans who couldn't read or write . . . If there is a need in America today, it is for Schweitzers among us . . . For at Lambaréné I learned that a man does not have to be an angel to be a saint."

This is a paeon of emotional praise with which few would wish to argue, for it is personal, sincere and brilliantly conceived. And if Cousins over-balances in favour of Schweitzer the man, then it is his right to do so. Where, however, it is easy to take issue with him is in his assumption that a myth is more important than the reality; for here Albert Schweitzer himself would differ. The Doctor spent too many weary months searching and sleuthing for the reality of the historical Jesus to support such a doctrine. So we are left, those who wish to see the scales fairly weighted, with the question of the legend of Albert Schweitzer *as apart from* the man, and in researching this we are not helped by our distinguished American author any more than by the many adulating flatterers who have written lesser works.

Does Cousins honestly believe, as an experienced journalist and editor, that generations to come will be satisfied with the roseate picture left by such biographers? He says with convincing self-assurance that history will overlook most things in a man; but what of T. E. Lawrence of Arabia? Was ever a man so besmirched by reaction to his over-glorified legend? Have not the greatest figures of their times been judged by what has been gathered in their train, rather than by the truth of their histories? What mankind desires to believe about one of their number will become him in time, if only when he is dead and buried. Thus the separation process of legend from man rises above the evangelical cries, even of Mr. Cousins, to the very throne of truth. In re-assessing the worth of Albert Schweitzer, we may believe in that.

FIFTEEN

IS SCHWEITZER A CHRISTIAN?

SOME YEARS ago, one of the highest-browed magazines in Europe held a poll to establish which figures, dead or alive, were thought by its readers to be the most exceptional all-rounders of known time. In the trio chosen, Albert Schweitzer was linked with Leonardo da Vinci and the phenomenal German poet, philosopher and scientist, Johann Wolfgang von Goethe. This was no sentimental impulse on the part of the egg-heads, but an appreciation of a man whom they must have regarded as the most accomplished of his age. Those who voted for him were unlikely to be misled by the popular image of him at work in Lambaréné, a simple and self-sacrificing leper doctor. They knew of his other attainments, in particular his importance as a theologian. They recognized that his work in this field had been criticized, notably in Britain and Rome, as radical to the point of heresy; yet they still voted for him. The fact must be weighed in any consideration of Albert Schweitzer.

For whatever may be argued about the value of Schweitzer as a jungle doctor, his standing as a theologian is considerable. The notions that such revolutionary German theologians as Hegel and Johannes Weiss had dared to demolish before him, Schweitzer brilliantly succeeded in pulverizing into academic dust. His one consistent theme, that Jesus did not claim to be the Messiah, but believed Himself the man chosen by God to lead mankind into the eventual spiritual Kingdom, was not new. But his approach was so dynamic that it caught the attention of English scholars. As a result his early theological books were translated and published in Britain—*The Mystery of the Kingdom of God* in 1905; *The Quest of the Historical Jesus* in 1910; *Paul and His Interpreters* and *The*

Mysticism of Paul the Apostle later. They caused an explosion of controversy that can still be heard rumbling in the middle distance. As Dr. Micklem, Principal of Mansfield College, Oxford, said: "The publication of Dr. Schweitzer's book (*The Quest*) was like the explosion of a vast bomb in the theological world. It finally blew up the nineteenth-century liberalistic interpretation of the life and teaching of our Lord."

The dust has now dropped out of the air, and we can see that the bomb was in two parts. The first was Schweitzer's analysis of the many religious historians who had previously charted the life of Christ. He shrewdly proved that no theologian should ever attempt such a survey. In the second part, he went on to do what he had warned could not be done, to describe Christ's life as it had actually occurred. The result was the failure (a vague and contradictory analysis) that he had prophesied.

To encompass the area of centuries and scholars which the study entailed, Schweitzer brought armfuls of books to his room, arranging them in piles on the floor. Each stack represented the available research for a particular chapter. (He recalls in his memoirs that his most anxious task was preventing an industrious Alsatian charwoman from tidying them away!) Thereby, he contrived to do a job that had never before been attempted. And from all this industry and eye-strain emerged a triumphant study which will live as a scholar's guide to the life and ministry of Jesus. It is a colossal re-cap of all the New Testament historians from Reimarus to Wrede who, in Schweitzer's opinion, had failed. Hermann Samuel Reimarus was the bitter philosophical Hamburg Jew whose work on religion had been cautiously hidden during his lifetime and only published after his death in 1768. W. Wrede was less interesting, but came as a punctuation point at the end of the radical school of theologians, mainly Germans, who had attempted their own map of Jesus's times. Schweitzer had taken their writings apart, shown up their weaknesses, and with skill and irony proved that the whole "Lives of Jesus" movement faced an impossible quest.

English theologians received this part of the work with acclaim.

F. C. Burkitt, regarded as the doyen of English New Testament scholars, wrote an enthusiastic foreword to the English translation. It was published in a dozen languages, and became an international best-seller. A high tribute to its durability can be seen today in the naming of America's most recent theological movement "The New Quest" in honour of Schweitzer's *Quest*. In the words of a leading British theologian: "*The Quest* is a major theological work, an incredible piece of analysis written in rather a fine, slightly ironic style, and remarkably interesting."

It was, however, not as original to the German-speaking scholars who had been fed the strident rationalism of George Wilhelm Friedrich Hegel, that early nineteenth-century philosopher and theologian who not only began the habit of taking snuff but is also held to be part-responsible, intellectually, for the birth of the Prussian and Nazi forces in Germany. His study of Jesus as a normal but extraordinary man, the purely human son of Joseph and Mary, unquestionably influenced Schweitzer, who told Norman Cousins that he had always thought of Hegel as one of his most influential teachers. The Doctor respected Hegel's influence on Goethe. If he fell short of believing, as Hegel did, that everything serves progress ("the passions of rulers and of peoples") he was nevertheless deeply affected by the earlier revolutionary's cry that "What is reasonable is real, and what is real is reasonable." The first major part of *The Quest of the Historical Jesus*, in so far as it set out to put the record straight, hung on this belief.

But in the last sixty of its 400 or so pages, the book switched over to reveal a side of Albert Schweitzer's character that is rarely seen. By doing what he had shown to be impossible, he clearly indicated that he did not see himself as other men. He was above them. Having satisfied everybody, as it were, that the instrument was unplayable, he now proceeded to play it with gusto. "The first part of the book had been decisive," says a contemporary theologian, "then, ridiculously, he tried to do exactly what he had decided could not be done. He sat down to write his own true history of the life of Jesus. No wonder it was—and is—regarded as something of a joke!" As a student at Oxford, this scholar was advised by his tutor to "read, learn and inwardly digest *The Quest*—so that you may never make the same mistake!"

In essence, Schweitzer's "Life" differed little from that of Johannes Weiss and others who had identified Christ's faith in the coming of the spiritual Kingdom with the ancient belief of the Jews, now known as "eschatological Judaism". According to this, a man would be born on earth as a Messiah. At the coming of the Kingdom, which they expected in their lifetime, he would lead all mankind into the heavenly world. But Christ, in Schweitzer's view, came to believe that only by His own sacrifice could the Kingdom be achieved. He would then appear resurrected, as the Son of Man. When His death failed to achieve this, His followers reached the conclusion that His belief had been right, but His timing wrong. The Kingdom, they thought, *would* materialize, but not immediately. Christ *would* be seen as the Son of Man, but only in due time.

The important consequence of this, for Schweitzer, was that he could revere Christ as a truly remarkable man, yet see his example as one which any other exceptional man might follow, perhaps with the hope of ultimately similar favours from God. "Anyone who ventures to look the historical Jesus straight in the face and to listen for what He may have to teach him in His powerful sayings, soon ceases to ask what this strange-seeming Jesus can still be to him. He learns to know Him as One who claims authority over him," wrote Albert Schweitzer in his autobiography. But did he *mean* Christ, the son of God, with a capital letter even to his pronoun? For that is how it appeared in the English version of his book *My Life and Thought* published here by Holt. It is pertinent to ask, for in 1950, when Colonel E. N. Mozley published *The Theology of Albert Schweitzer*, the Doctor added an epilogue in which he used no such reverential capitals, and in which he said: "To me, however, Jesus remains what he was. Not for a single moment have I had to struggle for my conviction that in him is the supreme spiritual and religious authority, though his expectation of the speedy advent of a supernatural Kingdom of God was not fulfilled, and we cannot make it our own."

The most direct of Schweitzer's inquisitors, Norman Cousins, indeed discussed these views with him recently, reporting that Schweitzer told him: "Jesus Christ did not proclaim Himself to be the Son of God; His mission was to awaken people to the Kingdom of God which He felt to be imminent."* Another visitor, the Danish surgeon Østergaard-Christensen, told a revealing story of how he was with Schweitzer when he received a book by a Norwegian professor in which a chapter was headed by the question: "Albert Schweitzer—a Christian?" Schweitzer, said Christensen, smiled, shook his head slightly and remained silent. The surgeon remarked, in his account of the story: "It was a reply without words, but its meaning was clear: Who can know anything about that but me?"**

In fact, Schweitzer is an enigma. He declares himself to be a minister of the Lutheran (Christian) Church. Yet he has accepted membership of the Unitarian-Universalist sect in the U.S.A., which is Trinitarian. Not surprisingly, there have been outspoken attacks on his religious views, notably from the Free Church of Scotland. On September 3 1956 it was reported that this Church's *Monthly Record* described the sanitary conditions at Lambaréné as "atrocious, owing to the Doctor's religious aversion to the killing of life, even of germ-laden insects . . . Schweitzer is more a Hindu-Buddhist than a Christian . . . As far as Christian teaching goes at Lambaréné, it practically does not exist . . ." The same attack criticized Schweitzer's "abandonment of the New Testament's conception of Christianity", warning that those who fall into this error "eventually abandon every recognizable tenet of Christian faith and every vestige of Christian practice".

Yet Schweitzer was giving his life to the practice of what appeared to be a purely Christian form of existence. Only his ideas were at fault. To Cousins, he candidly admitted: "In my effort to get away from intricate Christian theology based on later interpretations, I developed some ideas of my own. These ideas were at variance with the ideas that had been taught me. Now, what was I to do?

* *Dr. Schweitzer of Lambaréné*
** *At Work with Albert Schweitzer*

Was I to teach what I myself had been taught but which I now did not believe? How could I, as the principal of a seminary, accept the responsibility for teaching young men that which I did not believe? But was I to teach that which I did believe? If I did so, would this not bring pain to those who had taught me? Faced with these questions, I decided I would do neither. I decided that I would leave the seminary. Instead of trying to get acceptance for my ideas, involving painful controversy, I decided I would make my life my argument. I would advocate the things I believed in terms of the life I lived and what I did. Instead of preaching my belief in the existence of God within each of us, I would attempt to let my life and work say what I believed." In that statement, recorded in Cousins's book *Dr. Schweitzer of Lambaréné*, there is a clear key to the Doctor's inner thinking.

That Schweitzer came into prominence theologically at an opportune time, must not be overlooked. From the middle of the eighteenth century, the question had been asked with increasing daring: did things happen as people, including the apostles in their gospels, say they did? By the end of the nineteenth century, the whole image of the established figure of Jesus which had been left by earlier teachers seemed out of focus. As a result, a swarm of learned and complicated Lives of Jesus was published, especially in Germany. It has been said that many of these works were more than a little inspired by personal motives, that "whatever your own particular whim, you fitted it to Jesus". This was just as true in England, where Thomas Hughes, author of *Tom Brown's Schooldays*, wrote his convictions of fair play and the rugger-field into a work entitled *The Manliness of Christ*, published in 1879.

By the turn of the nineteenth into the twentieth century, the idea that Christ's life was not as traditionally portrayed was supported by serious scholars. It had become conventional to oppose the version dutifully accepted for centuries. At this time Johannes Weiss expressed the opinion that Jesus had believed he would emerge as the Messiah not during his lifetime on earth but at the coming of the Kingdom. And it was this view that Schweitzer expanded and elaborated in *The Quest*. What helped to make his book so remarkable, as well as the thoughts contained in it, was the extraordinary youth of the author. Schweitzer was in his middle twenties when he began it. Such an advanced and provocative work might well have crowned a distinguished career.

Yet in that final part of the book which offered Schweitzer's own interpretation of Christ's life, there was little more than an intellectual impression created out of flimsy evidence. If the first two thirds of the volume were magnificent, the consummation was egregiously ineffectual. The reader was left to form his own interpretation of the indeterminate phrases and conclusions. Schweitzer revealed himself as an historian under the influence of hero-worship for the great German theologians and philosophers who had preceded him. All that can be said is that, in failing to make Christ's life emerge satisfactorily from his creation, he proved the point of his earlier dictum.

This is not to denigrate *The Quest*, which remains a phenomenal achievement by one so young, as well as a theological classic. No theologian has ever written such a considerable and important book at such a slight age. The spirit of the times may have been against him, in that it leaned heavily towards veneration of the established "greats". But his youth and radical character forced him to rebel against convention. Nietzsche and Ruskin were regularly beating bounds outside which it was dangerous for any scholar—let alone an unfledged tyro—to tread. Schweitzer, though imbued with respect for such writers, felt himself forced by the strength of his conviction to break away; to join the rebels behind the intellectual barricades of his day. In doing so, he out-did his contemporaries and altered both the pattern of theological learning and of his own vital design. By succeeding in being acclaimed in Britain, and translated, as Weiss had not been, into the languages of other countries, he earned a high and universal mark of esteem.

At about the same time, a French theologian, the Roman Catholic Alfred Firmin Loisy, was writing and publishing a remarkable interpretation of Christ's life. Both he and Johannes Weiss were greater scholars than Schweitzer. And both expressed views which supported an understanding of Jesus based on the times in which he lived, hence on the Messianic expectations of the Jews. But Schweitzer carried exploration of this path to its final goal. As an English theologian has said: "There were better men on the same track, but Schweitzer out-distanced them. He set the problem for the whole of theology when he showed that Christ was a first century Jew with all the attitudes and beliefs of his times."

There is little doubt that Schweitzer intended his life of Jesus to be definitive; to put an end to the senseless study once and for all. In it, he hewed out a rough and visionary carving of the essential periods of Christ's life, forcing it to work in its author's imagination if not in his readers. At one point in the argument, Schweitzer turned a panoramic eye on the entire map of events, writing with dramatic brilliance: "There is silence all around. The Baptist appears, and cries: 'Repent, for the Kingdom of Heaven is at hand.' Soon after that comes Jesus, and in the knowledge that He is the coming Son of Man lays hold of the wheel of the world to set it moving on that last revolution, which is to bring all ordinary history to a close. It refuses to turn, and He throws himself upon it. Then it does turn; and crushes Him. Instead of bringing in the eschatological conditions, He has destroyed them. The wheel rolls onward, and the mangled body of the one immeasurably great Man, who was strong enough to think of Himself as the spiritual ruler of mankind and to bend history to His purpose, is hanging upon it still. That is His victory and His reign."

Such fireballs could not go unextinguished. In Germany *The Quest* was said to be received "with passive hostility", though Schweitzer has always denied this. In Britain, Professor Sanday of Oxford and Professor Burkitt of Cambridge both acclaimed it, but other critics were anything but admiring. The Roman Catholics, especially, could hardly find scorn cool enough to pour on the book, as a review in *The Tablet* showed: "These two books (another work was dealt with at the same time, to reduce the importance of Schweitzer's) before us are samples of many modern efforts on the Life of Christ. His seamless robe is examined thread by thread. It is pulled this way and that, till we are almost under the impression that it is a patchwork of tatters. Schweitzer's work gives the history of the rending. Then, on the other side, an attempt is made to unravel the manufactured tangle. But was not His robe woven from the top throughout . . . ?" There were others who sneered that the book was "ingenious but unconvincing", though by far the larger number of reviews were favourable.

If the praise of Jesus as "the one immeasurably great man" seemed to smell of the same smouldering incense as Hegel's emotional idolatry, the unease that this created was quickly smothered. Yet Schweitzer's German character had been well served by his choice of subject. In the mortal Jesus he had found his superman. Inadvertently, he had also given relief to the *bourgeoisie* of his period by excusing their many extravagances on the grounds that the coming of the Kingdom was not to be expected in the immediate future. The important but little understood fact that emerged from *The Quest* was that Schweitzer believed Jesus's expectation of the end of the world pointed to an ethic; that we should be prepared for the day of judgement while observing strict rules of conduct and avoiding war, revolution, and even divorce. It led to his embrace of the ethical as the fabric of his own experiment in Christ-like living, the rule which was to govern more than fifty years of service at Lambaréné. Out of it grew Reverence for Life, originally invisible, later realized and recognized as encompassing the whole practical ideal.

He had not escaped entirely unhurt from opposing the Establishment in religious thought. "Both Johannes Weiss and I," he said, "have suffered severely through the compulsion which truth laid upon us to put forward something which was bound to offend Christian faith."* Until 1947 the B.B.C. refused to permit broadcasts containing "affirmations of widely differing beliefs", which ruled against Schweitzer's theological views ever being mentioned or read. Some of the more didactic of the old school of theology poured scorn on him. But in the main the "vast bomb" went off with little serious damage to its creator.

We are left with the absorbing consideration of how Schweitzer's theological convictions brought him to Lambaréné and to the laying

* Epilogue to *The Theology of Albert Schweitzer* by E. N. Mozley

aside of his brilliantly-started academic career as a theologian, as well as his other talents. In a lecture he gave on *The Problem of Ethics in the Development of Human Thought* Schweitzer said: "The respect we owe to our own life would be hypocrisy without our being true to our own self. As we respect our own life, we must, at the same time, abstain from all temptations to deny our personal convictions in certain situations, and we must make all efforts to become better and nobler in terms of humanity." It was essentially in support of humanity, but also of his own convictions, that Dr. Schweitzer sailed for the African jungle in 1913. His biographer, Dr. George Seaver, summed up his definition of the historical Jesus and its effect on his development thus: "It is the delineation of a figure, stark, august, tremendous—like the figure of Epstein's 'Christ'. And so he would have it left. He would not invest it with any theological nimbus to veil its heroic grandeur, he would not adorn it with any picturesque fancies to blur its sharp-edged outline. And having etched it thus he turns away, away from the historical Jesus of His own age, to find Him as He is in ours—not in the study or the cloister, but in the field of self-renouncing action in lowly service to the least of His brethren."*

What he turned towards was a ready-made crucible. He sought a practical field wherein he could carry out his own experiment. He found it among the primitive Africans of his day. That they were men and women, not beasts or insects, mattered to him little. His ambition was to serve, to build and to deliberate. Out of his action of renunciation would spring a message for a civilization that was doomed, but could still pay attention. "To be different from the world," he has said, "that is our spiritual destination. By acting according to it, we live our existence instead of suffering it." If he had not mapped out the path trodden, in his belief, by Jesus Christ nearly 2,000 years ago, it is doubtful if he would ever have envisaged such a mission.

But whether or not his version of Christ's existence will prevail against future scholars is another matter. As a definition of the motivation of Christ, it often appears vague and ambivalent. An

* *Albert Schweitzer, the Man and His Mind*

"immeasurably great man" is not a deity; yet Albert Schweitzer sees all Christian benefits flowing through Him and His example. In accepting His overlordship, he gives to Jesus the same reverence that he gives to the spirit of God which he believes is in all men; and no more. If his credo thereby leaves the observer bewildered, it does not destroy the undoubted value of Schweitzer's standing as an historical explorer in the field, and as a critic of past historians. We can only judge him, pending the arrival of his unfinished *Kingdom of God*, on the known facts. He appears as a reformer, opposing bigotry, cant, and conceit in Christian understanding. As such, he has brought Christ down to the level of any man who, like Schweitzer, serves humanity.

Half a century has passed since Schweitzer published his theological beliefs. He has added little to them. In November 1934 he concluded an article in the American journal *The Christian Century* with these words: "We wander in darkness now, but one with another we all have the conviction that we are advancing to the light; that again a time will come when religion and ethical thinking will unite. This we believe, and hope and work for, maintaining the belief that if we make ethical ideals active in our lives, then the time will come when people will do the same." Would he echo these hopeful words today, in the atomic age, when nearing the end of his life? Norman Cousins and I both asked him the question: "Are you glad you came to Lambaréné?" In both cases Albert Schweitzer replied that he was. To Cousins he added that he had taken some forty years to reflect on the answer, and there was not the slightest doubt or hesitation in his reply: he was very glad indeed.

In the light of what we have seen were Schweitzer's reasons for going there in the first place, the question has to be asked: is his gladness due to a sense of accomplishment? For, if Schweitzer has modelled his life on the life of Jesus, and if Jesus was no more than a man, then it is conceivable that other men might do as well in God's eyes. It is conceivable, too, that Albert Schweitzer's theological reasoning may have prompted his whole, grand experiment in seeking such favour for himself.

SIXTEEN

PHILOSOPHER OF DOOM

HAVING ESTABLISHED his creed, Schweitzer looked for a means of sending his message abroad into the world he had relinquished. In 1900, when a student of twenty-five, he had begun to amass material for a series of philosophical books which he called *The Philosophy of Civilization.* It grew in his mind that here was a vehicle to carry his message; to explain and amplify his belief in the ethical practice of righteousness, as well as in mere allegiance to it. Here was a means by which he would be able to publish the essence of his Reverence for Life credo in its world context; attacking the "life diminishers" as another philosopher has called them; rallying mankind for a return to virtue. Thus philosophy was to be the pulpit from which Schweitzer's views would be preached to the world outside Lambaréné. In philosophy, the theologian, artist and healer in him would find a common voice.

For all its grand design, this crusade was a flop. Much of the writing remains to be done. There is little hope of triumph for Schweitzer's ultimate convictions. The greater part of the message of Reverence for Life has spread no farther than the river-bank at Lambaréné, where it is unlikely to survive the Doctor's death. Only two of the four promised volumes of his philosophical cycle have so far been published. The balance is either unwritten or encased in the Doctor's trunk at Lambaréné, fading, and occasionally being nibbled at when removed by the tamed animals with which he surrounds himself. The mental picture of one of these beasts taking back into the jungle in its belly some fragment of what might be one of the world's greatest documents is painful but not improbable.

To return to what exists, namely the two volumes published in England and Germany simultaneously in 1923 as *The Decay and The Restoration of Civilization* and *Civilization and Ethics*, the first question is whether, in the intervening period of forty-one years, they have established a lasting reputation as a philosopher for their author, already a Doctor of Philosophy. We have the word of Bertrand Russell that they have not. On January 14 1958 I asked Earl Russell whether he considered that Schweitzer, in his *Philosophy of Civilization* thus far published, had made any significant contribution to modern philosophy. His reply was categorical: "I don't believe he is understood to have made any significant contribution." To a subsequent question asking how Schweitzer ranks as a philosopher in the eyes of contemporary philosophers, Russell replied: "It is news to me that he ranks as a philosopher at all." Even more surprisingly, Bertrand Russell admitted that he had not read any of Dr. Schweitzer's philosophical writings. Thus there is no support from Britain's leading philosopher and mathematician; only an ignorance which appears to be deliberate.

What do the works themselves say? It is too much to expect common knowledge of their meaning, because few people have read them. They must be explained. And this is not made simpler by the inconsistency of a philosophy of doom that nevertheless demands an expectation of salvation. "If everyone will turn to humanity and humane thoughts," Schweitzer told me in Lambaréné, "then my philosophical teachings will succeed, despite everything; as Christ's teachings succeeded after His death." Let us consider what elixir lies in them that will have such power.

In the Preface to the first volume of the *Philosophy*, Schweitzer summarizes the battle-plan he proposes to adopt: an attack on the materialistic mania of civilized man. To prepare the ground, he writes a verbose definition of civilization and his own place in it. "It is only in his struggle to become ethical that man comes to possess real value as a personality," he writes. "It is only under the influence of ethical convictions that the various relations of human society are formed in such a way that individuals and peoples can develop in an ideal manner. If the ethical foundation is lacking, then civilization collapses, even when in other directions creative and intellectual forces of the strongest nature are at work."

Schweitzer continues: "This moral conception of civilization, which makes me almost a stranger amidst the intellectual life of my time, I express clearly and unhesitatingly, in order to arouse amongst my contemporaries reflection as to what civilization really is . . ." From this point in the intellectual wilderness, Schweitzer proceeds to denounce the "self deception" of modern man, the "collapse" of his civilization, the "superficial" character of modern philosophizing, the "unfree" economic position of the modern individual and the "under-developed condition" and "lack of spiritual independence" in man of today. It is a gloomy prognosis reminiscent of the Old Testament prophets, and of some contemporary evangelists who call on sinners to repent or be consumed. "We are living today under the sign of the collapse of civilization," writes the Doctor in his opening sentence; it is hardly a message of cheer from the man who banished himself to save us all.

But in subsequent chapters of his works, the restoration of our abysmal mode of living is shown to be just faintly possible, though only through the reform of almost everything in sight. Since civilization is basically moral, that is to say ethical, in its constitution, we have nothing to fear if we will only respond to the natural forces within us. While ideals—or, rather, "civilization-ideals"—have withered into uselessness, there is still the escape route of unswerving, ethical observance. And side by side with this austere remedy for our many blemishes is the conviction, expressed firmly by Dr. Schweitzer, that a false understanding of the universe is at the root of all our troubles; a false understanding provided, it should be noted, by other contemporary philosophers. As a result: ". . . we crossed the threshold of the twentieth century," writes Schweitzer, "with an unshakeable conceit of ourselves . . ."

Thus misdirected, modern man has plunged to his consequent doom ("It is clear now to everyone that the suicide of civilization is in progress . . ."); has enmeshed himself in a false pattern of living, thinking and being. Humanitarian aims, ethical values and virtues have been swept aside in the torrent. Helter-skelter, we have all been sent hurtling towards an extinction that will, nay is bound to, annihilate us. There is only one slender hope: that we turn towards a finer, clearer and better theory of the universe, in which Dr. Schweitzer's creed of Reverence for all—even poisonous—Life triumphs over such petty and selfish considerations as preservation of our own human species. "The future of civilization depends, therefore, on whether it is possible for thought to reach a theory of the universe which will have a more secure and fundamental hold on optimism and the ethical impulse than its predecessors have had," he writes. It is hard to believe that the prophet of doom really means "optimism".

The American Negro writer, James Baldwin, said in a television interview recorded at the time of the racial troubles in the Southern U.S.: "I can't be a pessimist, because I'm alive. To be a pessimist means that you have agreed that human life is an academic matter. So I'm forced to be an optimist; I'm forced to believe that we can survive whatever we must survive . . ." Schweitzer's view is that man must be an optimist only in the strict control of an ethical philosophy; otherwise he is doomed. Without his ultimate ethic of Reverence for Life, there is no question of survival. It is a commanding, indeed a dictatorial, philosophy but one in which he profoundly believes. In his autobiography, the Doctor reflects that two perceptions cast their shadow over his existence. "One consists in my realization that the world is inexplicably mysterious and full of suffering, the other in the fact that I have been born into a period of spiritual decadence in mankind. I have become familiar with and ready to deal with each through the thinking which has led me to the ethical world and life-affirmation of Reverence for Life. In that principle my life has found a firm footing and clear path to follow."*

The second volume of Schweitzer's incomplete *Philosophy* takes us farther into the depths of this self-analysis, asking: "Why does the will-to-live experience itself in this way in me alone? Is it because I have acquired the capacity of reflecting on the totality

* *My Life and Thought*

of Being? What is the goal of this evolution which has begun in me? To these questions there is no answer. It remains a painful enigma for me that I must live with reverence for life in a world dominated by creative will which is also destructive will, and destructive will which is also creative."* It goes far, too, in establishing Schweitzer's rules for practising his creed of Reverence, warning the farmer who may have mown down a thousand flowers in his meadow as fodder for his cattle that he must never knock the head off a flower on his way home in "wanton pastime". To take such life except under pressure of necessity is, in the Doctor's opinion, to commit a crime.

Yet nobody, it seems, is or can be wholly free of anti-Reverence. "I too am subject to division of my will-to-live against itself," he says frankly. "In a thousand ways my existence stands in conflict with that of others. The necessity to destroy and to injure life is imposed upon me. If I walk along an unfrequented path, my foot brings destruction and pain upon the tiny creatures which populate it. In order to preserve my own existence, I must defend myself against the existence which injures it. I become a persecutor of the little mouse which inhabits my house, a murderer of the insect which wants to have its nest there, a mass-murder of the bacteria which may endanger my life. I get my food by destroying plants and animals. My happiness is built upon injury done to my fellow-men . . ."*

In the grip of this despair he explains that, as there are wheels within wheels, so there are ethics within ethics; and "ordinary ethics seek compromises". Man must be the judge of when they should be granted. In the case of Reverence for Life there is no compromise, only an understanding of the acute difference between wanton and necessary injury. Conveniently enough, the Doctor manages to excuse his medical "murders" on these grounds, though with compassion for the pests he is butchering. "Every time I have under the microscope the germs which cause the disease (sleeping sickness)," he says in his autobiography, "I cannot but reflect that I have to sacrifice this life in order to save other life." An un-

* *Civilization and Ethics*

enviable dilemma, from which even his most profound philosophical ruminations have so far failed to save him entirely.

It is not yet the time to form a conclusion about this hypersensitivity, nor to comment on the obvious parallel between what Schweitzer wishes, and what he finds, to be true; yet it is worth pausing to take stock of all that it may mean. Until he conceived the theme of Life Reverence, the Doctor was trying to write the music of life with one hand, and without full control of the keyboard. He was narrow in his philosophy, merely expressing in practical form what he had discovered to be the way of existence of his "immeasurably great man" Jesus. Suddenly, there occurred the flash of illumination which gave him his policy, or main-spring, of philosophical and ethical living. Ever since, he has been saving ants and mosquitoes with a relish and apparent conviction that has done nothing, certainly, to diminish his stature in the eyes of an impressionable world. What he writes about it, what he says in his two published volumes of the *Philosophy*, is merely the wrapping. The ethic is a living thing, and at Lambaréné it can be studied for its effect on human conditions. The visitor may perhaps be pardoned for wondering whether man or some lesser organism is better fitted to survive its universal application.

The idea of Reverence for Life came to Dr. Schweitzer in direct line of descent from another thesis he had evolved, that of Reverence for Truth. When in 1913 he wrote a medical paper on the mental background to Jesus, psycho-analysing Jesus's known behaviour, he developed this principle as a logical conclusion of a scientific analysis. It was, he stated, the highest demand that could be made of man that he should recognize, observe and reverence Truth throughout his life. Some sediment of this pronunciation may have filtered down into his thinking as he later pondered the creation of an ethic suitable to his philosophy.

When it came to him the Doctor was, he tells us, sailing sluggishly up the Ogowe River on a mission of mercy in September 1915. The wife of a missionary had fallen seriously ill and he was on his way to treat her. The journey was long, stiflingly hot and uncomfortable so that, when not taking his share of the native passengers' communal cook-pot (he had left too hurriedly to pack adequate food), he escaped into deep and concentrated thought. For hour upon hour the problem rolled about in his mind, refusing solution. He knew that what he sought was a practical expression of his moral, scientific and religious beliefs, yet no amount of mental projection would take him further. Then he began to notice the passing vegetation on either bank. Much of it was rotting; some had been born recently; other parts were in the grip of death. The whole presented a vast panorama of the life-death cycle in which man was as subject as the smallest plant or insect. The comparison was attractive, since here too death was unfolding at the expense of life and not always at life's extremity. Here in the jungle there were as many savageries and cruelties as in the so-called civilized world of man, which he so deplored for its wars and material vendettas. Here, too, the lack of reverence for the will to live—the right which every vital particle is given at least to feel—was bringing wholesale slaughter and suffering. What use his hospital, treating a few wounds and ailments, when so much carnage occurred wantonly in the natural kingdom? The answer came with the crunch of revelation: *reverence for life*.

Schweitzer, as he pondered the implications of his discovery, grew increasingly excited by it. It was as though his ethic had been given into his hand like a key. The door that had held fast against his intrusion into the whole realm of philosophy and practical religion had suddenly sprung back on its hinges, admitting him. Everything he truly believed and fostered occupied a place in the design which it offered; no longer would he lack purpose in treating men of little value to themselves or others. No more would he have to begrudge the time spent healing animals when so much more important work was to be done. Here was a cause that placed no life higher than another in its right to survival, that offered the ultimate balance between the will to live and the sacred right to do so. He completed his journey in a daze of delighted abstraction, dwelling on his new-found treasure.

As he thought about how he had made his discovery, the Doctor realized that without the anguish which had consumed him for days and weeks it could never have happened. Thus he reached a second conclusion, that ideals and all philosophical virtues spring from thought. He had taken three days of the river journey to reach his mental goal, and in the process had covered sheet after sheet of paper with disconnected jottings (where are they now? Their value as curiosities alone would be considerable). When inspiration came, he was idly watching a herd of hippopotami; historically, they must rank in importance to humanity with the worms in Darwin's garden at Downe. "Now I had found my way . . ." he wrote. "Now I knew . . ."*

There were, to be sure, a few loopholes to be caulked before the blazing new slogan, and all that it represented, could be put into regular service, but these were soon dealt with. Where a problem, such as pain, offered a challenge, it was lopped off with the injunction to "man who is truly ethical" to be content to leave it unsolved. Since the world was inhabited by evil, he must do good "and thus step for a moment out of the incomprehensible horror of existence". It was a far-reaching battle-cry.

How it appealed to such upholders of public morality as those enthusiastic huntsmen and women, the crowned heads of Europe, is an interesting reflection. In Britain, Prince Philip does not today go out of his way to observe reverence for the lives of the game-birds he shoots, despite his royal wife's decoration of Dr. Schweitzer. The Christian churches do not commend the protection of rodents, nor take up cudgels against the destruction of pests. In an age when man may judicially take his fellow's life on the scaffold, there are many anomalies in Schweitzer's creed. Only in Lambaréné has the ethic taken root; and only there, it is believed, for the Doctor's lifetime. But for Schweitzer it became a transcending expression of everything his almost-rejected philosophy was struggling to say.

"I am thrown, indeed," he wrote, "by Reverence for Life into an unrest such as the world does not know, but I obtain from it a blessedness which the world cannot give. I begin to learn the secret of spiritual self-assertion. I win an unsuspected freedom

* *My Life and Thought*

from the various destinies of life. At moments in which I had expected to find myself overwhelmed, I find myself in an inexpressible and surprising happiness of freedom from the world, and I experience therein a clearing of my life-view."*

With this fresh clarity and understanding, Schweitzer found it easier to forgive those who scorned his new-born ethic, as well as those who failed to register the proper respect for his universal law of life-protection. He knew that all truth is laughed at until it becomes widely recognized. But only in his later years has he been forced to accept the improbability of his doctrine being adopted in a world committed to the nuclear bomb. One of his helpers, the young American Fergus Pope, told me in December 1961 that the Doctor had been persuaded two years before to join the world crusade for nuclear disarmament. According to Pope it had taken another American a whole week to convince Schweitzer that the campaign was essentially an expression of his ethic. Even then, he had agreed only grudgingly. Yet today he is believed to spend more time in working for this cause than in administering his hospital and other duties.

Olga Deterding, as one of his helpers, wrote in a British journal a few years ago that in the several years she had spent at Lambaréné, Dr. Schweitzer had made her aware of the terrible dangers presented to the human race by nuclear tests. "Nuclear warfare, which threatens the whole human race with extinction, is to him the most terrible thing which has ever been conceived . . ." she said. Almost as if his philosophy of the doom of civilization in 1900 had demanded it, the Doctor had found his anti-ethic in the nuclear menace.

As long as seven years ago he wrote a *Declaration of Conscience* for the American journal edited by his admirer Norman Cousins, in which he warned: ". . . Our descendants . . . are threatened by the greatest and most terrible danger. That radioactive elements created by us are found in nature is an astounding event in the history of the earth and of the human race. To fail to consider its importance and its consequences would be a folly for which

* *Civilization and Ethics*

humanity would have to pay a terrible price. We are committing a folly in thoughtlessness. It must not happen that we do not pull ourselves together before it is too late. We must muster the insight, the seriousness, and the courage to leave folly and to face reality . . ."

Miss Deterding pleaded, more emotionally, for the same cause: "If a dedicated old man is prepared," she wrote, "after a full and exhausting day, to work through the night on behalf of humanity from the depths of Equatorial Africa, then surely we, from the comfort of our twentieth-century homes, can do something ourselves. In all humility, I suggest we try to follow his example in taking a stand now against the nuclear destruction of our world."

Thus the ethic of Reverence for Life had expanded into a crusading campaign to abolish the nuclear threat from a world that had already signed its death warrant by failing, as early as 1900, to see the universe as it really was; from a civilization still not free of the Reformation; and from a mankind blinded by self-interest, materialism and cruelty. Schweitzer's pessimism had been turned into undreamed channels of purpose by his persuasive American guest. In place of a unique and personal philosophy which few heeded, he had suddenly acquired a position in staff headquarters of the anti-nuclear command. Even Bertrand Russell, the most gifted prophet of nuclear doom, could no longer ignore the direction of Schweitzer's thinking. They walked the same path. When I asked the Doctor in Lambaréné whether Russell had been right in resigning from Britain's Committee of One Hundred, his reply was complimentary: "The good bull," he said, "does not run with the herd."

What may seem odd in this connection is Schweitzer's reticence. He has seldom lacked words to describe his convictions, yet we hear little from him in the way of denunciation, or attack. He told me he would make one more pronouncement. He was waiting until he judged the time ripe to do so. But at the time of writing this book, some six months after seeing him, there is still only silence; and the test-ban treaties are not fully implemented. If Schweitzer means business, it might be said, he should at least show more support for those who are prepared to march, rebel and go to prison for their belief that the bomb must be banned. That he does not do so should not be taken as a mark of faulty courage, but of his distaste for campaigns run by others.

One essential element of Schweitzer's philosophy is that it was created by *him*. He is the only leading exponent of it, just as Ghandi was the sole master of applied passive resistance. For Schweitzer, this is crucial to any consideration. He has lived out his life in independence of authority other than his own, except when he worked at his studies. It would be surprising if this had not brought traces of megalomania. In his case, a man possessed of German authoritarianism and influenced by Hegel, Kant and Wagner, the effect has been to create an unyielding reserve towards all mass-participation. "In a way," the Doctor told Norman Cousins and Mrs. Clara Urquhart during their discussions with him at the hospital, "the two of you in coming here have broken down my resolve not to involve myself in anything remotely concerned with political matters. But as I said the other day, the problem goes beyond politics. It affects all men. All men must speak. Some way must be found to bring about an increased awareness of the danger . . ."*

That conversation took place more than seven years ago, and the effect of Albert Schweitzer's intrusion on to the political scene has so far been anything but dramatic. As he looked out at the windy sky, unusual for the time of year and raising the question, he thought, of whether atomic explosions were altering the conditions of the world's weather and crops, he told Cousins sadly: "All things are now possible. Man can hardly even recognize the devils of his own creation." In the legend of the practical philosopher of Lambaréné, it is sometimes difficult to recognize the champion who will identify these "devils" for mankind.

* *Dr. Schweitzer of Lambaréné* by Norman Cousins

SEVENTEEN

THE BACH BOOK

IN MUSIC, the same curious shadow seemed to fall on Schweitzer's work. The infant prodigy of nine who played his father's church organ during a service at Günsbach, who published a deeply-perceptive study of J. S. Bach at thirty, has made little change in the established order of things. There has been a reluctance, particularly in Britain, to adopt his doctrines, though they have been respected as academically interesting. In more than half a century since his book, *J. S. Bach*, was published in two volumes in this country there has been no hint of the great revolution of attitude towards the composer which it invoked.

In it, he lambasted the huge orchestras and massed choirs of the period. He admonished contemporary musicians for playing Bach's works too fast. He pleaded for the use of boys', rather than women's voices in the choirs. In everything he said, he was principally right—to no avail. These "crimes" are still committed here and elsewhere (except in Germany where some of his prayers have apparently been listened to with more attention).

As we look into this slender, colourful strand of the Doctor's complex genius, the reason for its failure becomes clear. Schweitzer had asserted himself too much. The same arbitrary vigour that brought his radical theology, his demanding philosophy, and his provocative administration of Lambaréné into controversy was present again in his musical work. The same compulsion to make his life an argument had isolated his views, just as it had forced a gulf between him and the world in each of the other directions to which it has turned. "Schweitzer," says a leading British expert, "is respected more today as a musician than as a musicologist. It is doubtful whether his *J. S. Bach* is widely studied at such schools as the Royal Academy of Music; though this may well be because students read few of the classics today, and accept as little guidance as possible."

This expert had helped the Doctor during some of his organ recitals in this country. He was surprised to note that the man who insisted on strict performance techniques observed few of them himself. "What he did was in contradiction to everything he had written," he explained. His account of a performance given by Schweitzer only a few years ago was illuminating: "The old Doctor approached the parapet which rose to a height of some three feet from the floor between him and the organ. He astonished the press and everyone else by vaulting clean over it. Then he sat at the organ and pulled out each stop in turn. Where the sound pleased him, he let the stop remain out. Where it did not, he replaced it. Then he played. We had all expected Bach, but instead he favoured us with Widor. It was clear that this composer had had an enormous influence over him. As an Alsatian, Schweitzer has always suggested the two races of his country's ancestry, French as well as German. This has led to a certain mixture of temperament. But on the occasion we are talking about he played more as a Frenchman, very slowly and ponderously. It was rather magnificent. I have not heard any recent recordings of his organ-playing, but I have been told that they tend to be stiff and wooden. Yet what can one expect? He has had little time to keep in practice."

Musicians in England are generally agreed that the Doctor's playing is of greater academic than aesthetic interest. But his written work on Bach was of special significance, because it went beneath the biography to lay bare the thoughts and problems of the great composer whose son had died a drunkard, his wife destitute. "Schweitzer's greatest contribution was that he psycho-analysed Bach," said a prominent scholar. "He revealed the inner motivation of much of what Bach has written, allowing students to appreciate his genius in a new and subtle way. It was an enormous gift to music."

Yet it was a gift that established its author more as a curio than as an eminence. Schweitzer was never a virtuoso on the organ. He held theories about phrasing which were, and are, considered extremely odd among his contemporaries. Certainly, he himself could make sense of them, and did so; but they rarely appeal to the present-day student or professor.

One of his pet theories was, so I am told, to insist that everything in music began, correctly, after the first note. He insisted that the second note was the fundamental starting point of any score. As in so many more of his radical views on other subjects, this seemed quaint and eccentric to the majority of musicians who heard him argue the case. "Sometimes," said a great admirer of his, "Dr. Schweitzer puts his finger right on the thing, but it has to be admitted that at other times he wanders off the track normal musicians and musicologists follow. When he railed against the use of women choristers for alto and soprano parts in the Bach Cantatas and Passions, for instance, he was far away from the view most people have today; even if Bach did always use boys himself in these parts."

But his appreciation of how the great *St. Matthew Passion* should be performed was significantly right. "Today," an expert declared, "we go on doing a perfectly hideous parody of this noble piece of music in Britain. In Germany, they are more alive to its beauty and have followed Schweitzer's advice. Here he has been largely ignored, and we are the worse for it."

It is curious that, in the realm of organ building and restoration, his authority has been of less practical value to present-day organ designers and makers. One of our leading designers admits that he not only has never read, but has never heard of, Schweitzer's essay, *The Art of Organ-Building and Organ-Playing in Germany and France*, first published in 1906. Since this was Schweitzer's only known publication on the organ-building industry, apart from his frequent criticisms, reported in the press, of any instrument which he felt was lacking in the harmony and beauty of the best eighteenth-century organs, there is little to judge him by. He is often described as the greatest of all experts on old organs (the seer who "cures old niggers in the jungle, and old organs in Europe" as he likes to joke about himself), but his knowledge is largely unavailable, except in his single essay referred to above and in his more general writings.

Like a boy born on a small island who finds the sea an immediate and instinctive ally, Albert Schweitzer had inherited and absorbed musical appreciation during his earliest years. His father's father was an organist. His mother's father had not only played, but had been fanatically interested in organs and organ-building. On his death, grandfather Schillinger had left the Schweitzer family his old square piano, and here Albert, aged five, was given his first lessons by his father. "He had," he wrote in his autobiography, "no great technical skill, but improvised charmingly."

Albert's improvisations were as ready, though perhaps less charming to his teachers. "I did not play much from notes," he wrote once, "my delight was to improvise, and to reproduce songs and hymn tunes with an accompaniment of my own invention. So now, when in the singing lesson the teacher continually played the hymn-tune with one finger and no accompaniment, I found it far from pleasing, and during the interval I asked her why she did not play it properly with the harmony. Then in my enthusiasm I sat down at the harmonium and played it straight away to her out of my head, but with harmony in several parts. Then she became very friendly with me, and used to look at me in a new and unusual way, but went on herself always picking out the tunes with one finger only. Then it occurred to me that I could do something which she could not, and I was ashamed of having made a show before her of my ability, which I had till then taken as something which I possessed as a matter of course."*

All through his impressionable youth, he was constantly being exposed to thrills and shocks as the result of his phenomenal musical appreciation. In his second year at school he reports that he had to "hold on to the wall to prevent myself from falling" when he overheard a vocal duet through the open door of a neighbouring classroom. He remembered the emotion of this experience clearly in

* *Memoirs of Childhood and Youth*

later life. It was the same when he first heard the brass chorus of a military band. The young Schweitzer almost fainted "from excess of pleasure". Only violin music at first failed to cast any spell over him, taking many years to attract him with its delicate, less militant beauty.

While living with his Aunt Sophie and Uncle Louis in Mülhausen during his schooling at the Gymnasium, young Schweitzer was strictly held down to his musical studies. After midday dinner he had to perch on the piano stool and work at scales and exercises until it was time to run off to school again. In the evenings, as soon as he had finished his homework, the piano was again invoked as a necessary piece of discipline. His aunt constantly reminded him of the value he would one day find in his music, though she can have had no idea of the truth of her prophesy. In fact, his organ recitals were to pay for much of his early work in Lambaréné, and to provide the fees for his examinations while studying as well as other necessities.

But at this stage in his development it was hard to recognize the ability which would one day appear in this phenomenal student. Schweitzer was a vague boy, given to day-dreaming. His music-master at Mülhausen, Eugen Münch, was irritated by his refusal to follow his teachings and accused him flatly of being "a boy with no feelings". It was this gibe that brought Albert to his senses, sending him home determined to study, if only to astonish the master. When he returned for the next lesson, he tells us that he played "just as my very soul bade me", and enjoyed the triumph of seeing surprise and delight creep over his teacher's face. Shortly afterwards, he was allowed to graduate to the playing of Bach.

The organ was Schweitzer's first and only real love in the performance of music. He had nursed an ambition since he could remember to play one of these mighty and soul-stirring instruments. At times he had been permitted, through the kindness of his father's organist, Daddy Iltis, to play as his substitute, and at the age of nine to take his place during an entire service. But the full realization of his dream came when he was fifteen; for at this time Eugen Münch, himself a great organist, invited him to take lessons on the great organ, complete with three keyboards and sixty-two stops, which adorned St. Stephen's Reformed Church, Mülhausen. As he sat at this magnificent instrument, entrusted by his teacher with the playing of Brahm's *Requiem*, Schweitzer felt a rare pleasure. "For the first time," he wrote in *Memoirs of Childhood and Youth*, "I knew the joy, which I have so often tasted since then, of letting the organ send the flood of its own special tones to mingle with the clanging music of choir and orchestra."

To Münch, Schweitzer admits a debt on two counts: the introduction his teacher gave him to Bach, and the inspiration brought by the organist's death to write and publish his first written work, a small appreciation of Münch which appeared in Mülhausen in 1898. This should not suggest to music scholars that the celebrated Berlin teacher had contributed to Schweitzer's radical assessments of Bach, which were peculiarly his own. It was not in Schweitzer's nature to conform in music any more than in other subjects.

It was on June 18 1893 that he scraped through his leaving examination with the single distinction of having obtained an "Excellent" in history. The same October an uncle in Paris managed to persuade the Parisian organist and composer Charles Marie Widor to consider Albert as a pupil. As has been said, Widor was fussy about his students, normally restricting them to members of the Organ Class at the Conservatoire. But when he had heard Schweitzer play, he agreed to take him. "The introduction was for me an event of decisive importance," Schweitzer wrote. "Widor led me on to a fundamental improvement of my technique, and made me strive to attain to perfect plasticity in playing."*

Nevertheless, the association began anything but auspiciously. Schweitzer was to attend Widor's studio in the morning of a particularly sunny day. The good weather had brought crowds on to the Paris streets and boulevards to watch a procession of Russian sailors. Jostled and obstructed, Schweitzer arrived late at the master's house. Doubtless the impatient, temperamental Widor found it hard to imagine that such a thankless pupil would ever turn out well. Yet only a few years later he was listening in amazed

* *My Life and Thought*

rapture as Schweitzer played Bach to him in a way he had never before heard attempted.

It was Widor, too, who persuaded him to write the book on Bach. At first, Schweitzer was wary of the suggestion, knowing that his studies at Strasbourg University would take up all his time. Widor listened, nodded sympathetically, then told him: "You are right. But what can one not do with order and the will?" So for six years, during which he often existed on only one meal a day so that he could pay his fares and expenses to hear the music of Wagner in Bayreuth, Albert Schweitzer worked on his manuscript. At times Widor actually feared that he was starving, and insisted on taking him off to his favourite restaurant for a meal. For the most part Albert struggled on alone, working incredibly long and exhausting hours at his various studies.

When the book appeared in 1905, it contained an introduction from Widor, who exclaimed: "As we read Monsieur Schweitzer's book, it seems to us that we are present at the inauguration of a monument . . ." This was high praise from the man who had taught him much of what he knew, but it was nothing to the ovation the book received in the world of music. It seemed that here was an interpretation that would transcend even the exhaustive biography of Friedrich Spitta, the celebrated German hymn-writer. Schweitzer had discovered the poet in the composer and exposed it. The result was held to be magnificent.

Today we are back to regarding Spitta's two volumes as the standard work on the subject, despite Schweitzer's uncanny analysis of Bach's promptings and psychiatry. If the book is tremendously worthy, it is little read. The impression I have gathered from British musical circles is that Schweitzer's study is incomplete; a limitation he admitted himself in its conclusion, saying: "The problem of interpretation is far from being solved . . ."

Having written such a triumphal book, one might have thought that its author would be able to take a breathing space and to give himself wholly to his other studies which now included medicine. But the first publication had been composed and written in French, at Widor's request. Now the Germans clamoured for a translation, which Schweitzer was flattered enough to agree to. The painful moment of realization came when he set about translating his own work, to find that it was impossible to use the same phrases and expressions in both languages. Only one alternative existed and he accepted it without complaint. He sat down and re-wrote the whole book. Schweitzer's musical biographer, Charles R. Joy, tells an illuminating story of the magnitude of this task. "Once in later years he picked up the German edition and turned the pages thoughtfully. 'Did I really write this?' he asked, with a look of bewilderment on his face."*

At the University, Schweitzer studied music under a Professor Jacobsthal, a reactionary for whom no composer since Beethoven existed. Such narrow-mindedness amused his pupil, who nevertheless admired his ability in pure counterpoint. Another influence on Schweitzer at that time was the brother of his old teacher at Mülhausen, Ernest Münch, who was both an organist and conductor of Bach concerts. With such a man he was able to share his enormous passion for Bach and Richard Wagner, whose *Tannhauser* had so thrilled him as a boy of sixteen.

Two years before the turn of the century he was again in Paris, spending the winter working at his music; preparing his dissertation for his Doctorate of Philosophy at the same time. The great Widor was now so excited by his pupil's progress that he accepted him without fee. He studied the organ and the piano, in which instrument his teacher was J. Philipp who later became a professor at the Conservatoire. Simultaneously, he was a pupil of Franz Liszt's pupil and friend, Marie Jaell-Trautmann, who had retired from her position as a star of the concert hall and was now studying Touch in piano playing. It was due to her that Schweitzer was able to change and improve his whole hand and fingering, but he had to avoid letting Philipp know that he was going to her. The two had poor opinions of each other. Thus, in the mornings he played with Marie, using her method. In the afternoons he adapted to Philipp's conventional fingering.

Returning to Berlin in 1899, Schweitzer was disappointed to

* *Music in the Life of Albert Schweitzer*

find the organists of that city lacking in true plasticity of style, Widor's most precious attainment. Also, the organs of Berlin had not the fineness of those at St. Sulpice and Notre-Dame. Still, there was work to be done, and Schweitzer obtained a post as deputy to Professor Heinrich Reimann, the organist of the Kaiser Wilhelm Memorial Church, on the strength of a letter of introduction from Widor. Association with this learned man led to a meeting with the art and intellectual world of Berlin; painters, sculptors and writers as well as musicians. At this time the great university of the city had attracted a dazzling corps of intellects and talents which delighted Schweitzer. It was, so he says, the finest period of the city's existence. It was still a smaller, more provincial city than Paris but, for this reason, was intellectually more closely-knit. He found that it required no great effort to be accepted in its society.

At the end of the year he had to return to Strasbourg to take his degree in philosophy. And there he remained, a paying guest in the College of St. Thomas which he so loved. The work now occupying him, beside his music, was for his Licentiate in Theology. Having obtained it, he was granted the post of preacher at the Church of St. Nicholas as Curate which brought five pounds a month and freedom to work at both science and music. It even provided him with the unaccustomed luxury of holidays. In the summer he returned to Paris to continue his studies under Widor. There, in 1905 when his book on Bach came out, he met Romain Rolland the musician who later became his staunch friend.

In Strasbourg, Schweitzer had already made the acquaintance of Frau Cosima Wagner, the second wife of the composer. Through her he became a close associate of the Wagner family. During his visits or, as he calls them, "pilgrimages" to Bayreuth for the music festivals, he spent a great amount of time with them, discussing the work which Frau Wagner was then doing in preserving the traditions of Bayreuth. These contacts added to his store of musical knowledge, but they also sharpened an intellect that was already acute. Yet they did nothing to change the pattern of his prejudices.

Schweitzer was essentially a traditionalist, both in his adherence to the rules of interpretation expressed by the composers, and out of a professional prejudice in favour of the past. He became attracted to the round bow for the violin, used in Bach's time. He resented modern orchestrations of Bach's works where they differed from the composer's original instructions. In his attitude to organs and organ-building he expressed a reactionary fondness for eighteenth-century instruments, believing that nothing as good had been constructed since that period; a critical view that led him to write the essay which is today so little known on the art of organ-building. It also sent him off in search of old organs which might be restored, so that he could thwart the progress of the factory builders at least as far as his knowledge and strength would allow.

Whether these activities were wholly successful is questioned by at least one English expert. Some recordings were issued of music played on organs that Schweitzer had brought back to life in Strasbourg, and they have been heard in this country. They have not always been favourably commented on. "To me, they sounded very, very peculiar," said an English organ designer recently.

Schweitzer admits his abstraction for this work of recovery. "I was curiously affected by the organs which were built towards the end of the nineteenth century," he writes. "Although they were lauded as miracles of advanced technical skill, I could find no pleasure in them."* It bothered him not at all that he seldom expressed his views about the new organs without receiving "laughter and jeers" from other organists and builders.

By 1927 he was able to announce in an article: "Today the fight is won. Scientific experts in organ-building and old organs, like Ernst Schiess of Solothurn and Hans Henny Jahnn of Hamburg, are actively rebuilding old organs. In the Institute of Musical Knowledge at the University of Freiburg in Baden, Professor Willibald Gurlitt and his pupils are engaged in research into old music and old organs. Societies have arisen for the preservation of old organs. We had not dared to hope that a young generation would carry on so soon and so strongly what we had undertaken

* *Music in the Life of Albert Schweitzer* edited by C. R. Joy

in Vienna against the spirit of the time. With deep emotion I think of those who shared with us the work of those wonderful days but were not permitted to see the triumph of the idea."*

Also, his great debt to music for the pleasure it had given him since early youth was fully paid with his book on the distinguished composer, Johann Sebastian Bach, who had been rewarded so little in his own lifetime. The Schweitzer biography may be ignored by students in England and elsewhere, but it is a musical achievement of the first rank. It is, curiously, his single uncontested triumph which legend has failed to distort.

* *Music in the Life af Albert Schweitzer* edited by C. R. Joy.

EIGHTEEN

HOW GOOD A DOCTOR?

SO WE come to medicine, and the bloom on Schweitzer's multi-floral stalk that is as much a paradox as the man. For Schweitzer is known for his medical healing. He is respected as a jungle surgeon. The dignity of "Doctor" when used before his name by millions of people refers only to this profession. Yet it is the field in which he has shown the least talent and will leave the slightest mark. So far as he has allowed anyone outside Lambaréné to know, he has contributed little to the study and control of tropical diseases. His "forest hospital" as he likes to term it, stands for practically nothing in the eyes of Science. The whole period of fifty and more years of unique practice among African primitives, is likely to leave little of value to medicine.

To the legend, however, it serves as a handy hook on which to suspend tales of the Doctor's great skill with knife and pill; a natural exaggeration, since photographs have been shown in their scores presenting the Doctor, gowned and masked, his face as sympathetic as a Rembrandt mourner, apparently at work in his operating theatre at Lambaréné. Reports of the long hours of medical and surgical work in the hospital have become newspaper and magazine clichés. His own memoirs and autobiographical books give an impression of unceasing vigilance in ward and consulting-room, of delicate and intricate work with the knife, and of absorption in the study and control over the pests and germs of the tropics.

The effect of all this has been a distortion of the truth. For although Dr. Schweitzer has done good medical work at his hospital, he has done it rarely and with less and less regularity over the years. Indeed, the total of his medical participation in the record of Lambaréné is astonishingly slight; though, perhaps unintentionally, he has done nothing to correct the imprint made on men's minds outside the hospital of a hard-working doctor and surgeon. Thus he is partly responsible for the creation of this false part of the legend of Lambaréné.

What do we know of his medical experience? Such flashes as appear in his books are deliberately understated; yet they offer interesting details of the picture. We learn that in 1905 Albert Schweitzer, the dazzling scholar of theology, philosophy and music (already a doctor twice over) went to the Dean of the Medical Faculty at the University of Strasbourg, where he was himself a member of the teaching staff, asking to be enrolled as a medical student. No wonder Professor Fehling would have preferred, as Schweitzer says, to hand him over to his colleague in the Psychiatric Department to see if his mind was in order. The request, coming from a man of thirty with the world already made to his design, must have sounded bizarre to the point of lunacy.

Having studied for five years under a team of distinguished professors (then among the best in the world) Schweitzer sat his examinations. Scientific lessons, he says, had been a spiritual experience in the use of hard fact which he accepted eagerly, and not for themselves alone. "I felt them to be needed for my own intellectual development," he wrote later. Thus the scholar had learned from the precise thinking of the laboratory something which was to be useful far outside the practice of medicine.

Meanwhile, as he studied, he fought fatigue brought on by the numerous roles he continued to play. He was writing his books, preaching and teaching. He could no more bring himself to give up these interests than he could wait to qualify before impatiently commencing preparations for his journey to Africa. Holidays, which other students enjoyed at leisure, were to Schweitzer times of toil. He went to Paris to study music. But during term-time there was only the narrow world of vivisection, of sinks and stinks, and the long nights of incessant cramming. By 1908 he was "going through the worst crisis of fatigue that I can recall during the whole of my life". It was hardly surprising, though he had by then been persuaded to abandon most of his outside work, that he found the struggle murderous. Somehow, he got through the end-of-year examinations, and passed on to the less exhausting clinical study which followed. Here his main teachers were replaced by others, and a number of new interests attracted him. During lessons on drugs and their uses, he felt a special fascination, recognizing that here was a new and potent ally to take with him into the African jungle. What would he not need to treat the frightening conditions he would encounter there?

In October 1911 Schweitzer sat his State Medical Examination, having earned the fee by performing an organ recital. It was afterwards, on that cold evening when the last scratch of his pen, the last puff of the Bunsen, had ended the ordeal, that he was paid that lasting compliment to his endurance by Madelung: "It is only because you have such excellent health that you have got through a job like that." A year of practical work was ahead, during which he was to write his thesis for a Doctorate; but the worst was over. He had passed. And by a happy chance he was able to isolate a medical aspect of his theological studies for the thesis: an analysis of all that had been published about the medical side of the mental derangement of Jesus, believed in by the previous writers. As might be expected of the author of one of theology's most distinguished contemporary works, his paper was well-received.

Thus, as a qualified medical man, Schweitzer was able to begin his curious mission. In Lambaréné, there were black-skinned men who died in pain for want of a doctor. He was to feel enormous gratification at being able to spare them, at least, the long and terrible suffering. While Mme. Schweitzer gave anaesthetics, and a trusty African, Joseph, assisted at the more gruesome tasks wearing long rubber gloves, the fledgeling surgeon made his first lonely slices at the rot and poison of life. Within a short time he was able to report that he had performed several operations, and that in every case the patient had lived.

Working alone, without medical colleagues, soon tested the many weaknesses which every doctor has when only recently qualified.

In 1923 he was in Europe, taking a course in obstetrics and dentistry. His wife, his one loyal woman nurse, had collapsed and he was pleading with a friend, the American-born Mme. André Rieder, to let him take her medical student son, Noel Gillespie, back to Africa with him as an assistant. Since Mme. Rieder had devoted herself to his cause in England following her husband's death, there was little danger that he would be refused.

Together, the two white men—one forty-nine, one less than twenty—returned to Lambaréné to begin the worst of Schweitzer's many struggles with the jungle, the huge rebuilding of the hospital already described. Imagination sees them at this time with a saw in one hand, a hypodermic in the other. Indeed, this may have been no exaggeration. Schweitzer was ready to excuse himself more and more from the medical side of things during this period, and the habit was never broken. Ever since, he has been a rare member of the actual medical team.

It seems that, for all his many talents, he showed little brilliance either as a surgeon or doctor. He has never claimed any such distinction, but his writings give an oddly heroic elevation to everything he has done, even the treating of slight wounds. Schweitzer's skill and technique is today rated, by medical men, as "no more than that of a middling G.P.". It is a proficiency which he conceals by showing it in use as seldom as possible.

"During the last twenty years the Doctor has practised very little medicine or surgery himself," wrote his American helper, Fergus Pope, in a British medical journal. "He wants always to know about anything going on which is out of the ordinary but otherwise medical and surgical matters are left to the staff. His time has gone towards enlarging, improving and running the hospital community." A doctor who worked at the hospital quite recently confirmed this. "Those who have actually seen Schweitzer in the performance of his medical duties are rare birds indeed," he has written. "The simple fact is that Schweitzer's medical work has always been at an unbelievable minimum." Both these views tally, with the result that a myth held by half the world is blown away. But this is not the whole story.

A close perusal of the medical records at Lambaréné, started in 1924, reveals that Schweitzer actually performed only a few operations during four brief periods at the hospital. Yet continual references in his autobiography *My Life and Thought* suggest that he was attending a large number of surgical patients. Those who know the history of the hospital say that it has been the same in pure medicine as in surgery; the Doctor has done very little of either.

While it has always been entirely up to Schweitzer to decide how much doctoring he does, it is strange that a totally false impression should have grown up in the world that he is a toiling, humble, negro doctor. It seems that his real use of Lambaréné has been much the same as an actor's use of a set, a backdrop with living "props" against which he could conduct his experiment in ethical living. The actual healing, he has been content to leave to others. "I saw him touch one patient during nearly two years there," a Lambaréné doctor told me, "and that was coincidental with the sudden arrival of a guest, and possibly related to this. Otherwise he never touched nor took a visible interest in any of the patients. Absolutely no surgery, at present, is done by him. One might as well add that he practises absolutely no medicine now, also. I once showed him a sick patient for his suggestions (when I first arrived). He looked at him, grumbled something under his breath, and turned and walked out, saying he would talk with me tomorrow. I thought the patient would live only for a matter of hours!"

The role of administrator-in-chief to a community as large as Lambaréné is not to be shrugged off, however. That a man in his late eighties is capable, under the equatorial sun, of running such a concern is barely credible.

We must accept the fact that Schweitzer did not have any great stomach for healing men's bodies, while his time could better be used in trying to patch up their doomed souls. Also, one cannot run a community as large and sprawling as Lambaréné without discipline. Schweitzer likes to keep all power in his own hands, rarely if ever passing it to any other person. He has therefore been more than amply occupied with the work of administering his village-size colony. When not concerned with the purchase and storage of manioc, rice, bananas and other staples of the hospital diet, the provision of drugs, dressings and similar medicaments for the patients, the continual supervision of buildings, their decoration and maintenance, as well as the fresh construction of new premises and even roads, he has had plenty to do at his lonely desk. Letters lie in small mountains, waiting to be answered. There was an amusing story put around not so long ago that Schweitzer was then only two years behind in his correspondence, and that recently he had been astonished to read in a previously unopened cable that the first man had been launched into space. In truth, it is known to be virtually impossible to reach him through normal communications unless one has "a spy in the camp", so to speak. The favourite approach, used by most of the Lambaréné veterans, is to address letters to one of the senior nurses, then to ask her to pass messages on to the Doctor. In this way it is possible to by-pass the queue of letters, papers and even telegrams said to be stacked in date order at the hospital, and answered mainly by members of the staff, who pretend that the Doctor has seen and commented on the letter.

No doctor with knowledge of the administration of a large hospital would expect Schweitzer to have time to practise as well as supervise medicine at Lambaréné. The question that has disturbed medical circles for some time is whether the old Doctor, who qualified well over half a century ago when Joseph Lister was still alive, is capable of managing each department of his crowded life with the same care and knowledge. Surgeons know that Lambaréné is a place where it is possible, once the Doctor has agreed to let them visit him, to try experiments that might be frowned on under stricter management. They can be sure that cases will be forthcoming, and that any unfortunate failure will be overlooked by the public gaze. And the nub of the reason is that Schweitzer will not always know whether they are doing what is orthodox or not.

If this widely-held view is justified, perhaps the most upsetting of all criticisms of Schweitzer's own experiment is that it can inadvertently attract other experimenters. While his designs are on the minds and spirits of man, the doctors and surgeons he entertains and permits the facilities of his hospital are concerned with the flesh. It may be argued that in this way Lambaréné is further contributing to the improvement of the human condition; for will not the surgical and medical experiments conducted there result in useful new techniques of healing? This is not to be denied. Beside its truth, however, must be placed the distress felt by at least one conscientious nurse who has worried over a patient unfortunately fated to become an "experimental failure", and now unable to walk.

Professional justification for this is not in question. It is not to be said that anything in the least unethical takes place behind the mesh-screened walls of the operating theatre, or among the straw-covered bunks of the wards. Nor would Dr. Schweitzer's high moral principles allow themselves to be smothered where he knew of risks being taken for the purpose solely of experimentation. The germ of anxiety here is due to his possible weakness when it comes to knowing what is proper to try and what is not. When a man has practised no medicine or surgery in the modern fields from which some of his distinguished colleagues and visitors come, he is unlikely to rank with them in knowledge of the latest techniques. Should they tell him that such-and-such a method is now considered well worth trying in this case, or that so-and-so path of diagnosis and treatment is the most up-to-the-minute thing, how can Schweitzer be in the position which, as Chief Administrator of Lambaréné, he should be in, to argue and if necessary disagree with them?

"At Lambaréné," states an official Gabonese brochure, listing the country's achievements, "the celebrated Dr. Schweitzer welcomes and cares for the many sick people attracted by the fame of his hospital." It is perfectly true that he welcomes them. That he cares for them himself is more in doubt. Whereas years ago the Doctor knew most of his patients by name, and took a delighted interest in their peculiarities, today he sees them only as a black tide of humanity running at his feet. As old age and fresh concerns have possessed him, he has slowly but increasingly given up the time he used once to give to patients. When I saw and talked to him in his pharmacy, in the heart of the building where healing and treatment were going on on all sides, his first injunction to me was "not to talk about the hospital, only the world outside".

It is fair to add a note about the hospital; for this appears to run itself about as harmoniously as a transit camp for primitive displaced persons. The rhythms of the wards are self-generating, under the strict gaze of Nurse Ali and Nurse Mathilde. And, while it is impossible to delineate exactly between these and the domestic side, where families and attendants of the sick live in a typical, backward-village community, the impression is that African natives who have survived the jungle can adjust to anything. As to the medical nature of the hospital, there have been many interesting comments by expert witnesses. After his visit, during which he had performed a number of intricate plastic surgery operations on victims of leprosy and elephantiasis, Mr. Jack Penn, F.R.C.S. of Johannesburg, South Africa, wrote an article, published on September 3 1956 in Vol. 18 of *Plastic and Reconstructive Surgery* and printed in the U.S.A., in which he described some of the medical and surgical conditions as he found them. It is particularly worth noting, because Mr. Penn had recently returned from Hiroshima, Japan, where he had operated on burns inflicted by the world's first wartime atom bomb. He was not blind to the suffering of poverty-stricken Africans, having seen much of it in his own country and elsewhere. He knew his profession and its techniques as few other surgeons can claim to do.

Penn wrote: "Although Dr. Schweitzer provides the impetus which keeps this unit moving he is, nevertheless, greatly beholden to his staff who have helped him through all his vicissitudes." He made no reference to the Doctor's work as doctor or surgeon. His sole tribute was to his achievement in having erected the hospital and leper village: "Dr. Schweitzer is undoubtedly an excellent carpenter," said Mr. Penn, in strange praise of his older colleague. Privately, when talking to friends in Johannesburg later, Mr. Penn gave a personal opinion that hundreds of hospitals and mission stations provide a better service for the underprivileged; that Schweitzer's hospital is of no importance *as* a hospital.

Penn further hinted that Schweitzer's great failing was his "refusal to delegate authority". As the old Doctor does little or none of the medical and surgical work himself, that suggests a frustrating situation for those doctors who serve him. Mr. Penn was not unaware of this, and it was one reason why he expressed the view to a friend that "the whole place will collapse on Schweitzer's death".

But Penn was struck, as others have been, by the paradox of Lambaréné's modern Gabonese state hospital which has recently been expanded—in staff and equipment—to meet the growth of its patients. While Schweitzer plainly lacked the most advanced medical facilities (and talents for using them), he was greatly respected in jungle villages hundreds of miles away. Men and women reached him during Penn's visit who had come from places never visited by a white man. The Doctor's fame as a healer had reached them via drum-beat messages and word-of-mouth. It was also possible, of course, that they had heard of the hand-outs provided by Marion and other philanthropists. But the fact was that they came, queued for treatment, and took their medicine from a white doctor in defiance, often, of their local "medicine man" or witch doctor. It was a fact that could not be disputed.

In England, we are just becoming aware of Africa's giant stride into the twentieth century. The growing insistence among the emergent nations on proper hygiene and medical operations is already demanding something far more civilized than Lambaréné. But until the stream of patients from the interior begins to dry up Schweitzer and his followers are justified in claiming that Lambaréné is far from redundant.

Yet the anomalies, and the curious way in which Schweitzer does nothing about altering them, persist. As Penn noted, and wrote: "All the patients at Lambaréné have chronic ulcers of the feet. The jungle paths never get the direct sun, moisture is everywhere and they are probably teeming with organisms. In my view, the problem will not be solved until every native here is provided with sandals. A gift to Dr. Schweitzer's hospital of a thousand pairs of leather sandals may do more good than all the antibiotics now so freely given."

This is the crux of the criticism levelled at Dr. Schweitzer, M.D.—that he is much less concerned with preventing the tribulations which ignorance and custom have stamped on backward Africans, than in healing them. He is believed by everyone who knows him well to possess enormous funds of donated money which could be turned to this work. If he wanted sandals, and was prepared to ask for them, they would pour into his hospital by the boat and plane load. The days when he had to struggle to raise funds for his early work by performances and pleas are no more. Today his is said to be among the richest hospitals in the world, and its potential for adding to its wealth is unlimited. Schweitzer has only to raise a finger in America alone.

There are those who suspect that his well-established American Fellowships, now spreading over the civilized globe, control the funds subscribed to them, and that therefore the Doctor is little more than a paid servant of these wealthy charitable combines. But this is not so. I am assured by a doctor who worked at Lambaréné that Schweitzer has only to ask for any sum of money and it is put into his hand without question. I am told that he holds controlling power over all funds and donations subscribed. When a nurse or doctor, after loyal service, is provided with costly air tickets and a sum of money to cover a long holiday and further training period, presumably these sums are drawn from one of these accounts. When the Doctor's daughter, Rhena Eckert, asks her father for cash to continue the good work she does for him in Europe, that must also be listed among the outgoings. Where Schweitzer's personal exchequer ends and his public one begins must be a puzzle. But I am not alone in thinking that the Doctor, for all his protestations about being unsuited to add two and two in matters of business, is shrewdly aware of every last penny in the financial score.

The world may ask, with respect, why he sits on so much of his capital when it could be turned to medical account? Why there is no blood transfusion service; no doubt costly, imported and needing the facilities of up-to-date refrigeration and electrification, but none the less possible? And why does use of slow methods of the past persist, when a modern world is asking to share its riches with the poor whom Albert Schweitzer has so nobly brought to its notice? Only one person could answer, but he chooses to ignore such questions, or treats them with contempt.

NINETEEN

THE SUCCESSOR

AN OFFICER of the United States embassy, waiting for the ferry boat to Lambaréné town, had stopped to pass the time of day under the hot sun. Within a few minutes he and his companion were talking about the Doctor and his hospital, which they knew and had visited from time to time on their rounds. They agreed that its life was limited. Scratching his arm where a mosquito had bitten it, the officer said: "When the old man dies, it'll just wash down into the river. It's the only shrine there is to a god that ain't immortal. When he dies, *it* dies for sure."

All over Africa it is possible to hear the same blunt prophesy about the future of Lambaréné. It cannot outlast Schweitzer, say the realists. He is the mainspring and when he goes, it goes. For many of those who make these forecasts, the spoken thoughts are reflections of their own subconscious hope to see the jungle finally triumph over the man who has held it back for more than half a century. For others, it is a logical outcome of something they understand to be a simple, natural rule. When a great man comes along, a tremendous leader, then the strength of his empire is the strength of his own power to reign. In Schweitzer's case, there are surprisingly few outside his own camp followers who would bet on the hospital surviving his death.

But in a poor district of London last year was a young man, an American, who may prove them all wrong. His name is Fergus Pope. He is dark, lean, wiry and with the face of a longer-suffering film actor. In what he once said there may be a key to a possible future for Lambaréné. "Before any jungle starts rolling over the hospital," he said, "it'll have to roll over me."

The question of a successor intrigues many of those who have inquired into the secrets of Schweitzer's life and work, but not one of them has yet found an answer to it. The Doctor is gruffly diffident about discussing the matter. His staff know nothing of any wish he may have. It would be naïve to imagine that they do not think of the day when *le grand docteur* will be no more; perhaps with personal anxiety. But there was a time, quite recently, when it was generally thought that Dr. Percy, Schweitzer's once-trusted assistant, would be ready to take over. That passed with his departure. Today there are no doctors on the staff who could command the kind of loyalty and service needed to keep the "shrine" alive, save perhaps this one, lone American.

By the time this book comes out Pope will be adding experience, doing a year's surgical work in tropical hospitals elsewhere. But his one wish, his sole reason for having studied medicine, has always been to obtain a post at the hospital and there to walk in the steps of the man he acknowledges as a master, Albert Schweitzer.

This American is a fanatical individualist, whose lean jaw-line, brooding eyes and hollowed, blueish cheeks bear witness to the struggle that has gone on inside him. In 1951, aged twenty-one, he devoured books by Gandhi and Schweitzer, reaching a decision that his own soul was hungering for a similar purpose. He chose Schweitzer because he was alive, and because: "Gandhi was probably more saintly, but the Doctor is both a practical man and an idealist. His vision is something a practical man can attain with his own hands, something of practical value. He has shown me how much *I* can do."

Between Pope's theorizing and his actually taking part in the saintly life of Lambaréné there was a gap of several years; an interesting period, when the forces which now possess him were brought to maturity. At the time when he was reading Schweitzer, he was on the point of leaving a small American university to join the United States Air Force, which he did voluntarily, anticipating the Korean war draft. He was fit enough, and appeared warlike enough, to be trained as a pilot. For a while he behaved exactly like any other good-looking young American going into battle. He was not particularly religious or ascetic in his habits. A colleague says that he was inclined to favour the lighter side of life, and was "a normally quiet guy, maybe a little reserved, who would wake up whenever a party got going". He was popular with his comrades and attractive to a number of unmarried girls on the base. Not one of them would have believed, had they been told, that twelve years hence Fergus Pope would be setting off into the jungle to work at the side of the world's most illustrious negro doctor.

The war was dragging on, with casualties on both sides inevitably rising. Where at first it had seemed merely a skirmish with a few ill-equipped Asiatics, now the Americans were aware of the enemy they were up against, the toll of war. At such a time, a man may think more deeply than ever before about his role in life and his responsibilities for it. Pope was fully trained. He had been assigned combat duty as co-pilot of a Super-Fortress bombing aircraft. He was waiting for an order to move with his squadron to Japan when the impact of Albert Schweitzer's Reverence for Life creed got through to him in the most urgent way. He all at once realized that he could not, would not, drop bombs on living, civilian beings for no other reason than the merciless need of war.

Having made up his mind to fix a limitation on the violence he would inflict on the living in the name of battle, Pope saw his Commanding Officer and explained his feelings. He was particularly fortunate in having an officer to deal with who showed a humane understanding of his situation. Instead of recommending that the pilot be court-martialled for refusing to do his duty in the face of the enemy, he released Pope to await medical, psychiatric and other investigations. These were as thorough as America's tough military and medical experts could make them, but they failed to find any chink of cowardice or weakness of spirit in Pope's character. He was strongly, indeed courageously, determined not to drop bombs on others; that was all. Finally, when it had been agreed that he was no shirker, but a man possessed of unusually idealistic notions about the sanctity of human life, his interrogators withdrew. Pope was posted to non-combat duty in Cheshire, England in 1954, when he was twenty-four years old. His job was to include giving talks and holding discussions on current affairs, which naturally involved attitudes to war and peace; an almost laughable solution to the militarists' dilemma, were it not so habitual.

His flying duties were to glide out over the North Sea on weather survey flights and patrols; long, undisturbed periods of flying during which he had plenty of time to think. When not at the controls, he could read. In the evenings, as he took his class in Current Affairs, his liberal views first shocked, then outraged his fellow officers. Ultimately, he came near to being ostracized by many of them for what they felt to be his un-belligerent attitude during wartime. Perhaps that was the moment when Pope first deliberately set himself on the hard road to Lambaréné. He resigned from the Air Force and settled for a while in England.

He had made English friends, among them a witty playboy barrister whose brother, Baron, had become a famed social photographer and friend of Prince Philip and other members of the British royal family. With Baron's brother, the late Jack Nahum, he enjoyed a high-life which was both intellectual and gay. For a while Pope found nothing incongruous in spending some of his evenings playing, dancing and talking with pretty young English girls while at other times he buried himself in his rooms and read weighty books on philosophy and religion late into the night. Friends bear witness to the fact that the two bachelors enjoyed many high-spirited evenings in the north country town where barrister Nahum had a flourishing practice. But the social side of his life was superficial to the purpose forming inside Pope's heart; the urge to see Dr. Schweitzer at work, as well as to read what he had written about himself and what others had written about him. How was he to realize such a wild dream?

There was only one way that offered a practical solution, if he was prepared to do it, and he was. He must make the journey across land, learning the ways and customs of Africa as he went so that he would not arrive a total "greenhorn" at the hospital. As an ex-bomber pilot, even with the right ideas, he realized that he was far from being the sort of person they would welcome.

So the journey, he thought, would give him experience and, at the same time, save the high cost of any form of paid travel. Having decided this, he bought a jeep with money saved from his Air Force pay and stocked it with 700 lb. of equipment, mainly books.

On an icy February 1 1956 he drove away from a farewell party in Chelsea, London, to begin his mission into the heart of Africa; and an accident halted him in the first few miles. The jeep was too loaded to handle easily on the frozen Dover Road, and Pope was inexperienced in driving it in its laden condition. He overturned the vehicle and had to leave it, fortunately unhurt himself, to be repaired before he could set off again.

This time he succeeded, landing in France intact and in good spirits to begin a journey that is both severely testing and highly dangerous. From Spain, via the Straits of Gibraltar, Fergus Pope crossed into Africa. He was soon leaving his tyre-tracks on the drifting sand of the Sahara Desert. Within a couple of days he was lost in blinding sand-storms, the prey of marauding Touaregs whose camel tracks he crossed. More than once, so he later told a friend in Lambaréné, he barely escaped without a fight. To anyone who knows the Sahara, the wonder is that he survived. It took him three months to cross the forest and jungle and desert lands to reach the border of Ghana and the final stretch of his journey.

In fact, arrival at Lambaréné was far from the end of Pope's travels. Dr. Schweitzer's greeting was brusque: "I don't like surprises. Why didn't you let me know you were coming?" As he could speak no German or French, the young American was at an impossible disadvantage. But what was so bitterly obvious was that he was also no use. He could not claim to be builder, architect, locksmith, nurse, doctor, or surgeon. He knew nothing of the ways of hospitals, or of the behaviour of primitive people. After a few days rest, he went on his way.

Such a rebuke would have turned away less stubborn men for good; but Fergus Pope is a Pennsylvanian whose upbringing had conditioned him to face obstacles with determination. His mother, a Christian Scientist, had been separated from his father by divorce when he was two years old, since when Fergus had not set eyes on him. His mother taught the boy, his elder brother and two sisters, that self-reliance and stubbornness in the face of difficulty are essential qualities. As he retreated from his first encounter with the Doctor, Pope saw that the failing had been all on his side. He had come intent on helping, but without the languages or skills needed. Having appreciated his mistake, he set about remedying it.

In southern Africa, he sold the jeep and spent the money on keeping himself and buying a course in French lessons. When he was accomplished enough in the tongue to do so, he wrote the Doctor a long and apologetic letter, asking finally: "May I come back and serve you? In any capacity, however humble . . ." Schweitzer might have imagined he had seen the last of the lean, young American whose jeep had been the first motorized vehicle to enter Lambaréné in the lifetime of the hospital. When Pope's letter arrived, he was obviously touched, perhaps a little amazed, at his perseverance. He wrote agreeing to provide the wished-for post.

This time the American spent two months working alongside Schweitzer, discovering something of the meaning of Lambaréné and the Doctor's experiment. But his contact with the Doctor was frustratingly slight. There were weeks when he rarely spoke to him, and days when he only saw him at meals, the enshrined father-figure of his well-disciplined and ordered table. Pope, who had been given ample handiwork tasks to do, such as mending broken locks and helping with carpentry and building construction and decoration, began to understand that such service was not enough for his desire. It was not that he believed, he says, that he merited a more important place in the hospital's affairs. But he wanted to be of more service. "I never hope to obtain salvation," he has said, "only to burn my hands stretching towards it."

In other ways, the experience was satisfying and refreshing because it showed that his earlier, distant appreciation of what the hospital was trying to do, "what it all means" as he put it, had not exaggerated. The *raison d'être* of Lambaréné seemed to Pope to be ideally against the spirit of the times with which he, like Schweitzer, was in disagreement. So here was a strong link. And were there not perhaps other ways in which he resembled the great man who had drawn him to the jungle? Certainly, Pope was only in his late twenties, while the Doctor was over eighty; but Schweitzer, too, had turned from the main stream of life at almost exactly the same age as Pope was now turning from his. Also, it was a parallel to his own spiritual dilemma that Schweitzer had experienced in renouncing the world of rampant materialism. As Albert Schweitzer had astonished his contemporaries by taking up the study of medicine at the age of thirty when he was already established in other fields, could not Fergus Pope, with less qualifications it was true but with an equally strong ambition, and at the same age, do the same? The answer brought him away from Lambaréné ready in his will to attempt the biggest assault course of his life.

First, he needed the academic status of a Master's degree in his own country, and for this he returned to his interrupted university studies in the States, qualifying without difficulty. Then he came again to England where he enrolled at St. Bartholomew's teaching hospital in London as a medical student. The six-year course was to test his powers of endurance even more than the sacrifices and travels he had already made. Fergus Pope kept the memory of the Doctor of Lambaréné clearly etched in his mind, and allowed nothing to deject him. Slowly, with the difficulty an older man always finds in studying a new subject, he absorbed the necessary knowledge and ability. At Bart's, where he finally qualified in the autumn of 1963, he gained a reputation as a quiet, saintly man. "Nobody knew him well," a contemporary has said, "though some worshipped him." And, if this seems surprising in the unsentimental society of medical students, it must be added that Pope had already mastered one of Dr. Schweitzer's arts: the ability to charm people without giving himself to them.

He married while he was a student, and the girl he chose was as suitable to his dedicated life as Schweitzer's uncomplaining wife had been. So here again was a similarity, or a deliberate emulation. Ruth Pope was an Austrian girl who had suffered in a Nazi concentration camp. Like Mme. Schweitzer, she was Jewish. She adored her husband as Hélène Schweitzer must have adored her Albert. The knowledge that his life—and hers—was pledged to service in the heat and squalor of the jungle did not depress her. Only when one of their two small children sickened during a visit to Lambaréné did Ruth Pope's determination to stay at her husband's side falter. She has said that she disagrees with Fergus here, believing that the youngsters would do far better at a European school. But for her husband, the best school is the school of life and nowhere, he believes, is it more comprehensive than in Lambaréné.

And Pope's dedication leads along rough paths in other directions, paths few women would accept for their small European children. It is not surprising that Ruth Pope has misgivings. Her husband supports the view that in marriage man is the horse, his wife and family the cart. Thus where he goes, they must follow. He would be happy to see his children grow up in Lambaréné, learning their lessons from his wife and himself, picking up the languages of the Africans of the area. Ruth would prefer either an Austrian or an English school, but she may change her mind when her family is complete. Saying that they are unlikely to have any more children themselves, they plan to adopt several children of different nationalities, an Indian and a Chinese among them.

In everything they did while in London, the Popes were rehearsing themselves for their future roles in the jungle. They lived in a slum house in London which they bought jointly with Ruth's concert-pianist mother and in which they rented out rooms to pay for their own frugal upkeep. They cooked and ate simply, in one room, had no car, inadequate heating and few possessions. "Money means absolutely nothing to me," Fergus Pope has said. But, like Schweitzer, he is already supported by outside contributions and sees these as perfectly justified. His brother, a chemist turned business man, puts aside a small sum each month to help Fergus.

Thus far, the picture is of a man who has determinedly modelled himself on Schweitzer, adapting his own style to the Doctor's. But if the question is to be asked, will Fergus Pope succeed Schweitzer as the chief administrator and guiding light of Lambaréné? there are other factors to be taken into consideration. Most important is whether Pope sees himself as the Doctor's successor, to which the answer is a qualified "maybe". Asked if he wishes to assume the leadership one day, Pope has said: "If one has the qualities, then one can lead. I certainly see the possibility of something greater developing out of my work at Lambaréné." But he told a man who had been in Lambaréné that he would willingly work *with* another doctor, though not *under* one, if Schweitzer were to die.

Pope is equally guarded about any discussion he may have had with Schweitzer about his future role. This could be because, at least until recently, he had not reached such a position of intimacy with *le grand docteur* as his story suggests. Conflicting views are held in the hospital about his ultimate role in the hierarchy, but few of the experienced staff will admit the possibility of his becoming "Number One" in the same sense as Dr. Schweitzer. "The Doctor doesn't regard him as a true 'insider'," one veteran said, "because he doesn't speak enough French to allow the subtleties of intelligent conversation, and he does not seem to have the same sense of humour as the Doctor, if he has one at all." It is an interesting corollary of this that Schweitzer continues to give a Dutch-avuncular lecture to those doctors who leave his service, and whom he does regard as "insiders", advising them to return so that they will be eligible to carry on in his place one day. "I am an old man," he will tell them with his usual winning charm, "I cannot go on for ever . . ." This is undoubtedly, if unfortunately, true. The future of the hospital will have to be decided in one way or another without too much delay.

The most probable action to be taken on Dr. Schweitzer's retirement would be an appointment by the President of the Albert Schweitzer Fellowship in New York, Dr. Emery Ross. It is unlikely at present that he would appoint fellow American Fergus Pope because he has not yet made much of a contribution to Lambaréné, nor gained the Doctor's full confidence. But, if Pope's plans materialize, he is certain to gain increasingly in stature. Nobody else has, or is likely to have, his single-minded dedication and love of Schweitzer and his ideals.

What Pope planned to do, once he qualified as a Doctor of Medicine, was to spend one year practising surgery in the centre of Equatorial Africa, but outside Lambaréné. With this experience and the knowledge of ways in which similar tropical diseases and ailments are handled elsewhere, he could return to Schweitzer to serve him; this time, as a fully-fledged surgeon and doctor. From there, the path seemed to lead upwards towards the throne, though the young American, now thirty-three years old, will not admit it.

Asked whether Dr. Schweitzer had, in his knowledge, made any provision for the future of Lambaréné after his death, Fergus Pope said not so long ago: "Oh yes, he has made provisions. But as to appointing a successor he would not do that. And as for all this talk of the jungles rolling over the hospital after he has gone, that will be left to those who are still alive, won't it?"

Twice already Pope has taken his wife and children, the elder now five, to Lambaréné with him. He has gone during vacations from the medical course at Bart's; purely to keep in touch with the hospital and its progress. Slight pock-marking of one side of his face suggests that he may have contracted a tropical fever while there, but he does not mention this even to friends. He is a secretive, shy and reserved man, who hints at more than he actually says. For instance, he has hinted at having had many private talks with Dr. Schweitzer, but has refused to give an inkling of what was said. He agrees that he is interested in dedicating his life to Lambaréné for more reasons than those contained in the surface function of the hospital, i.e. the healing of the sick and the relief of pain. But he will not go so far as to say what it is he really seeks in this vocation. If it is religious, it will not have been influenced by his mother's Christian Science. He says he was led by her to accept this faith blindly until he was thirteen, "when I rebelled and had nothing more to do with it". Yet something of the spiritual crusader hangs about him, and it is possible that it is because rather than in spite of his lack of sectarian allegiance that this obviously highly religious man is attracted to the humanist practices of Lambaréné, backed as they are by the superior theological persuasions of Dr. Schweitzer.

Indeed, if Pope has been able to follow Schweitzer in worshipping Jesus as an exceptional man, then he may have found a grail at Lambaréné which would be hard to find anywhere else. The strict observance of the Lord's Prayer (understood by Schweitzer as a supplication of the eschatological Jews of Christ's time); the readings from the New and Old Testaments and Schweitzer's sermons thereon; the Sunday Church service for the mission-converted Africans; these are all devotions of the common order of Christianity. Yet there is no church or chapel. The Doctor does not worship conventionally when in civilized Europe. And the atmosphere at Lambaréné is far more scientific than spiritual. If anyone is worshipped there consistently, it is Dr. Schweitzer.

Pope certainly understands Schweitzer's curious religious position far better, or more tolerantly, than many established churchmen. He stresses the value Schweitzer places on Christ as an exceptional *man* ("someone who was misled; who believed that the world would end, and it didn't, and He was wrong; but still a unique man"). He accepts the Doctor's view that Christ must be seen as a man of His time, and that His sayings and predictions are based on this temporal consideration. It seems that he regards Schweitzer as part saint, part enigma, and wholly the man he has been seeking as a leader since his own moral crisis of the Korean war.

What is also interesting, and perhaps more significant, is that he claims to see medicine as "a trade, like any other". In this he comes surprisingly close to what must be assumed to be Dr. Schweitzer's view, since the Doctor has advanced so little in this field and taken so small an active part in it. Politically, too Pope is as liberal as Schweitzer towards the claims of East and West, if not more so. It is unusual to meet an American with this intellectual tolerance towards Communism, but his way of life would be unthinkable without it. He and his wife are both sympathetic towards all ideas and their expression and, like Schweitzer, recently joined the campaign for nuclear disarmament. The Popes made more than one protest march across England, taking their young children with them.

The strength of spirit which it requires to carry off one's beloved wife to the sickly heat of the jungle was first clearly demonstrated by Dr. Schweitzer, but Fergus Pope is quite as capable of this act of self-discipline, and he includes his children. He knows, from experience, that very young children are less likely to contract dangerous illnesses in the tropics. But when they reach the ages of nine or ten, then they become increasingly vulnerable. What will he do at that time? Perhaps it will depend on the reluctance which his wife has already shown to keeping her children buried in the black depths of Africa.

If a last word is needed to stress the suitability of this young, extraordinary American for the role he will not admit to be seeking, the role of Dr. Schweitzer's successor at Lambaréné, then it must be his attitude to the Doctor's primitive equipment. With obvious feeling, Fergus Pope has said: "What would be the use of an electrically-operated instrument for testing urine—the latest and most expensive gadget there is—if half the patients hadn't enough to eat?"

The beckoning conclusion is that Pope sees a future for Lambaréné as a primitive, deliberately old-fashioned hospital where the native sufferers will continue to be guinea-pigs to a central, intellectual experiment in living. He sees himself indulging a similar passion for service as *le grand docteur*. But it is a service that has no place in a world without extreme poverty and ignorance, so that the progressive march of Africa must either by-pass it or, as seems more likely, roll it into the river. If such a man were to be trusted with the hospital which Dr. Schweitzer has made a beacon to the world, then his personal store of courage and strength would indeed be tested by the times.

TWENTY

VERDICT

As we now prepare to reach our verdict, the many pros and cons in Schweitzer's character form, perhaps, a confusing pattern. When Dr. Johnson wrote, about a doubtful foreign priest, "wherever human nature is to be found, there is a mixture of vice and virtue, a contest of passion and reason" he might have been warning us in advance about the Doctor whose inconsistencies have created one of the most perplexing enigmas of our time. How shall we sum up the qualities of this extraordinary man? Let us briefly recall the facts, as we have seen them.

We first noted the peculiar aura of mystery—one critic called it "an international taboo"—veiling Schweitzer and his hospital. Why it is thought necessary to project the image of a toiling, humble, negro doctor, when in fact Schweitzer is far from being merely this, remains a mystery. The strange silence that falls on the departed seems to support an egocentric design. Schweitzer has seen to it, for whatever reason, that his legend alone remains the brand image of Lambaréné.

Then there is his curious attitude to progress, most noticeably where it affects the health and comfort of his staff and patients. It is hard to commend, on the excuse given by the Doctor that "simple people need simple healing methods". Harder still to comprehend his apparent reluctance to put to this use the funds now enriching his hospital charities. The most likely explanation is that the Doctor wishes to remain in sole command of an artificially isolated colony.

His classification of "insiders" and "outsiders" gives support to this. So, too, does his quaint misuse of time. Perhaps, as much as anything, this shows his weakness for fundamental power over his fellow men.

There is the suggestion that Schweitzer is a self-deluded man, a bigot whose false example of the "white man's" charity has created a thorn in the side of emergent Africa. Well, his distrust of civilization is apparent and he is certainly not optimistic about the future of the self-governing Africans. But what is more significant is that he apparently sees no future for his hospital, or for any other in primitive Africa, unless he is running it himself in his old-fashioned way. He has refused to allow money to be raised in America for the creation of a Schweitzer hospital after his death. He has more than once declined to accept gifts which would have brought Lambaréné into the modern age. Let these facts be noted carefully.

Yet much of the rumour about waste and inefficiency at the hospital is untrue, as a witness has shown. Schweitzer's peculiarity here is that he pretends to understand nothing of the material reckonings of life, while being known to close associates as a shrewd and tough bargainer. He not only charges native patients for drugs, but persuades them to sell him their produce "on the cheap".

We see, too, that he is oddly careful about his own health and protection—eating scarce hens' eggs and bathing only in boiled water—while his staff risk infection and put up with a poorly balanced diet. The main accusation which critics like Mrs. Jane Rouch level is that he stands in the way of hygiene and progress. On the facts, this is hard to deny.

Nevertheless, Schweitzer's capacity for self-propaganda—his knack of "backing into the limelight"—is considerable. It has produced an Image curiously at odds with the reality, supporting his own contention that "to know me, people must come to Lambaréné". Face to face, he emerges as an autocratic political persuader, rather than a humble doctor. He utters gloomy advice to the Western powers, hinting at approaching doom. He appears tinged with tolerance for the Russian viewpoint, hostile to American defence plans. His satisfaction with the example he has created at

Lambaréné clashes oddly with his essential belief that civilization is about to commit suicide.

But a look at his early life and influences explains much. He was born in an age of Germanic ascendancy, over-shadowed by such thinkers as Goethe and Hegel. In this connection, we observe that Schweitzer has never made any prolonged attempt to master the English tongue, though he professes to love England (where his radical theology was first accepted and praised). He found little to admire in the spirit of Paris before the Kaiser's war, preferring the intellectual circles of Berlin. His own decision, to give up the world for a life of service, was in keeping with the highest ascetic principles of the German idealists.

The reason for his act of self-sacrifice, too, seems linked to his love of exclusive power. He had tried his hand at helping the poor of his own country, only to find that such service—and its fruits—had to be shared. Consequently, he sought a dominion which would allow him absolute control. He found it in Africa, among the savage and cannibal primitives of Lambaréné. Yet even here he found it necessary to remove his hospital from the mission which first gave him sanctuary, so as to be free of all outside authority.

Perhaps the harshest criticism is that he failed as a family man through dedicating himself to his ideal. Mme. Schweitzer, the nurse he married so opportunely, could not keep pace with him. Her ill-health and loneliness, as well as her husband's separation from his only child, were not as important, apparently, as the task he had set himself. Indeed, it seems that his visits to Europe and his family were only possible when he needed to raise funds for the hospital. And when the growing throng of admirers persuaded him to return to them.

This is not to say that he did not have to make enormous personal sacrifices. He had given up his beloved music; his important, if controversial, position in the world of theology; his attempt to make his philosophical writings known; and his preaching. These were extraordinary acts of selflessness, though it is possible that he had crammed more than was good for him into the brilliant early years. We must weigh this possibility, since it may have coloured his whole motivation. Was he escaping, in going to Lambaréné ahead of the storm which his radical opinions were bound to provoke? If this were true, it would offer a more convincing reason than those he has given.

It is a curious fact, too, that women have been attracted, while men have more often been put off, by his forceful personality. His "benign dictatorship" can be accepted by most women, while men are inclined to question the need for such autocracy. With the help of women he was able, in his early days, to advance both socially and culturally. Despite his contempt for money and materialism, he was easily charmed by women of wealth and noble blood. And when he needed help in the jungle, following his exhausted wife's collapse, women soon offered their services. It is important to realize that the legend of Lambaréné was partly created by these silent, self-effacing, and often heroic "jungle brides".

But in the case of men, we glimpse Schweitzer's most significant failing: his inability to foster close personal relations with individuals. His chosen successor left him. Most doctors and surgeons stay only for the limit of their original tour of duty. The Doctor allows them too little freedom, and almost no chance to make changes. This frustrates many of the younger and more eager among them. The example of how he prevented one enthusiastic helper from cultivating wild bees is particularly revealing. For it prompts the question, whether he refuses to let others exercise their ideas for fear of losing even one part of his total power?

Schweitzer answers, when he chooses, that his life is intended to be "an argument". It is nowhere more provocative than in his tolerance towards young, lovely and wealthy women. Does he know that their gifts and "hand-outs" appeal to the primitives who, he boasts, walk past more modern hospitals to come to his? If not, then it is difficult to understand why he allows these women to stay. Many are untrained in nursing. Often, they appear to seek personal satisfaction in secluding themselves at Lambaréné. The conclusion that they are flattering attendants on a man who once gave up a circle of similarly rich and beautiful women in Europe is hard to dismiss.

Also there are the eccentrics, again mostly women. If Mr. Graham Greene is right, such tragically deranged psychopaths as "leprophils" (those who would "wash the feet with their hair rather than clean them with something more antiseptic") may be attracted to Schweitzer and his leprosarium, as well as virtuous women who suffer from nothing worse than an excess of religious zeal. Has the Doctor, knowing the awful depths of these people's craving, done enough to place his hospital above the level of their eyes? Has he made it sufficiently clear that his is a place of healing, not a shrine for those who may be gullible? The question really is whether Schweitzer shows a lack of strength as an administrator in welcoming such unorthodox helpers.

The novice who comes to work at Lambaréné faces an unreal atmosphere, and several unattractive customs. Yet it is usual for women nurses to settle down happily. They learn to accept the Doctor as part overlord, part deity and part parent. Only rarely do they question the need for the primitive conditions under which they must live, still less the disciplined and austere routine of their service. But the question here is whether Schweitzer's autocracy and Victorianism are as necessary today as they were fifty years ago? Now that the hospital is rich, and its creator famous, what prevents Schweitzer from improving and modernizing conditions for these noble and dedicated helpers?

Even more disturbing is the strange way the Doctor has ignored the deeds of his most heroic helpers. Their work has added to his legend. Their reward has been obliteration. It is rare to hear mention of any of the many brave nurses who performed such selfless tasks as the supervision of savage lunatics, or the care of the leper village. We see here—and it is an unattractive vision—how his own Image has been fostered at the expense of these unsung heroines.

His attitude to them is as hard to explain as his shortcomings as a family man. One must ask whether the sacrifices of his wife and daughter were necessary. Is it justifiable to attempt a way of life that reverences all living things, and yet bring loneliness and suffering to one's own flesh and blood? The tragic career of Mme.

Schweitzer is barely mentioned in his writings. While the Doctor's admirers excuse the omission on the grounds of personal reticence, the question hangs in the air.

Meanwhile, the legend of Schweitzer the "jungle saint" has been allowed to expand. Those who have written of their visits to Lambaréné, as well as the Doctor's biographers, are largely to blame. From the chorus of adulation rising from their works, it is obvious that Schweitzer has been poorly served by his flatterers.

But once again one asks why he has allowed these false impressions to gain circulation. If, as his theological writings suggest, he went to Lambaréné to serve his own aim and purpose, not *primarily* to heal sick primitives, this would explain it. But how much did his radical religious beliefs influence his choice of a career? So far as can be seen, the ambition to make his life "an argument" from which men would turn to thought and an ethical existence was due to these beliefs. But did Schweitzer, once he had proved to his own satisfaction that Jesus Christ was no more than an "immeasurably great man", logically conclude that any other man—himself not excluded—might gain equal favour in God's eyes? Did he, and does he, see himself as a latter-day Jesus, showing the world by his example the way to eventual salvation? It seems, both from his revolutionary theological books and his revealing statements to friends, that he both did and does. Whether or not he has the right, therefore, to regard himself as a Christian is a provocative point.

Though he succeeded so well in other directions, and was granted the Nobel Peace Prize and the Order of Merit, Schweitzer's philosophy has been coolly received. Bertrand Russell dismisses him. It seems that thinkers find it hard to accept his contradictory assumptions that civilization is doomed, yet that universal Reverence for Life can save us all. This combined optimism and pessimism has proved too much for ordinary men. So we know only of his work in this field that he threatens to be great, not that he is. At present, his unfinished works are with him in the jungle.

Where music influenced him most was in providing a comfort for his solitude. Alone in the jungle, he has been able to relax at the touch of a keyboard. His work on Bach was distinguished, though of relative importance. But more important to our understanding of Schweitzer are his own reflections on the thrill he felt when first listening to the militant Wagner and the full brass of a military band.

Medically, the Doctor appears to have added little to knowledge of treating the African primitives. His own practice has been surprisingly slight, though he has allowed another impression to prevail. We have the word of expert, modern doctors that Lambaréné has no value as a hospital; that its patients could easily be treated elsewhere. Lack of a blood transfusion service handicaps the work of healing, although funds exist which should be more than sufficient to provide it. Most disturbing is the rumour that surgeons and specialists use Lambaréné as a place in which to conduct unorthodox experiments. It must be asked whether Schweitzer is competent to prevent this, since he is out of touch with the advances of modern medicine. If not, then the question of why he refuses to establish a team of trained and up-to-date colleagues is all the more pressing.

There is also the question of whether Schweitzer is really so interested in curing Africans as is imagined. He has made few strides in the branches of medicine and surgery most vitally needed in his situation. His reputation among educated local Africans is contemptuously poor. An American journalist, Jon Randal, reported in 1963 that one upper-class African in Lambaréné told him: "I'd rather die unattended than be humiliated at Dr. Schweitzer's hospital."* While local whites prefer using Schweitzer's hospital to the antiseptic building in Lambaréné town run by the native administration, this may be prejudice on the other side. And the Doctor refuses to budge an inch in his belief that Africans are too immature to be treated as other human beings. "You cannot change their mentality," he said recently. Which means, if one accepts the views expressed in his books, that you must never trust them, expect gratitude from them, or ask a fair return in the form of work for what you have given them.

* *Time*: June 21 1963.

"Schweitzer cares nothing for the Africans, and nothing for medicine," said a writer who had visited Lambaréné. The facts may not support this completely, but they do hint at its possibility. If the African had meant more to his innate scheme, Schweitzer could have encouraged the growth of medical services on the lines of Lambaréné throughout the primitive regions.

Within the Gabon Republic there are new and potent forces for improvement. Schweitzer is unimpressed by them. The fact that America's Peace Corps is reportedly building primary schools all over the country, that a handful of the Gabon's best medical students are already qualifying as doctors in France, does not alter his conviction that the African cannot run his own show as well as a trained European. So he continues to boot their backsides and to address them by the imperious "tu" of French parents and governesses. As one writer summed it up: "He lives in the Africa of 1913, hardly knowing or caring that a continent and a century have passed him by."

Yet, with it all, he is a man above men. Nobody can meet him, can shake that large, softening hand and look into those mocking eyes, without liking him. "Here is a mixture of gentleness and strength taken to an extreme . . ." wrote the South African novelist and historian, Rayne Kruger. "That powerful, craggy face hints at a man of commanding physical strength, proved by his miraculous survival in one of the most disease-ridden places on earth. It belongs to a man with as romantic a story as anyone could wish for: a brilliant young man who denounced everything Europe promised his immense intellectual and artistic gifts to bury himself in Darkest Africa and there, literally surrounded by cannibals and gorillas, fight diseases and witchcraft. And he has won Success with a very large S indeed . . ."

He has certainly won universal acclaim. Repeatedly—in broadcasts, books and speeches—Schweitzer has been treated with the utmost veneration. "The most revered figure of our time . . ." said Sir Michael Redgrave on the B.B.C. recently. It was, perhaps, over-exalted praise but the public have grown accustomed to hearing terms which lavish on him the sanctimonious adulation once given to medieval monarchs; though it is these tributes that are most likely to destroy the real value of his legendary reputation by bringing a reaction of disgust. It must be remembered that he was awarded both the 1952 Nobel Peace Prize, and the Order of Merit founded by King Edward VII in 1902 as "a mark of distinction for really eminent men and women". He *is* a really eminent man, whose "sublime defects", when understood, only add to the fascination of his character.

As to the value of his hospital, and its right to a place in the future of Africa, these are harder to commend. The stain left on the heart of most black Africans by "the white man's burden" will not rub off lightly. "When you have succeeded in dehumanizing the Negro," said Abraham Lincoln, "when you have put him down and made it impossible for him to be but as the beasts of the field; when you have extinguished his soul in this world and placed him where the ray of hope is blown out as in the darkness of the damned, are you quite sure that the demon you have roused will not turn and rend you?" Who can be quite sure of this? Or, indeed, hopeful that such monuments to white man's patronage as the Schweitzer Hospital will be tolerated a moment longer than they have to be. At present, and during his lifetime, the "shrine to the only god that ain't immortal" will be allowed to remain; may even be respected by many of the African leaders; though for others it is "a living insult". When the great Doctor goes, the place where he has conducted his experiment will almost certainly disappear.

This is a sorrowful thought, yet there are practical compensations to place alongside it. Would the area have felt so anxious to build its own health services without Schweitzer's irritating example of what can be done? If he had not cared for the sick who came to him, would not their plight have gone unheeded in the majority of earlier, and some of the later, cases? Would the beacon of self-denial and service which shone from Lambaréné have touched men's hearts, if he had not insisted on preserving his own identity in an increasingly anonymous world?

It is often complained that Schweitzer has attracted all the attention which many dedicated men and women all over Africa, performing equally magnificent and selfless service, should have shared. Yet their names are known to no more than a handful of people. This is a harsh truth, but a lack of wit, wiles or wisdom through which others might have used propaganda to advantage need not blind us to the strong appeal of Schweitzer's own very special case.

Even accepting that Schweitzer has occasionally twisted the world's tail to suit his purpose, this is not usually deplored in a materialistic age. And Schweitzer has made no claims to be above reproach, either in his behaviour or in his most personal character. It is, indeed, his admission of failure as a man that may concern us most. For either directly or undirectly it is the spring from which the river of life has risen and flowed.

Schweitzer chose, out of his own conceit, to give his life to the jungles of Africa; to service of a harsh and penitent sort. He placed second those who suffered from his thwarted career, or those who—like his dutiful wife, Hélène—stumbled along in his path. He over-rode all personal feelings for others, as for himself. Who can say that his mission was more important than the feelings of the woman he had married, and their only child? When he wrote: "Because my life is so liberally spotted with falsehood, I must forgive falsehood which has been practised upon me; because I myself have been in so many cases wanting in love, and guilty of hatred, slander, deceit, or arrogance, I must pardon any want of love, and all hatred, slander, deceit, or arrogance which have been directed against myself . . ."* was he not thinking of these two women who had known and shared so little of the man nearest to them? Was he not torn from time to time in the depths of his beloved primeval forests, when the throb of conscience told him that his duty did not only lie in working out his personal theory, but in responsibilities to those outside as well?

If so, the world has been shown little of his remorse. For profound reticence on all personal matters is built into his Alsatian heart like a grille. What has stayed chained and mute behind it

* *The Philosophy of Civilization: Vol. II*

for so many years will never be revealed, so that we can only guess what it might be. How we do so is important to our verdict. Perhaps it is also true to say that our verdict is important in a world which has too often mistaken the legend for the man.

BIBLIOGRAPHY

Out of My Life and Thought, by Albert Schweitzer (Henry Holt and Co. 1949).

On the Edge of the Primeval Forest, and *More From the Primeval Forest*, by Albert Schweitzer, two volumes in one (Macmillan 1961).

Memoirs of Childhood and Youth, by Albert Schweitzer (Macmillan 1949).

The Philosophy of Civilization, Part I (The Decay and Restoration of Civilization); Part II (Civilization and Ethics), by Albert Schweitzer (Macmillan 1949).

Music in the Life of Albert Schweitzer, translated and edited by Charles R. Joy (Beacon Press 1961).

The Theology of Albert Schweitzer for Christian Inquirers, by Lt.-Col. E. N. Mozley (London, A. & C. Black 1950).

At Work With Albert Schweitzer, by L. Ostergaard-Christensen (Beacon Press 1962).

Dr. Schweitzer of Lambaréné, by Norman Cousins (Harper & Brothers 1960).

Albert Schweitzer—The Man and His Mind, by George Seaver (London, A. & C. Black 1949).

The Road to Lambaréné, by Waldemar Augustiny (Frederick Muller 1956).

The True Book about Albert Schweitzer, by John Merrett (Soccer Associates, New Rochelle 1961).

Dr. Schweitzer, O.M., by Nina Langley (London, Harrap 1956).

With Dr. Schweitzer in Lambaréné, by Clara Urquhart (London, Harrap 1957).

Days With Albert Schweitzer, by Frederick M. Franck (Henry Holt and Co. 1959).

The files of *Associated Newspapers Ltd.*

The files of *The Times*.

The files of *Time* magazine.

INDEX